THE ESSENTIAL WRITINGS OF JAMES WELDON JOHNSON

Edited and with an Introduction by
Rudolph P. Byrd

Foreword by Charles Johnson

THE MODERN LIBRARY
NEW YORK

2008 Modern Library Trade Paperback Original

Published in the United States by Modern Library, an imprint of The Random House Publishing Group, a division of Random House, Inc., New York.

Grateful acknowledgment is made to the following for permission to reprint previously published material:

Alfred A. Knopf, a division of Random House, Inc.: Introduction by Carl Van Vechten to *The Autobiography of an Ex-Coloured Man* by James Weldon Johnson, copyright © 1927 by Alfred A. Knopf, Inc., and copyright renewed 1955 by Carl Van Vechten. Reprinted by permission of Alfred A. Knopf, a division of Random House, Inc.

University of Illinois Press and Michael S. Harper: "Portrait of James Weldon Johnson" from *Honorable Amendments: Poems* by Michael S. Harper, copyright © 1995 by Michael S. Harper. Reprinted by permission of the poet and the University of Illinois Press.

Viking Penguin, a division of Penguin Group (USA) Inc.: Chapter 2 and Chapter 7 from *Along This Way* by James Weldon Johnson, copyright © 1933 by James Weldon Johnson and copyright renewed 1961 by Grace Nail Johnson. "Noah Built the Ark" and "The Judgment Day" from *God's Trombones* by James Weldon Johnson, copyright © 1927 by The Viking Press, Inc., and copyright renewed 1955 by Grace Nail Johnson. "Saint Peter Relates an Incident of the Resurrection Day" from *Saint Peter Relates an Incident* by James Weldon Johnson, copyright © 1917, 1921, 1935 by James Weldon Johnson and copyright renewed 1965 by Grace Nail Johnson. Used by permission of Viking Penguin, a division of Penguin Group (USA) Inc.

Sondra Kathryn Wilson: "Chronology" from *Lift Every Voice and Sing,* edited by Julian Bond and Sondra Kathryn Wilson (New York: Random House, Inc., 2000); *Do You Believe in Ghosts?* and *The Engineer,* both by James Weldon Johnson from the James Weldon Johnson Memorial Collection of Negro Arts and Letters, Yale University, New Haven, CT; "Native African Races and Culture" by James Weldon Johnson from the John F. Slater Fund No. 25 (1927); "The Dilemma of the Negro Author" by James Weldon Johnson from *The American Mercury,* December, 1938; "Race Prejudice and the Negro Artist" by James Weldon Johnson from *Harper's Magazine* 157 (1928); and *Negro Americans, What Now?* by James Weldon Johnson (New York: The Viking Press, 1934). James Weldon Johnson's writings are reprinted here with the permission of Sondra Kathryn Wilson.

ISBN 978-0-8129-7532-1

Printed in the United States of America

www.modernlibrary.com

2 4 6 8 9 5 3

To

Georgia Lyles Saunders, Blanche Lyles Solomon,
Ingrid Saunders Jones, Cecelia Corbin Hunter

and

in memoriam

Garth Tate

Portrait of James Weldon Johnson

Michael S. Harper

The rolled cigar: Nicaragua politics,
the jazz age sequestered 'round midnight;
NAACP business around the clock.

His novel a mystery,
certainly "autobiographical"
in the sense that he wrote it.

Carlo let loose on the Harlemites;
he flicks the switch of the publishers,
eats cognac, eats champagne,
his Iowan teeth like headlights
from Jay Gatsby's coupé.

Reading for the cigarmakers
is not laughter, and not to be laughed at;
good cigars are a novelty
to tourists, but for quality,
white and black, the best
leaf for the book,
smelt of print,
and away from the print,
stylized segregation.

Housing patterns are to be cashed in on;
Strivers Row are bungalows
compared to plantations;
for immigrants,
just off Ellis Island,
they are goldmines
and golden business.

From the Atlanta Archives
four coattailed *sports*
are about to go out on the road.

Hair parted, not a smoker
in the bunch, Weldon tunes up
his infield for the orchestra:

This is GA; it is a town
Du Bois walks in; commercial peachtree
is not the apple of his eye;
he remembers the Seminoles
above all Indians; railroads
are a checkered experience,
chaingangs, turpentine wards,
bring him the blues. He begins to read in Georgia.

The Caribbean calls to understand
revolution; Garvey gets to town
just in time; in Niagara, over the falls,
the braintrust works out strategy.
In eighty years we'll be ready to tackle
Latin America; *Plessy* v. *Ferguson*
is barely cold. The marshals of progress
turn their phases on stock prices;
the stock is paper or it's meat.

Foreword

Charles Johnson

When we look at a life as luminous as that of James Weldon Johnson's, there are countless ways we might discuss his enduring contributions to the literary culture and political life of this nation, but perhaps one appropriate starting point for describing this multidimensional man straddling the nineteenth and twentieth centuries, the place that will help us most at the dawn of a new millennium, is by acknowledging that he was in the truest, the noblest, and purest sense of the phrase an American "Renaissance man." (The pun is intentional, of course, given the pivotal role he played during the Harlem Renaissance.) But how *does* one become a Renaissance individual? Does his capacious life and character contain some truth about the art of living in a multiracial world that is useful to our children and ourselves?

In other words, what was there about this man, born just eight years after the Emancipation Proclamation, that enabled him to create so prolifically and serve so widely during the era of Reconstruction, then in the most entrenched period of American apartheid—the 1920s and '30s—when the opportunities for black people were so painfully circumscribed, when the Great Depression fueled European fascism, the rise of racial eugenics, and black lynchings throughout the South? How in such a racially restrictive world could Johnson confess that he once had an "unconscious race-superiority complex"?

Happily for us, Johnson provides in his *oeuvre* a few tantalizing clues from which we might coax an answer. Surely it helped that while he had friends of many races, he was "reared free from undue fear of or esteem for white people as a race," and possessed a profoundly felt spiritual faith, as revealed in the words of his best-known creation, "Lift Every Voice and Sing." Added to which, and of equal importance, when he was a student at Atlanta University, "The ideal constantly held up to us was of education as a means of living, not of making a living. It was impressed upon us that taking a classical course would have an effect of making us better and nobler, and of higher value to those we should have to serve. An odd, old-fashioned, naïve conception? Rather."

But perhaps the wisdom at the heart of this pedagogical model that urged students to be lifelong learners so that they could unselfishly serve others, to value the contributions of those who came before them, and to see themselves as being capable of similar achievements, is not as odd or naïve as Johnson claims. In his time, as well as ours, anyone belonging to a racial and ethnic minority in a predominantly white, Eurocentric society must learn at a very early age to "read" all manner of phenomenon from the nuanced and polyvalent standpoint of a bifold consciousness. Lately, I have been calling this an "Aleph consciousness." I borrowed this term from Jorge Luis Borges' short story "The Aleph," where he describes the *aleph* as "the place where . . . all the places of the world, seen from every angle, coexist." It is the first letter of the Hebrew alphabet, and of its shape Borges says that it "is that of a man pointing to the sky and the earth, to indicate that the lower world is the map and mirror of the higher." From its vantage point, Borges says, one can see "simultaneously night and day." The biographies of our most preeminent and intellectually impressive black predecessors—"Race" men like Frederick Douglass, W.E.B. Du Bois, Richard Wright, Ralph Ellison, and Martin Luther King Jr.—disclose how they developed this expansive vision and catholicity as their existential posture before the world. It is an antidote to everything that racism, intolerance, and bigotry represent: the narrowly parochial, the culturally provincial, and at its core this posture is unabashedly integrationist, implicitly honoring the interconnectedness of all life.

Those who embraced an Aleph consciousness were determined that nothing of significance in our world would be lost on them. Despite racial discrimination, they saw all endeavors as their real possibilities, and the global achievements of the past as their inheritance. Never complaining about their studies not being "black" enough or relevant to the lives of African Americans, they learned how to absorb the products of the Greek and the Judaic, the Roman, French, British, and, unlike their white counterparts, the black American and African as well. To emotionally empathize and project themselves behind the eyes of ancestors as diverse as Homer and the Beowulf poet, Goethe and Synge, Olaudah Equiano and Paul Laurence Dunbar. (Little wonder, then, that Johnson briefly had a "race-superiority complex.") For children of color, an Aleph consciousness has always been not only necessary for daily survival in a predominantly white country, enabling them to navigate successfully through America's institutions—schools, jobs, social situations—but also for a broadly humanistic path to personal and professional excellence. In it there is something delightfully Emersonian, a feeling that "[i]t is our duty to be discontented with the measure we have of knowledge & virtue, to forget the things behind & press toward those before." It is difficult for me to believe that anyone can encounter Johnson's biography, which reads like the life story of two or three men, and not immediately recall Emerson's celebration in "Self-Reliance" of the distinctly American character represented by "the sturdy lad from New Hampshire or Vermont, who in turn tries all the professions, who *teams* it, *farms* it, *peddles,* keeps a school, preaches, edits a newspaper, goes to Congress, buys a township, and so forth, in successive years, and always, like a cat, falls on his feet."

In this important volume made possible by the outstanding literary scholar Rudolph Byrd, the superb example of the art of living represented by James Weldon Johnson, that sturdy lad from Jacksonville, Florida, appears vividly on every page, prodding us to reflect deeply on how we, as Americans, might bring the wisdom and rich legacy he has left us into a dangerous yet promising new century.

Seattle, September 2006

Contents

PART FOUR: CULTURAL CRITICISM

PART FIVE: AUTOBIOGRAPHY

PART SIX: POLITICAL WRITING

Introduction

Rudolph P. Byrd

The rolled cigar: Nicaragua politics,
the jazz age sequestered 'round midnight;
NAACP business around the clock.

His novel a mystery,
certainly "autobiographical"
in the sense that he wrote it.

—MICHAEL S. HARPER,
"Portrait of James Weldon Johnson,"
from *Honorable Amendments*

"I find that looking backward over three-score years does not lessen my enthusiasm in looking forward," writes James Weldon Johnson in the final paragraphs of his autobiography, *Along This Way*. "What I have done appears as very little when I consider all that the will to do set me as a task, and what I have written quite dwarfed alongside my aspirations; but life has been a stirring enterprise with me, and still is; for the willingness is not yet over and the dreams are not yet dead."[1]

The Modern Library's *Essential Writings of James Weldon Johnson* spans three-score years of Johnson's richly lived life. Through the selection of representative works arranged in chronological order, this volume seeks to capture the depth and range of his artistic, cultural, and political interests. Notwithstanding his own modest estimation of his corpus, the volume is a record of Johnson's impressive achievements in several modes of expression, as well as convincing evidence that for him life remained a "stirring enterprise."

Johnson was born in Jacksonville, Florida, in 1871. His education as a race man, in his case, as a cosmopolite and the unafraid advocate of African America, began in his boyhood. From his mother, Helen

Louise Dillet, born in 1842 in Nassau, Bahamas, and reared in New York, Johnson developed a deep appreciation for poetry and music. "She was my first teacher," he recalls, "and began my lessons in reading before ever I went to school."[2] Most evenings his mother would read to James and to Rosamond, his younger brother, such classics as *David Copperfield.* This initiation into the world of letters nurtured Johnson's imagination and provided him with an almost tangible sense of the existence of dimensions beyond his present dimension. As his mother was "the first colored woman public school teacher in Florida," she was a pioneering figure in a profession that he would join in later years.[3] Along with providing her son with a model of leadership through education, Helen Louise Dillet was also a "nonconformist and a rebel" who never accepted the operations of the color line.[4] Doubtless, his mother's example of erudition and resistance were extremely important to Johnson as he developed into manhood.

From his father, James Johnson, born a freeman in 1830 in Richmond, Virginia, Johnson developed a love of reading. James Johnson gave his first-born a library comprised of children's literature, which he kept until his death. As the headwaiter of Jacksonville's St. James Hotel, "the most famous and the most fashionable of all the Florida resort hotels," the father introduced his son to the glamorous and mannered world of society.[5] As Johnson senior possessed "a working knowledge of the Spanish language," which aided him in the execution of his duties at the St. James Hotel, the younger Johnson soon developed an appreciation for foreign languages and, later in life, fluency in Spanish.[6] His father's ability to negotiate successfully a world of culture bearing the imprint of a foreign language deeply impressed Johnson. As a consequence, reading and writing were taken up as desirable pursuits, along with the study of foreign languages and the race rituals of Victorian society.

Beyond the home, there were certain important lessons about culture and race that Johnson imbibed as a member of a self-conscious African American community in an increasingly segregated society. As a boy in Jacksonville in the late nineteenth century, he recalls that his first awareness of difference was derived from a particular kind of "religious experience [which] preceded any experiences of race."[7] Johnson is alluding to his journey as a Methodist to the mourner's bench at the age of nine and the debate that this state of being "consecrated to God" generated within his family. As an adolescent, Johnson came to the conclusion that he was not a Christian but rather an agnostic.

As race emerged as a factor in his existence, Johnson writes that his "early impressions constituted what might be called an unconscious race-superiority complex. All the most interesting things that came under my observation were being done by colored men."[8] There were many things that Johnson would have learned earlier if he had not been, as he observes, "restricted in play" by his parents. Initiated by degrees into what his colleague and friend W.E.B. Du Bois would poetically term "the veil" or the color line, Johnson would become more cognizant of race during his studies at Atlanta University Preparatory Division, which he entered at the age of sixteen, and later as a student at Atlanta University. "Here was a deepening, but narrowing experience; an experience so narrowing that the inner problem of a Negro in America becomes that of not allowing it to choke and suffocate him. I am glad," writes Johnson of his years at Atlanta University, "that this fuller impact of the situation came to me as late as it did, when my apprehension of it could be more or less objective. As an American Negro, I consider the most fortunate thing in my whole life to be the fact that through childhood I was reared free from undue fear of or esteem for white people as a race. . . ."[9] Johnson came of age before the formalization of separate but equal in the landmark case of *Plessy v. Ferguson* of 1896. In his most "plastic years" there emerges, in incremental fashion and through the lens of a community conscious of its value, an awareness in Johnson of the racially defined patterns that would over time congeal into the American system of apartheid against which he would valiantly do battle for most of his adult life.

Along with his parents and the community, which functioned as buffers against the "race prejudice [which] might have become a part of [Johnson's] subconscious as well as of [his] conscious self," Dr. T. O. Summers exercised a decisive influence upon Johnson's development.[10] According to Johnson, Summers was "the outstanding surgeon in Florida," and a member of Jacksonville's white elite.[11] Through a series of unexpected turns Summers hired Johnson as an assistant in the reception room of his medical offices in Jacksonville. At the time of their first meeting, Johnson was approximately seventeen or eighteen years old, yet he knew that he "had made contact with one of those mysterious forces that play close around us or flash to us across the void from another orbit."[12] In Summers, Johnson came "into close touch with a man of great culture. He was, moreover, a cosmopolite."[13] Well traveled and fluent in several languages, Summers initiated a relationship with Johnson that proceeded "on a high level," and, according to Johnson, " 'race' never showed its head. He neither condescended nor patronized; in fact, he treated me as an intellectual equal."[14] Summers welcomed Johnson into his library, exposing the young man to works by Montaigne and Thomas Paine, along with erotica by Boccaccio and Balzac. Here Johnson discovered a body of literature that was not available in the library of Atlanta University. Summers also gave Johnson "the first worthwhile criticism and encouragement [he] had yet received" of his poetry.[15] Johnson's employment with Summers ended when the former returned to Atlanta University in the fall to resume his studies. He recalls that "I was filled with regret at parting from Dr. Summers. The regret was mutual. He had formed a strong affection for me which he did not hide. I had made him my model of all that a man and a gentleman should be."[16] Johnson writes that he left Summers "with an older ambition clarified, strengthened, and brought into some shape—the ambition to write."[17] When the surgeon relocated with his family to another region of the country, they corresponded for "several years. Then one day I was shocked to learn that Dr. Summers had committed suicide. I was deeply grieved, for I had lost an understanding friend, one who was, in many ways, a kindred spirit."[18] Johnson memorialized Summers in his novel *The Autobiography of an Ex-Coloured Man* for there the surgeon appears as the protagonist's worldly and world-weary patron who commits suicide.

Given the constellation of influences encountered in the home and the worlds beyond it, Johnson was well prepared for the education he received as a boarder enrolled in the preparatory school and later as an undergraduate at Atlanta University. Johnson's course of study was in the liberal arts; his study of Spanish expanded to include French along with the required courses in Greek and Latin. Graduating in 1894, Johnson would pursue postgraduate studies in drama at Columbia University, earning a Master of Arts under the tutelage of the scholar Brander Matthews. While he valued his postgraduate training, Johnson believed that the education he received at Atlanta University was, in fact, the superior one. Recalling the philosophy of education at Atlanta University, Johnson writes: "The ideal constantly held up to us was of education as a means of living, not of making a living. It was impressed upon us that taking a classical course would have an effect of making us better and nobler, and of higher value to those we should have to serve. An odd, old-fashioned, naïve conception? Rather."[19]

Johnson sought to actualize this philosophy of education in his choice of vocation and in his many forms of service to the race. Soon after his graduation from Atlanta University, he returned to Jacksonville where he became principal of Stanton School, his alma mater, from 1894 to 1902. Within two years, Johnson transformed Stanton School, which offered instruction from the first grade to middle school, into Florida's first public high school for African Americans. In 1895, Johnson also established the *Daily American,* an afternoon daily that would be, in his words, "a strong weapon in the Negro's defence against racial inequalities and injustices."[20] In circulation for only eight months, the failure of the *Daily American* was Johnson's "first taste of defeat in public life."[21] While disappointed in the outcome of this experiment in journalism, he observed in *Along This Way* "that my biggest satisfaction has come from looking over the files of the paper. I have reread my editorials and seen that I would not feel called upon to make any apology for them today."[22]

Soon after the failure of the *Daily American,* Johnson turned his attention to the study of law. He did not attend law school but rather, adhering to the custom of the Old South, read law in the office of Thomas A. Ledwith, a member of the Jacksonville bar. In 1898 Johnson became the first African American to be admitted to the Florida bar. While proud of this achievement, the practice of law, pursued while still principal of Stanton High School, never held much meaning for Johnson.

In 1900 Johnson, together with his younger brother J. Rosamond Johnson, a classically trained composer and singer, composed "Lift Every Voice and Sing." This hymn was composed for a program sponsored by the black leadership of Jacksonville to celebrate the birthday of Abraham Lincoln. At the time of its composition, Johnson was principal of Stanton School. The elder Johnson wrote the words of the hymn, and the younger Johnson, as his older brother remembers, created the "noble setting of the poem."[23] Johnson's New York publisher, Edward B. Marks, made "mimeographed copies for us, and the song was taught to and sung by a chorus of five hundred colored school children."[24] In subsequent years, the hymn was adopted by the National Association for the Advancement of Colored People, and for generations "generally used throughout the country as the 'Negro National Hymn.'"[25] "The lines of this song repay me in an elation," writes Johnson, "almost of exquisite anguish, whenever I hear them sung by Negro children."[26] While the Johnson brothers considered "Lift Every Voice and Sing" an "incidental effort, an effort made under stress and with no intention other than to meet the needs of a particular moment," it has easily eclipsed in popularity and importance their earlier compositions.[27] As Johnson would observe more than three decades after the hymn's composition, "we wrote better than we knew."[28]

From 1902 to 1905, Johnson enjoyed considerable acclaim as a composer of light opera for the stages of vaudeville and Broadway. This accomplishment Johnson shared with his brother J. Rosamond, and with Bob Cole, a singer and composer. Known as Cole and Johnson Brothers, they were the originators of several songs, most notably "The Maiden with the Dreamy Eyes," "Under the Bamboo Tree," and the unforgettable "Sence You Went Away," reprinted in this volume. A dialect poem, "Sence You Went Away" was Johnson's first publication beyond those he wrote at Atlanta University and appeared in *Century* while he was still an undergraduate. Later set to music by his brother Rosamond, "Sence You Went Away" was recorded by a number of artists, including Paul Robeson. At the height of their vogue, the songs of Cole and Johnson Brothers were regularly performed in the United States and the capitals of Europe. Throughout his life, Johnson maintained his deep and abiding interest in light opera and other genres of music. In 1914 he became one of the founding members of the American Society of Composers, Authors and Publishers (ASCAP). Nearly a decade later, Johnson co-edited with J. Rosamond Johnson *The Book of American Negro Spirituals*, published in 1925, followed a year later by *The Second Book of American Negro Spirituals*. Johnson's superb preface to *The Book of American Negro Spirituals* is still regarded as a standard reference for those interested in the history, evolution, and significance of the spirituals.

Johnson wrote in all of the major genres of literature. Of special interest to readers will be *Do You Believe in Ghosts? A Darkey Comedy* and *The Engineer: A Drama in One Act.* Published here for the first time, these early and experimental works in drama reveal a young writer in search of both a form and his own distinctive voice. Written between 1894 and 1902, these plays constitute Johnson's earliest and it seems only experiments with drama, and anticipate the later experiments in this genre by such writers as Jean Toomer, Langston Hughes, and Zora Neale Hurston.

The Autobiography of an Ex-Coloured Man is one of Johnson's most celebrated works, completed during his tenure as Consul General in Nicaragua. Published in 1912, this experimental novel that masquerades as autobiography deftly explores the phenomenon of passing while creating a fascinating portrait of New York's black bohemia, and giving fictional significance to Du Bois's theory of black psychology or "double consciousness." Johnson's pioneering treatment of the mulatto would influence the depiction of this figure by the writers of the Harlem Renaissance as well as such contemporary writers as Charles Johnson.

As a poet, Johnson experimented with standard and dialect verse, and in both genres produced poetry of enduring beauty and force. His master poem "Fifty Years," published in 1913 to mark the fiftieth anniversary of the Emancipation Proclamation, is one of the noblest commemorative poems in the English language. Johnson's poems in dialect are no less praiseworthy. With the publication in 1927 of *God's Trombones,* he captured for all time the majesties of black folk speech while also honoring the almost mythic oratorical powers of the black folk preacher. In "Saint Peter Relates an Incident of the Resurrection Day," published in 1930, Johnson reflects upon the heroic contributions of the black soldier while also revealing once again the emotional range and power of black folk speech or vernacular speech. In these poems he reveals the limitations of dialect poetry as practiced by such poets as Paul Laurence Dunbar, as well as realizes the promise and beauty of vernacular speech first postulated by the Romantic poets. Put another way and in his own words, Johnson expresses beautifully "the racial spirit by symbols from within rather than by symbols from without. . . ."[29]

A formidable cultural historian, Johnson's cultural criticism is the point of departure for anyone seeking to understand the function and value of culture in American society in the first decades of the last century. In his prefaces to *The Book of American Negro Poetry,* the first anthology of black verse in English, published in 1922, Johnson makes the claim that a people are only as great as the literature and art they produce. He then proceeds to reveal the ways in which a new black art form such as ragtime is, in actuality, yet another manifestation of our national art and culture. These prefaces, the first published in 1922 and the second in 1931, also contain the evolution of Johnson's critique of the limitations of dialect poetry as well as fresh evidence of his enduring faith in the artistic possibilities of black vernacular speech. In such groundbreaking essays as "Native African Races and Culture," first published in 1927, Johnson points out the dangers of ignoring the African background in any evaluation of African American culture, and in the process rehabilitates the low view of African culture, held by both blacks and whites, in the United States of the 1920s. Of course, *Black Manhattan* is the apogee of Johnson's cultural criticism. In this cultural history spanning the colonial period to 1930, he documents the deep imprint of African American culture upon many aspects of the cultural life of Manhattan while concurrently offering trenchant assessments of the strengths and weaknesses of black leadership. In these texts Johnson provides us with a balanced reading of the evolution, successes, and possibilities of African American culture. In every case, his insightful examination of the complex formations of African American culture is buttressed by the claim of the centrality of African American culture to American culture. Collectively, these texts reveal Johnson as one of the chief architects of the Harlem Renaissance.

Johnson's political writings are no less compelling than his writings in other genres. His last and most substantial analysis of the barriers to full citizenship for African Americans is *Negro Americans, What Now?,* published in 1934, three years after his historic term as Executive Secretary of the NAACP. In this treatise Johnson writes "directly to my fellow Negro Americans on the American question which most deeply affects them."[30] In contemplating the barriers to full citizenship for African Americans, Johnson's objective is not to "formulate a complete and praticable program" but rather to "lay down certain lines along which a program may be worked out."[31] For Johnson, the contradictions of American democracy are not solely the problem of African Americans but rather they are set forth as a national crisis requiring a national solution. Johnson's progressive and radical stance on race and rights places him in the tradition of Maria Stewart, Frederick Douglass, and Du Bois. Now available to a new audience, readers of *Negro Americans, What Now?* will note the kinship of ideas and positions between Johnson and his several successors at the NAACP, Walter White and Roy Wilkins, as well as such figures as Dr. Martin Luther King Jr.

A man of a refined and complex sensibility, Johnson distinguished himself in remarkable ways as teacher, journalist, lawyer, writer, diplomat, and advocate for the full realization of the ideals of American democracy as the chief spokesman for the NAACP, the nation's oldest and most progressive interracial alliance. While providing superb leadership in these various vocations for his race and the nation, to summon again the language of his era, Johnson also realized his aspiration to express the strangeness and beauty of his own individual imagination as well as that of the race through the expressive arts. Put another way, in his lifetime Johnson achieved the status of a national leader of African America, while producing canonical works in the expressive arts, particularly literature. The only figure of his generation to whom the formidable Johnson might yield ground in these overlapping spheres is Du Bois, who outlived Johnson by twenty-five years. As a major figure of American culture, history, and politics of an earlier generation, Johnson is an intellectual of a stature we have not seen in American life since his generation. Joel E. Spingarn, president of the NAACP board, has left us with a very apt description of his friend and colleague: "But he is that unusual thing, a poet who is also an effective man of action."[32]

While on the surface a man of seemingly competing, discrete parts, in actuality, Johnson achieved a rare and complex synthesis in his life. What emerges from this synthesis is an humane and catholic view of the world and of the human condition that Johnson termed "cosmopolitanism." Speaking of what is required of us if we are to transcend race and the other forms of difference that have divided us as a nation, in *Negro Americans, What Now?* he asserts that the "accomplishment at once demands of both sides a considerable cosmopolitanism of spirit and intellect. It is easy to live within the strict limits of one's own group; one knows its language, its language of words and ideas; one knows all the questions that will come up and the answers; one does not have to extend himself. Social and intellectual intercourse," observes Johnson, "on even the outskirts of cosmopolitanism is a more strenuous matter; and that is one of the reasons why human beings prefer parochialism."[33] Without question, Johnson's enduring significance and relevance as both artist and humanitarian is grounded in his rejection of parochialism, and the several ways in which he embodied a "considerable cosmopolitanism of spirit and intellect." It is this hybrid, egalitarian vision of the world in which nothing is alien, in which the cultures of the world constitute our shared inheritance, and in which all are valued that is everywhere in evidence in the pages of this volume.

Bellagio, Italy

NOTES

1. James Weldon Johnson, *Along This Way* (New York: Penguin Books, 1933; 1990), 409.
2. Ibid., 12.
3. Ibid.
4. Ibid.
5. Ibid., 15.
6. Ibid., 17.
7. Ibid., 31.
8. Ibid.
9. Ibid., 78.
10. Ibid.
11. Ibid., 93.
12. Ibid., 95.
13. Ibid.
14. Ibid., 95.
15. Ibid., 97.
16. Ibid., 98.
17. Ibid., 99.
18. Ibid.
19. Ibid., 122.
20. Ibid., 139.

21. Ibid.
22. Ibid., 140.
23. Ibid., 155.
24. James Weldon Johnson, *St. Peter Relates an Incident: Selected Poems* (New York: The Viking Press, 1933), 98.
25. *Along This Way*, 155.
26. *St. Peter Relates an Incident*, 98.
27. *Along This Way*, 156.
28. Ibid.
29. James Weldon Johnson, "Preface," *The Book of American Negro Poetry* (New York: Harcourt, Brace and Jovanovich, 1922; 1931), 41.
30. James Weldon Johnson, *Negro Americans, What Now?* (New York: Viking Press, 1934), v.
31. Ibid., vi.
32. Joel E. Spingarn to Dr. Evan M. Evans, July 5, 1929, Series Number 1, Folder 454, Box 19, James Weldon Johnson Memorial Collection of Negro Arts and Letters, Yale University.
33. Johnson, *Negro Americans, What Now?*, 81–82.

ACKNOWLEDGMENTS

I wish to acknowledge the generous support of the Rockefeller Foundation, which provided support in the form of a residency at the Bellagio Study and Conference Center in Bellagio, Italy, during the fall of 2005. I also wish to acknowledge the support and cooperation of the Special Collections Library of the Robert W. Woodruff Library of Emory University, and also the Beinecke Rare Book and Manuscript Library of Yale University.

I also wish to express my sincere thanks and appreciation to Michael S. Harper, teacher and mentor, for his permission to reprint "Portrait of James Weldon Johnson" from *Honorable Amendments*.

I would like to thank Dr. Sondra Kathryn Wilson, literary executor of the Estate of Grace and James Weldon Johnson, for granting permission to reprint her excellent chronology and the texts that appear in this volume. Generous and supportive, Dr. Wilson believed always in the value of this project.

It is important to recognize the vital contributions of Judy Sternlight: a very able editor who embodies the best traditions of the art and craft of editing.

After all these years, Henry A. Leonard remains essential in more ways than I could have imagined and that I can enumerate here.

I am grateful to all.

James Weldon Johnson

A Chronology

1871 Born June 17 to James and Helen Louise Dillet Johnson in Jacksonville, Florida.

1884 Makes trip to New York City.

1886 Meets Frederick Douglass in Jacksonville.

1887 Graduates from Stanton School in Jacksonville. Enters Atlanta University Preparatory Division.

1890 Graduates from Atlanta University Preparatory Division. Enters Atlanta University's freshman class.

1891 Teaches school in Henry County, Georgia, during the summer following his freshman year.

1892 Wins Atlanta University Oratory Prize for "The Best Methods of Removing the Disabilities of Caste from the Negro."

1893 Meets Paul Laurence Dunbar at the Chicago World's Fair.

1894 Receives B.A. degree with honors from Atlanta University. Delivers valedictory speech, "The Destiny of the Human Race." Tours New England with the Atlanta University Quartet for three months. Is appointed principal of Stanton School in Jacksonville, Florida, the largest African American public school in the state.

1895 Founds the *Daily American*, an afternoon daily serving Jacksonville's black population.

1896 Expands Stanton School to high school status, making it the first public high school for blacks in the state of Florida.

1898 Becomes the first African American to be admitted to the Florida bar.

1900 Writes the lyrics to "Lift Every Voicc and Sing" with music by his brother, J. Rosamond Johnson. Meets his future wife, Grace Nail, in New York.

1901 Elected president of the Florida State Teachers Association. Nearly lynched in a Jacksonville park. This near lynching made him realize that he could not advance in the South.

1902 Resigns as principal of Stanton School. Moves to New York to form musical trio—Cole and the Johnson Brothers. As part of this trio he writes over 200 popular songs, many of which are used in Broadway productions.

1903 Attends graduate school at Columbia University, where he studies with Brander Matthews, professor of dramatic literature.

1904 Writes two songs for Theodore Roosevelt's presidential campaign. Becomes a member of the National Business League, an organization founded by Booker T. Washington. Receives honorary degree from Atlanta University. During this time he meets W.E.B. Du Bois, then a professor at Atlanta University.

1905 Cole and the Johnson Brothers go on European tour. Becomes president of Colored Republican Club in New York City.

1906 Accepts membership in the American Society of International Law. Is appointed U.S. consul to Venezuela by President Theodore Roosevelt.

1909 Is promoted to U.S. consul to Corinto, Nicaragua.

1910 Marries Grace Elizabeth Nail, daughter of well-known Harlem businessman John Bennett Nail, on February 3, in New York City.

1912 Publishes anonymously *The Autobiography of an Ex-Coloured Man,* probably the earliest first-person fictional narrative by an African American.

1913 Resigns from the consular service on account of race prejudice and party politics.

1914 Accepts position as contributing editor to the *New York Age.* Becomes a founding member of the American Society of

Composers, Authors and Publishers (ASCAP). Joins Sigma Pi Phi fraternity and Phi Beta Sigma fraternity.

1915 Becomes member of the NAACP. Puts into English the libretto of *Goyescas,* the Spanish grand opera, which is produced at the Metropolitan Opera House.

1916 Attends the NAACP conference in Amenia, New York, at the estate of J. E. Spingarn. Delivers speech, "A Working Programme for the Future." Joins the staff of the NAACP in the position of field secretary.

1917 Publishes volume *Fifty Years and Other Poems.* Publishes poem "Saint Peter Relates an Incident of the Resurrection Day." With W.E.B. Du Bois, leads over 12,000 marchers down New York's Fifth Avenue to protest lynchings and riots. Becomes acting secretary of the NAACP. Supports U.S. entry into World War I and fights against the atrocities perpetrated against black soldiers. Meets Walter White in Atlanta and persuades him to join the staff of the NAACP. Attends conference of the Intercollegiate Socialist Society in Bellport, New York; gives talk on the contribution of the Negro to American culture. With W.E.B. Du Bois, becomes charter member of the Civic Club, a liberal club that grew to be a strong influence in the life of black New Yorkers.

1918 Is responsible for an unprecedented increase in NAACP membership in one year, particularly in the South, making the NAACP a national power.

1919 Participates in converting the National Civil Liberties Bureau into a permanent organization, the American Civil Liberties Union.

1920 NAACP board of directors names him secretary (chief executive officer), making him the first African American to serve in that position. Publishes "Self-Determining Haiti," which draws on his earlier investigation of the American occupation there.

1922 Publishes *The Book of American Negro Poetry.*

1924 Assists several writers of the Harlem Renaissance.

1925 Receives the NAACP's Spingarn Medal. Coauthors, with J. Rosamond Johnson, *The Book of American Negro Spirituals.*

1926 Coauthors, with J. Rosamond Johnson, *The Second Book of*

American Negro Spirituals. Purchases an old farm in the Massachusetts Berkshires and builds a summer cottage called Five Acres.

1927 During the height of the Harlem Renaissance, *The Autobiography of an Ex-Coloured Man* is reprinted. (The spelling "coloured" was used to enhance British sales.) *God's Trombones* is published.

1928 Receives Harmon Award for *God's Trombones.* Receives D. Litt. from Howard University and Talladega College.

1929 Takes a leave of absence from the NAACP. Attends the Third Japanese Biennial Conference on Pacific Relations. Receives Julius Rosenwald Fellowship to write *Black Manhattan.*

1930 *Black Manhattan,* the story of African Americans in New York from the seventeenth century to the 1920s, is published.

1931 Publishes the revised and enlarged edition of *The Book of American Negro Poetry.* NAACP honors him by hosting a testimonial dinner in New York City attended by over 300 guests. Is appointed vice president and board member of the NAACP. Accepts Fisk University appointment as the Adam K. Spence Professor of Creative Literature.

1933 Publishes autobiography, *Along This Way.* Attends the second NAACP Amenia Conference.

1934 Is appointed visiting professor, fall semester, at New York University, becoming the first African American to hold such a position at the institution. Receives the Du Bois Prize for *Black Manhattan* as the best book of prose written by an African American during a three-year period. Publishes *Negro Americans, What Now?*

1935 Publishes *Saint Peter Relates an Incident: Selected Poems.*

1938 Dies June 26 as a result of an automobile accident in Wiscassett, Maine, nine days after his sixty-seventh birthday. Funeral held at the Salem Methodist Church in Harlem on Thursday, June 30. Is cremated.

Mrs. James Weldon Johnson (Grace Nail Johnson) died on November 1, 1976. Grace and James Weldon Johnson were interred together by Ollie Jewel Sims Okala on November 19, 1976, in the Nail family plot in Green-Wood Cemetery, Brooklyn, New York.

PART ONE

DRAMA

DRAMA

James Weldon Johnson wrote in the major genres of literature. The two one-act plays published here for the first time are evidence of a young writer's efforts to master all of the forms available to him. Johnson left behind no commentary on these plays. He seems to have written them and then set them aside as neither, it appears, was ever staged.

It seems reasonable to suppose that *Do You Believe in Ghosts? A Darkey Comedy* was written first, and very probably during the period when the young Johnson returned to Jacksonville in 1894 after his graduation from Atlanta University. The title page of the play contains Johnson's Jacksonville address. He would remain in the city of his birth until he moved to New York in 1902.

The nine-year sojourn in Jacksonville was a very productive period for the future Executive Secretary of the National Association for the Advancement of Colored People (NAACP). During this period, Johnson emerges as a leader in public education for, in 1896, he transforms Stanton School from a primary school to Florida's first public high school for African Americans. Johnson also undertakes and completes his legal studies, becoming the first African American admitted to the Florida bar in 1898. In 1900 Johnson and his younger brother J. Rosamond Johnson compose together their great hymn "Lift Every Voice and Sing." While testing his powers as a lawyer and a composer, Johnson continues to provide leadership in public education in

Florida for, in 1901, he is elected president of the Florida State Teachers Association. He holds this elected position for only one year. Johnson decides to leave Florida after being nearly lynched in a Jacksonville park: a life-threatening experience that revealed to him that Florida would not be the place for the realization of his potential. In 1902 Johnson resigns from his position as principal of Stanton School and moves to New York to pursue his interests in light opera, and where he would establish, with Bob Cole, a singer and composer, and J. Rosamond Johnson, the musical trio Cole and the Johnson Brothers. This, I would like to suggest, is the rich context for the composition of *Do You Believe in Ghosts?*

As a one-act dark comedy, *Do You Believe in Ghosts?* reveals Johnson as a young writer immersed in the cultural life and folk traditions of black Floridians. With more emphasis upon action than dialogue, a fact which gives the actors greater scope to demonstrate their art, Johnson provides us with a particular view into a community he knew and also sought to know better. The view is not stained by minstrelsy and other stereotypical representations of black experience of the period. Rather, Johnson writes with a certain economy and verisimilitude regarding black folk experience and folk beliefs. He anticipates Zora Neale Hurston, another Florida writer, as well as writers Sterling A. Brown, Jean Toomer, and Langston Hughes, who would transmute in alchemical fashion these situations and themes into art within the context of the Harlem Renaissance or New Negro Movement.

The Engineer: A Drama in One Act is the work of a maturing artist in search of forms that would give shape and expression to his restless, fertile imagination. In active pursuit of such forms, in 1903 Johnson enrolled in the Master of Arts program in English at Columbia University, where he came under the influence of Brander Matthews, professor of dramatic literature. Johnson very likely wrote this play during his one year of study as a graduate student. A love story with a bitter, tragic outcome, the play is distinguished by its carefully rendered dialogue. One other remarkable feature is Johnson's ability to capture within the conventions of the one-act play the shifting, complex emotional terrain of his characters, who are released from a ménage à trois through the self-righteous and deluded actions of the lead character.

Located in the James Weldon Johnson Memorial Collection at Yale University, these two plays reveal Johnson as an experimentalist working in one of the major genres of literature. They also are evidence of Johnson's formal and thematic interests at the time—folk drama, folk beliefs, folk culture, love, deception, the dark operations of the heart—all of which would be given a fuller and more sophisticated expression as he continued to develop as an artist. In these early works of drama, published here for the first time, we find evidence of a search for voice and form that fills out the portrait of Johnson as man of letters.

Do You Believe in Ghosts?

A DARKEY COMEDY

SYNOPSIS.

Pegleg Lee (a one legged man) is the "know it all" of the Lime Kiln Club.

One night, after an evening at the club, Brickyard Brown and Whitewash Jones start for home. Near a graveyard they stop while Brickyard lights his pipe. Whitewash looks over his shoulder and sees a ghostly apparition approaching, and, without giving any alarm to Brickyard, makes a quick getaway. The ghost sides up to Brickyard, who, still engaged in lighting his pipe, is all unscious of the change in companions, when, by degrees he becomes aware of it, he outruns the ghost in a race back to the club. There he relates his harrowing experience and all are awestruck except Pegleg, who declares--"Der ain't no such thing as a ghost."--They make a $5.00 wager, and Brickyard, because Pegleg cannot walk the distance, agrees to take him on his back out to the graveyard to convince him and decide the bet. At the crossroads they stop, the ghost appears; Whitewash throws Pegleg off his back and takes the road marked "5miles to Town"; Pegleg, followed by the ghost, takes the road marked "25 miles to Town." Pegleg outruns the ghost and beats #### Brickyard back to the club.

CAST.

PEGLEG LEE (The "know it all".)
BROTHER BRICKYARD BROWN
BROTHER WHITEWASH JONES
THE GHOST
Members of the Lime Kiln Club.-

(Note)----Whitewash Jones is a whitewasher by trade and his hat and clothes are so covered with lime that Pegleg mistakes him for the ghost in Scene No. 24---)

SCENE PLOT

INTERIORS

LIME KILN CLUB- 1- 3- 5- 11- 13- 15- 26- 28-

EXTERIORS

CLUB- 4- 25- 27-
ROADS- 6- 8- 9- 10- 17- 18- 20- 21- 22- 24-
CROSSROADS- 14- 16-
FIELD of BUSHES- 12-
CLOSE UP- 2- 7- 19- 23-

ACTION

Scene 1- INTERIOR LIME KILN SOCIAL CLUB-
Brickyard at side table dozes- bottle labeled "GIN" on table- Whitewash playing checkers with member- Checker board on box or barrel- Pegleg watching game- criticises moves of member- member registers "If you know so much about checkers, you win a game"- Pegleg takes member's place- All members group around- Whitewash jumps all over board- blocks Pegleg- Whitewash and all members give Pegleg the ha, ha,- - -laughter wakes Brickyard-

Scene 2- Close up of Brickyard-
Brickyard yawns- stretches- looks at watch-

Scene 3- Same as No. 1- (INT. CLUB)

Brickyard stretches- gets up- takes large drink- persuades Whitewash to go- Pegleg still studying checkerboard- Whitewash laughs slyly at Pegleg- gets up- Brickyard and Whitewash exit-

Scene 4- EXTERIOR CLUB (NIGHT)

Brickyard and Whitewash come from club- exit-

Scene 5- Same as No. 1- (INT. CLUB)

Pegleg studying board- Other members holding dancing contest-

Scene 6- ROAD and GRAVEYARD.

Brickyard and Whitewash coming toward camera joking- stop- Brickyard borrows match- lights pipe- Whitewash looks- sees ghost over shoulder- makes quick getaway- Whitewash- laughs heartily- Ghost stands close beside him- Brickyard sees something from corner of eye- not sure what it is- afraid to look-

Scene 7- Close up of Brickyard and Ghost.

Brickyard wants to look- rolls eyes- afraid to turn full on- expression going from curiosity to terror-

Scene 8- Back to No. 6- (ROAD and GRAVEYARD)

Brickyard makes sneak motion-to run- ghost mimics his movements- Brickyard gets square look- oh horror!- grabs hat- runs- ghost follows up road-

Scene 9- ROAD-

Brickyard runs through rapidly- ghost follows closely-

Scene 10- ROAD-

Brickyard runs through- ghost lagging behind-

Scene 11- Same as No. 1- (INT. CLUB)

Pegleg still studying board- others playing cards- Brickyard bursts in- tells about ghost- all members except Pegleg awestruck- Pegleg poo poos-

Scene 12- FIELD-
Whitewash running through bushes-
LEADER- "Der ain't no such thing as ghosts"

Scene 13- Back to No. 11- (INT. CLUB)
Pegleg expresses incredulity- bets $5.00 with Brickyard- Brickyard says "Come on"- Pegleg says "can't on account of leg".
CUT IN--- "Come on, I'll carry you."
Back to scene- Brickyard takes Pegleg on back and exits-

Scene 14- CROSSROADS- -Sign with two hands pointing opposite directions to read--"5 miles to town"--"25 miles to town."
Brickyard carrying Pegleg on back enters coming toward camera- sees sign- stops- points to different distances-

Scene 15- Same as No. 13- (INT. CLUB)
Members discussing affair-

Scene 16- Same as No. 14- (CROSSROADS with signs indicating different roads.)
Brickyard looks- points- Pegleg peers- shakes head- ghost in distance approaches- Brickyard throws Pegleg off back- runs in 5 mile direction- Pegleg scrambles up and runs in 25- mile direction- ghost follows Pegleg-

Scene 17- ROAD
Brickyard runs through-

Scene 18- ANOTHER ROAD-
Pegleg running through- stops- takes off hat- fans himself-
CUT IN--- "I sho' was going some to beat dat ghost."-

Scene 19- Close up of Pegleg-
Blowing and fanning- smiles and congratulates himself-

Scene 20- Back to No. 18- (ROAD)
Pegleg still fanning- ghost approaching- Pegleg starts to sit down- sees ghost over shoulder- runs- ghost follows-
LEADER- "But I'se gwinter go some mo'."

Scene 21- ROAD-

Pegleg hopping through- ghost growing weary-

Scene 22- ROAD-

Pegleg hops in- stops- puffs and blows- fans with hat-

Scene 23- Close up of Pegleg-

Fanning and blowing- notes some noise and commotion-

Scene 24- Back to No. 22- (ROAD)

Watches intently object moving in bushes behind him- Whitewashes runs thru bushes- he emerges into road running- Pegleg starts out afresh-

CUT IN--- "Lordy, dat ghost done run tell he's black in de face!"- - - Good-bye!"

Back to scene- Pegleg hopping through-

Scene 25- EXTERIOR of CLUB - Same as No. 4-

Pegleg hops in- bursts through door-

Scene 26- Same as No. 1- (INT. CLUB)

Members still discussing- Pegleg bursts in- great excitement-

Scene 27- EXTERIOR of CLUB- Same as No. 4-

Whitewash rushes in- bursts through door-

Scene 28- INTERIOR of CLUB - Same as No. 1-

Peg- Pegleg telling members- Whitewash bursts in- sees Pegleg- looks- points- rubs eyes- Speaks- feels Peg's leg-

CUT IN--- "Brother, how did you keep dat stump from catching afire?"-

Back to scene- both talking at once- stakeholder hands money to Brickyard- Brickyard gives it to Pegleg- Keep it- you deserve it- they shake hands- Whitewash - tongue hanging out falls in door-

CURTAIN

"The Engineer"

A DRAMA IN ONE ACT

Adapted by James Weldon Johnson

DRAMATIS PERSONAE

PAUL WESTON . . . . . An Engineer.
CORA . . . . His young Wife.

(*Humble room in Paul's cottage. Present time. Window to right. Door at back. Chimney at left.*)

CORA (*Seated near the chimney; she appears nervous and pensive. Suddenly listens at the window.*) --Let me see --- I thought I heard him coming---- But, no; he always lets me know by singing---- He won't be long now --- I want to see him come, and I'm afraid, for this will be the last night. I can't any longer. I've made up my mind. --- (*Pause.*)--- It's cold --- This fire don't burn. It don't give any heat --- Maybe it's because I can't feel it ---- The ice in my heart won't let me ---- Oh, I'm so wretched! The train will soon pass through the cut, and my poor Paul will be on it, shut up in that hellish engine, as he says, with his thoughts always on me. Oh I'm so wretched! This deception is weighing on me too much. I can't add any more days of sin to it. The last!--The last! ------- Hush! --- I thought I heard him singing again. --- No it is the wind. --- (*She remains pensive.*)

(*Enter Paul by the door, smiling and cheerful. He stops a moment contemplating Cora.*)

PAUL (*She little thinks that I am here.*)-----

CORA Oh, it's terrible! It's awful! Paul don't deserve this----

PAUL I wonder if she's thinking of me----who can tell----Who can tell what a woman thinks? --(*He approaches her quietly and puts his arms around her.*)--

CORA (*With surprise and terror.*) --Paul! Paul! Is it you?

PAUL Yes, darling, it's me!

CORA Oh, God!

PAUL It's me, your Paul. He who thinks about you all the time. Who can't live without you---But--What has happened? What's the matter? --Oh, yes, the natural fright and surprise of seeing me when you thought I was still in my hell --- so many miles away---

CORA Yes, yes --- that is it---

PAUL Just fright from joy, eh, sweetheart?

CORA You understand --- to see you at this time --- to see you home at this time --- (*Oh God!*)

PAUL I'll explain it to you, but you mustn't quarrel with me.

CORA What do you mean?

PAUL You must pardon me before hand---Do you pardon me?

CORA -- I pardon ---- you? ---- Pardon you?

PAUL Yes, for the sin of loving you so much, Listen!

CORA What have you done?

PAUL What has been in my head and my heart for a long time. To leave the hateful engine cab, which seemed to hold me like a slave.

CORA Eh?

PAUL Yes, at last I have done it. I've done it at last.

CORA Paul, have you gone crazy?

PAUL It's because I didn't want to go crazy that I did it --- But, you are still nervous?

CORA No --- no------

PAUL Well, by the suffering of your own heart imagine mine --- How did you feel - - - you who love me so--- to never see me at home? When up from the out you heard through the window the whistle of my engine like a moan --- a moan from me? How did you feel to see the train going by, indifferent to everything --- farther and farther --- groaning and roaring over the rails, which seemed to have no end? Didn't your heart go along with it? ----- Didn't you wish for wings to be able to follow it and keep my company? Then imagine how I felt ---- Shut up all night in that oven --- the wind cutting me and the fire burning me -- and going, ---- going, -- passing through the cut like a flash of lightning -- looking up and seeing my little house alone on the hill, thinking of my little wife here, and losing sight of it all, before the thought got through my mind. And then going and going, deafened by the rumble of the train, alone, always alone --- with no other hope than to arrive at a station --- and then not to see you --- to leave and arrive at another -- and still not to see you--- Do you think that was life?

CORA I think as you think --- as you say -- but what can be done,- it was your work -- Paul --it was your work.

PAUL But a work I don't love. I'll find a way. I'm young -- I'm strong. There are factories in the town. I'll work, but I'll work with you. That distance which the train put between us, I couldn't stand any longer. Don't you see that every minute of the run seemed to separate me from you by a century?

CORA Yes, I see, I see it all. I, too, want you always close to me. Oh, I wish that we never had been separated!

PAUL You don't know how strong it makes me to hear you say that. - (*Puts his arm around her waist, and leads her to a seat by the fire.*)-- Come, let's sit down -- Ah, this is warmth, not the infernal heat of the engine. But, why aren't you happy?

CORA I'm sad to-night. I don't know why, but, Paul, I'm sad.

PAUL How can you be sad when you have me here with you? What reason for sadness can be between us? I swear I don't know how I could wait so long without deciding. How many times haven't I said to myself--- "Great God! why do I lead this black life of a slave, when on the hill there I have what few men have, a home and love and light." --(*Noticing Cora who in spite of her efforts cannot keep back the tears.*) -- But, you're crying. Why what's the matter girl?---- Why're you crying?

(*In the distance is heard the voice of a man singing, who seems to be approaching the house.*)

VOICE "I know a girl who loves me
A girl for whom I pine;
I know a girl who loves me,
And I know her heart is mine."

CORA (*Giving a start and a low cry as soon as she hears the voice.*) --Oh!

PAUL (*With surprise.*) --What's that!

CORA Nothing ------ Nothing!

PAUL What's the matter girl? ---- Why are you frightened? (*Listens to song coming nearer with surprise and perplexity.*) --Who's going around here at this hour of the night?

CORA How do I know? --- How do you expect me to know?---- Paul

PAUL But you are trembling; Look at me!

CORA (*With a cry.*) --Paul!

PAUL (*Taking hold of her.*) --Cora! Cora! What is this? By chance you----? Is that man coming here----? What is this? Speak! Speak!

CORA I tell you I don't know --- I don't know---

PAUL (*With irony.*) --You don't know. Do you know why you're trembling? Why you can't look me in the eyes?

CORA I'll go and see --Let me go!-----

PAUL (*Very calmly.*) --No, you stay here! If the singer is coming here, let him come in!

CORA Paul! Paul!

PAUL (*Holding her fast, but keeping his eyes fixed on the door.*) --Quiet! You keep quiet. What are you afraid of?

CORA (*Swooning.*) --Paul, forgive me! Forgive me!

PAUL (*Thrusting her suddenly from him. She grovels at his feet in terror.*) --Forgive? I forgive you? --Oh, my God! ---- No, no, it's not true --- it can't be true ----I won't believe it --- (*Coming closer down to her.*) Tell me it isn't true, Cora. Tell me I'm dreaming.

(*The voice is heard singing nearer. Paul strains to listen. He trembles.*) --Ah! --- no, it's not a dream! ---Damn you! --(*He starts toward Cora as though to strangle her, but restrains himself*) -- No, not yet, not yet! --(*The voice approaches singing nearer still. Cora swoons. Paul goes mechanically towards the door, then struck by a new idea goes softly to a drawer searching for a weapon -- he finds none.*) --I've got no arms, why should I have when I never thought I'd need one. --(*Suddenly bursts into tears.*)-- Miserable -- I'm more miserable than these two wretches! --(*He pauses as the song begins again, now at the very porch of the house. Paul frenzied but determined slips cautiously out of the door. A moment later the voice of the singer, who seems to have reached the very door, is suddenly choked off in the middle of the third line of the song. Faint sounds of a struggle. Another pause. The shrill whistle of the locomotive is heard far off. Then heavy, rapid strides of a man are heard on the porch, receding farther and farther from the house until lost in the distance. Then the loud whistle of the locomotive and rumble of the train as it passes thru the cut. Another pause. Then footsteps approaching nearer and nearer the house 'till Paul, bearing the signs of a struggle and like a madman bursts into the room. He goes over to Cora, shakes her brutally and shouts.*) --Cora! Cora! Wake up!

CORA (*Coming to herself.*) --What? ----- What?----

PAUL It's me! It's me! Your Paul, as you used to call me. (*Answering a glance of Cora's eyes.*) --No, you needn't look for him. You'll never see him again. Don't look for him.

CORA What have you done?

PAUL What I had to do, kill him!

CORA Kill him?

PAUL Yes, kill him! What less! --(*Rapidly and dramatically*) I went out crazy, trembling with pain and anger, I met him already at the door --- I fell on him like a tiger. I clutched him around the neck, and strangled the infamous song in his throat. He tried to defend himself, his strength rallied, he was strong--- we struggled --- the struggle was unequal --- I had right and just revenge on my side, while he carried the weight of surprise and sin, and so I overcame him. Soon the train blew, far off --- I saw a terrible thought flash into his glazed eyes. Horrible! ---- It was his own idea. He gave it to me. I struggled with him to the edge of the cut and threw him over. He fell, just as the train --*my train* passed and there he is.

CORA (*With her hands over her eyes.*) --Horrible!

PAUL Horrible, you say. What shall I say?

CORA (*With fear in her eyes.*) --Paul!

PAUL Don't be afraid, I'm not going to kill you. No you shall stay here, alone, always alone --- weeping tears that will burn your eyes and into your heart. I'm going back down to the train --- to my loyal friend whom I left, but who revenged my wrong. Back to the iron platform --- to pass again and again, roaring and spitting out fire and curses over the black stain that his blood left on the rails. (*Laughing like a maniac.*) --Ha! Ha! Ha! --- Good-bye Cora!

CORA (*Struggling to her feet and screaming.*) --Paul! Paul!

PAUL Good-bye! --(*Exits slamming the door.*)

CURTAIN.

PART TWO

FICTION

FICTION: *THE AUTOBIOGRAPHY OF AN EX-COLOURED MAN*

In 1905 Johnson shared the first two chapters of *The Autobiography of an Ex-Coloured Man* with Brander Matthews, professor of dramatic literature at Columbia University. At the time, Johnson was a student of Matthews in the graduate program and they would develop what Johnson later described as "a warm and lasting friendship." Matthews admired the concept, the prose, and the proposed title of the novel, and also stated that Johnson had exercised sound judgment in "writing about the thing [he] knew best." Johnson continued to write the novel as Consul General of Venezuela, his first appointment in the consular service. The relaxed regimen of daily life in Caracas gave Johnson much time to write; indeed, the consular service was particularly attractive to Johnson because of the opportunities it afforded him to pursue his writing. When *The Autobiography of an Ex-Coloured Man* was published in Boston in 1912, Johnson was contending with a revolution in Nicaragua, where he was Consul General, his second and last appointment in the U.S. diplomatic service.

Prior to his experiments with fiction, Johnson had written primarily poetry and light opera. In the writing of *The Autobiography of an Ex-Coloured Man* he was struck by the expansive medium of prose. "The use of prose as a creative medium was new to me; and its latitude, its flexibility, its comprehensiveness," recalls Johnson, "the variety of approaches it afforded for surmounting technical difficulties gave me a feeling of exhilaration, exhilaration similar to that which goes with freedom of motion." After completing the novel, Johnson reconsidered the title at the behest of his younger brother J. Rosamond Johnson, who suggested the alternative *The Chamelon.* In due course, however, Johnson decided to retain the original title, notwithstanding the fact that his brother regarded it as "clumsy and too long."

Although the novel received uniformly positive reviews in the United States and England, Johnson was somewhat unprepared for the confusion the novel generated. Some reviewers were persuaded that the novel was a genuine autobiography; this Johnson believed "was a tribute to the writing." He also was amused by the speculations, fictions, and mystifications the novel set in motion among many black readers. Johnson once had the bizarre experience of "being introduced to and talking with one man who tacitly admitted to those present that he was the author of the book." A different species of confusion entered the world of letters when the novel was reprinted in 1927. Then at the height of his powers as head of the National Association for the Advancement of Colored People and an architect of the Harlem Renaissance, Johnson made the strategic decision to pull back the veil of anonymity and to reveal himself as the author. During this period in the novel's history, he received many letters from readers inquiring about "this or that phase of my life as told" in the novel. Johnson states that such confusion was one possible motivation for writing his autobiography, *Along This Way.*

While fiction, *The Autobiography of an Ex-Coloured Man* does contain autobiographical elements. First, the novel is set in Atlanta, the home of Johnson's alma mater, Atlanta University, now Clark-Atlanta University. As compared with his native Jacksonville, Atlanta disappointed Johnson: "The city was neither picturesque nor smart; it was merely drab." This disappointment is captured in the novel's unflattering descriptions of the city's red clay roads; what Johnson terms elsewhere as "the bloody aspect of Atlanta's highways." Further, the model for the novel's protagonist is based upon Johnson's childhood friend, roommate at Atlanta University, and former law partner "D—," or J. Douglas Whetmore. Like the protagonist, Whetmore worked in a cigar factory in Tampa, Florida, a family-owned business. Although Whetmore passed for white and married a Jewess, he never shunned Johnson or his other black friends. Describing the ways in which Whetmore maintained connections in both the black and white worlds, Johnson observed: "D— was, so far as I can remember, the only man I have known to 'pass'—and I have known numbers of them—without feeling it was necessary to 'pass up' his colored friends." Unlike his fictional counterpart, Whetmore would commit suicide, shooting himself in the heart. Relatedly, the portrait of black bohemia, which achieves its most concentrated expression in the treatment of the Club, is based upon Johnson's personal knowledge of a number of such clubs in Harlem, particularly one owned and operated by Ike Hines. Finally, the model for the protagonist's patron is Dr. T. O. Summers, a white surgeon in Jacksonville whom Johnson describes as his "model of all that a man and a gentleman should be." Like Summers, the patron's marked degree of alienation is manifest in his addiction to ether, which culminates in suicide.

Prior to the novel's reprinting by Alfred A. Knopf Publishers in 1927, Carl Van Vechten, a patron of the Harlem Renaissance and author of *Nigger Heaven* and other novels, wrote to Johnson in 1925 to share his estimation of the novel: "It is a remarkable book in more ways than one, but in no way more so than in the gentle irony which informs the pages from beginning to end. You have said everything there was to say and said it without passion. The book lacks, I think, sufficient narrative interest; the hero might have had more personal experiences, but after all you were chiefly concerned with presenting facts about Negro life in an agreeable form, through the eyes of a witness who had no reason personally to be particularly disturbed." The artist Aaron Douglass, who had been contracted by Knopf to design the book cover of the second edition, expressed the following views of the novel in a letter to Johnson: "I have just finished reading the book and I am carried away with amazement and admiration. Your depth of thought, breadth of vision, and subtlety and beauty of expression awakens in me the greatest admiration. I am amazed at the gigantic effort which must have been necessary for the writing and publishing of the book at such an early date." When Knopf decided to print yet another edition of the novel in 1937, Van Vechten, pleased about the novel's reception in the last decade, wrote to Johnson stating that the 1927 edition, with its author's preface and the introduction by Van Vechten, should stand unaltered. It is the 1927 edition that is reprinted here, along with Johnson's original preface and Van Vechten's introduction. Van Vechten ended his letter to Johnson with this prediction: "I foresee a long career for this little book which has already had so many adventures."

In his own correspondence with Johnson, the poet and critic Sterling A. Brown offered this assessment of the novel's achievement, one which expresses the justification for its enduring relevance and canonical status: In "*The Autobiography of an Ex-Coloured Man* [you reveal] a breadth of knowledge concerning the Negro problem in all its ramifications, and a power both analytic and prophetic. In this book might be found the germinal idea of many later books dealing with the Negro."

The Autobiography of an Ex-Coloured Man has achieved the status of a permanent work of literature for many reasons. First, Johnson reveals himself as an experimentalist for he masterfully combines the genres of fiction and autobiography. Further, the novel, which possesses aspects of the slave narrative, provides us with a means of mapping the evolution of the African American literary tradition. Relatedly, Johnson is in conversation with W.E.B. Du Bois's *The Souls of Black Folk*, for the protagonist embodies the "double aims" of Du Bois's theory of "double consciousness." Johnson also provides us with a pioneering treatment of black bohemia; thus, the novel serves as a model for many writers of the Harlem Renaissance who were searching for ways to capture and define the new cultural formations of black America. Johnson also complicates the portrayal of the social phenomenon of passing and the figure of the mulatto, thus preparing the ground for such works as Jean Toomer's *Cane*, Nella Larsen's *Passing*, Zora Neale Hurston's *Their Eyes Were Watching God*, Charles Johnson's *Oxherding Tale*, and Edward Jones's *The Known World*. Finally, Johnson's protagonist has come to symbolize aspects of African American experience within the shifting and complex framework of modernism. Johnson's protagonist and the dynamic, known world in which he moves are defined by hybridity, migration, dislocation, and alienation: elements that have defined the experience of persons of African descent since the Enlightenment, and that endow *The Autobiography of an Ex-Coloured Man* with a profoundly contemporary cast.

Summoning again and recasting Sterling Brown's 1937 assessment of Johnson's highly influential novel, "[I]n this book [one finds] the germinal idea of many later books dealing with the Negro." It is this catalytic dimension combined with Johnson's gift for narrative and the creation of a character who embodies many of the paradigmatic aspects of African American life and culture that accounts for the canonical status of *The Autobiography of an Ex-Coloured Man*.

INTRODUCTION TO MR. KNOPF'S NEW EDITION

The Autobiography of an Ex-Coloured Man is, I am convinced, a remarkable book. I have read it three times and at each rereading I have found it more remarkable. Published in 1912, it then stood almost alone as an inclusive survey of racial accomplishments and traits, as an interpretation of the feelings of the Negro towards the white man and towards the members of his own race. Written, I believe, while Mr. James Weldon Johnson was U.S. Consul to Nicaragua, it was issued anonymously. The publishers attempted to persuade the author to sign a statement to the effect that the book was an actual human document. This he naturally refused to do. Nevertheless, the work was hailed on every side, for the most part, as an individual's true story.

The *Autobiography*, of course, in the matter of specific incident, has little enough to do with Mr. Johnson's own life, but it is imbued with his own personality and feeling, his *views* of the subjects discussed, so that to a person who has no previous knowledge of the author's own history, it reads like *real* autobiography. It would be truer, perhaps, to say that it reads like a composite autobiography of the Negro race in the United States in modern times.

It is surprising how little the book has dated in fifteen years. Very little that Mr. Johnson wrote then is not equally valid today, although in those remote times he found it necessary when he mentioned Negroes in evening clothes to add that they were not hired! On the other hand it is cheering to discover how much has been accomplished by the race in New York alone since the book was originally published. Then there was no Harlem—the Negro lived below Fifty-ninth Street. To encounter the cultured, respectable class of Negro one was obliged to visit Brooklyn. In the very few years since this epoch the great city beyond the Park has sprung into being, a city which boasts not only its own cabarets and gamblers, but also its intelligentsia, its rich and cultured group, its physicians, its attorneys, its educators, its large, respectable middle class, its churches, its hospitals, its theatres, its library, and its business houses. It would be possible to name fifty names such as those of Paul Robeson, Langston Hughes, Charles Gilpin, Walter White, Rudolph Fisher, Countée Cullen, Florence Mills, Ethel Waters, Aaron Douglas, Taylor Gordon and Jean Toomer, all of whom have made their mark in the artistic world within the past five years.

When I was writing *Nigger Heaven* I discovered the *Autobiography* to be an invaluable source-book for the study of Negro psychology. I believe it will be a long time before anybody can write about the Negro without consulting Mr. Johnson's pages to advantage. Naturally, the *Autobiography* had its precursors. Booker T. Washington's *Up from Slavery* (1900) is a splendid example of autobiography, but the limitations of his subject matter made it impossible for Dr. Washington to survey the field as broadly as Mr. Johnson, setting himself no limitations, could. Dr. Du Bois's important work, *The Souls of Black Folk* (1903) does, certainly, explore a wide territory, but these essays lack the insinuating influence of Mr. Johnson's calm, dispassionate tone, and they do not offer, in certain important respects, so revealing a portrait of Negro character. Charles W. Chesnutt, in his interesting novel, *The House Behind the Cedars* (1900), contributed to literature perhaps the first authentic study on the subject of "passing," and Paul Laurence Dunbar, in *The Sport of the Gods,* described the plight of a young outsider who comes to the larger New York Negro world to make his fortune, but who falls a victim to the sordid snares of that world, a theme I elaborated in 1926 to fit a newer and much more intricate social system.

Mr. Johnson, however, chose an all-embracing scheme. His young hero, the ostensible author, either discusses (or lives) pretty nearly every phase of Negro life, North and South and even in Europe, available to him at that period. That he "passes" the title indicates. Miscegenation in its slave and also its more modern aspects, both casual and marital, is competently treated. The ability of the Negro to mask his real feelings with a joke or a laugh in the presence of the inimical white man is here noted, for the first time in print, I should imagine. Negro adaptability, touchiness, and jealousy are referred to in an unself-conscious manner, totally novel in Negro writing at the time this book originally appeared. The hero declares: "It may be said that the majority of intelligent coloured people are, in some degree, too much in earnest over the race question. They assume and carry so much that their progress is at times impeded and they are unable to see things in their proper proportions. In many instances a slight exercise of the sense of humour would save much anxiety of soul." Jim Crow cars, crap-shooting, and the cake-walk are inimitably described. Colour snobbery within the race is freely spoken of, together with the economic pressure from without which creates this false condition. There is a fine passage devoted to the celebration of the Negro Spirituals and there is an excellent account of a Southern camp-meeting, together with a transcript of a typical oldtime Negro sermon. There is even a lynching.

But it is chiefly remarkable to find James Weldon Johnson in 1912, five or six years before the rest of us began to shout about it, singing hosannas to rag-time (jazz was unknown then). It is simply astonishing to discover in this book, issued the year after "Alexander's Ragtime Band" and the same year that "The Memphis Blues" were published, such a statement as this:

"American musicians, instead of investigating rag-time, attempt to ignore it, or dismiss it with a contemptuous word. But that has always been the course of scholasticism in every branch of art. Whatever new thing the *people* like is pooh-poohed; whatever is *popular* is spoken of as not worth the while. The fact is, nothing great or enduring, especially in music, has ever sprung full-fledged and unprecedented from the brain of any master; the best that he gives to the world he gathers from the hearts of the people, and runs it through the alembic of his genius." So the young hero of this *Autobiography* determines to develop the popular music of his people into a more serious form, thus foreseeing by twelve years the creation of *Rhapsody in Blue* by George Gershwin.

Sherman, French and Co., published the *Autobiography* in Boston in 1912. When, a few years later, they retired from business it was out of print and, although constantly in demand and practically unprocurable, it has remained out of print until now when Alfred A. Knopf, justifiably, I believe, has seen fit to include it in his Blue Jade series. New readers, I am confident, will examine this book with interest: some to acquire through its mellow pages a new conception of how a coloured man lives and feels, others simply to follow the course of its fascinating story.

CARL VAN VECHTEN
New York
March 1, 1927

PREFACE TO THE ORIGINAL EDITION OF 1912

This vivid and startlingly new picture of conditions brought about by the race question in the United States makes no special plea for the Negro, but shows in a dispassionate, though sympathetic, manner conditions as they actually exist between the whites and blacks today. Special pleas have already been made for and against the Negro in hundreds of books, but in these books either his virtues or his vices have been exaggerated. This is because writers, in nearly every instance, have treated the coloured American as a *whole;* each has taken some one group of the race to prove his case. Not before has a composite and proportionate presentation of the entire race, embracing all of its various groups and elements, showing their relations with each other and to the whites, been made.

It is very likely that the Negroes of the United States have a fairly correct idea of what the white people of the country think of them, for that opinion has for a long time been and is still being constantly stated; but they are themselves more or less a sphinx to the whites. It is curiously interesting and even vitally important to know what are the thoughts of ten millions of them concerning the people among whom they live. In these pages it is as though a veil had been drawn aside: the reader is given a view of the inner life of the Negro in America, is initiated into the free-masonry, as it were, of the race.

These pages also reveal the unsuspected fact that prejudice against the Negro is exerting a pressure which, in New York and other large cities where the opportunity is open, is actually and constantly forcing an unascertainable number of fair-complexioned coloured people over into the white race.

In this book the reader is given a glimpse behind the scenes of this race drama which is being here enacted—he is taken upon an elevation where he can catch a bird's-eye view of the conflict which is being waged.

THE PUBLISHERS
[SHERMAN, FRENCH AND CO.]

The Autobiography of an Ex-Coloured Man

CHAPTER I

I know that in writing the following pages I am divulging the great secret of my life, the secret which for some years I have guarded far more carefully than any of my earthly possessions; and it is a curious study to me to analyse the motives which prompt me to do it. I feel that I am led by the same impulse which forces the un-found-out criminal to take somebody into his confidence, although he knows that the act is likely, even almost certain, to lead to his undoing. I know that I am playing with fire, and I feel the thrill which accompanies that most fascinating pastime; and, back of it all, I think I find a sort of savage and diabolical desire to gather up all the little tragedies of my life, and turn them into a practical joke on society.

And, too, I suffer a vague feeling of unsatisfaction, of regret, of almost remorse, from which I am seeking relief, and of which I shall speak in the last paragraph of this account.

I was born in a little town of Georgia a few years after the close of the Civil War. I shall not mention the name of the town, because there are people still living there who could be connected with this narrative. I have only a faint recollection of the place of my birth. At times I can close my eyes and call up in a dreamlike way things that seem to have happened ages ago in some other world. I can see in this half vision a little house—I am quite sure it was not a large one—I can remember that flowers grew in the front yard, and that around each bed of flowers was a hedge of vari-coloured glass bottles stuck in the ground neck down. I remember that once, while playing round in the sand, I became curious to know whether or not the bottles grew as the flowers did, and I proceeded to dig them up to find out; the investigation brought me a terrific spanking, which indelibly fixed the incident in my mind. I can remember, too, that behind the house was a shed under which stood two or three wooden wash-tubs. These tubs were the earliest aversion of my life, for regularly on certain evenings I was plunged into one of them and scrubbed until my skin ached. I can remember to this day the pain caused by the strong, rank soap's getting into my eyes.

Back from the house a vegetable garden ran, perhaps seventy-five or one hundred feet; but to my childish fancy it was an endless territory. I can still recall the thrill of joy, excitement, and wonder it gave me to go on an exploring expedition through it, to find the blackberries, both ripe and green, that grew along the edge of the fence.

I remember with what pleasure I used to arrive at, and stand before, a little enclosure in which stood a patient cow chewing her cud, how I would occasionally offer her through the bars a piece of my bread and molasses, and how I would jerk back my hand in half fright if she made any motion to accept my offer.

I have a dim recollection of several people who moved in and about this little house, but I have a distinct mental image of only two: one, my mother; and the other, a tall man with a small, dark moustache. I remember that his shoes or boots were always shiny, and that he wore a gold chain and a great gold watch with which he was always willing to let me play. My admiration was almost equally divided between the watch and chain and the shoes. He used to come to the house evenings, perhaps two or three times a week; and it became my appointed duty whenever he came to bring him a pair of slippers and to put the shiny shoes in a particular corner; he often gave me in return for this service a bright coin, which my mother taught me to promptly drop in a little tin bank. I remember distinctly the last time this tall man came to the little house in Georgia; that evening before I went to bed he took me up in his arms and squeezed me very tightly; my mother stood behind his chair wiping tears from her eyes. I remember how I sat upon his knee and watched him laboriously drill a hole through a ten-dollar gold piece, and then tie the coin around my neck with a string. I have worn that gold piece around my neck the greater part of my life, and still possess it, but more than once I have wished that some other way had been found of attaching it to me besides putting a hole through it.

On the day after the coin was put around my neck my mother and I started on what seemed to me an endless journey. I knelt on the seat and watched through the train window the corn- and cotton-fields pass swiftly by until I fell asleep. When I fully awoke, we were being driven through the streets of a large city—Savannah. I sat up and blinked at the bright lights. At Savannah we boarded a steamer which finally landed us in New York. From New York we went to a town in Connecticut, which became the home of my boyhood.

My mother and I lived together in a little cottage which seemed to me to be fitted up almost luxuriously; there were horse-hair covered chairs in the parlour, and a little square piano; there was a stairway with red carpet on it leading to a half second story; there were pictures on the walls, and a few books in a glass-doored case. My mother dressed me very neatly, and I developed that pride which well-dressed boys generally have. She was careful about my associates, and I myself was quite particular. As I look back now I can see that I was a perfect little aristocrat. My mother rarely went to anyone's house, but she did sewing, and there were a great many ladies coming to our cottage. If I was round they would generally call me, and ask me my name and age and tell my mother what a pretty boy I was. Some of them would pat me on the head and kiss me.

My mother was kept very busy with her sewing; sometimes she would have another woman helping her. I think she must have derived a fair income from her work. I know, too, that at least once each month she received a letter; I used to watch for the postman, get the letter, and run to her with it; whether she was busy or not, she would take it and instantly thrust it into her bosom. I never saw her read one of these letters. I knew later that they contained money and what was to her more than money. As busy as she generally was, she found time, however, to teach me my letters and figures and how to spell a number of easy words. Always on Sunday evenings she opened the little square piano and picked out hymns. I can recall now that whenever she played hymns from the book her *tempo* was always decidedly *largo*. Sometimes on other evenings, when she was not sewing, she would play simple accompaniments to some old Southern songs which she sang. In these songs she was freer, because she played them by ear. Those evenings on which she opened the little piano were the happiest hours of my childhood. Whenever she started toward the instrument, I used to follow her with all the interest and irrepressible joy that a pampered pet dog shows when a package is opened in which he knows there is a sweet bit for him. I used to stand by her side and often interrupt and annoy her by chiming in with strange harmonies which I found on either the high keys of the treble or the low keys of the bass. I remember that I had a particular fondness for the black keys. Always on such evenings, when the music was over, my mother would sit with me in her arms, often for a very long time. She would hold me close, softly crooning some old melody without words, all the while gently stroking her face against my head; many and many a night I thus fell asleep. I can see her now, her great dark eyes looking into the fire, to where? No one knew but her. The memory of that picture has more than once kept me from straying too far from the place of purity and safety in which her arms held me.

At a very early age I began to thump on the piano alone, and it was not long before I was able to pick out a few tunes. When I was seven years old, I could play by ear all of the hymns and songs that my mother knew. I had also learned the names of the notes in both clefs, but I preferred not to be hampered by notes. About this time several ladies for whom my mother sewed heard me play and they persuaded her that I should at once be put under a teacher; so arrangements were made for me to study the piano with a lady who was a fairly good musician; at the same time arrangements were made for me to study my books with this lady's daughter. My music teacher had no small difficulty at first in pinning me down to the notes. If she played my lesson over for me, I invariably attempted to reproduce the required sounds without the slightest recourse to the written characters. Her daughter, my other teacher, also had her worries. She found that, in reading, whenever I came to words that were difficult or unfamiliar, I was prone to bring my imagination to the rescue and read from the picture. She has laughingly told me, since then, that I would sometimes substitute whole sentences and even paragraphs from what meaning I thought the illustrations conveyed. She said she not only was sometimes amused at the fresh treatment I would give an author's subject, but, when I gave some new and sudden turn to the plot of the story, often grew interested and even excited in listening to hear what kind of a denouement I would bring about. But I am sure this was not due to dullness, for I made rapid progress in both my music and my books.

And so for a couple of years my life was divided between my music and my school-books. Music took up the greater part of my time. I had no playmates, but amused myself with games—some of them my own invention—which could be played alone. I knew a few boys whom I had met at the church which I attended with my mother, but I had formed no close friendships with any of them. Then, when I was nine years old, my mother decided to enter me in the public school, so all at once I found myself thrown among a crowd of boys of all sizes and kinds; some of them seemed to me like savages. I shall never forget the bewilderment, the pain, the heart-sickness, of that first day at school. I seemed to be the only stranger in the place; every other boy seemed to know every other boy. I was fortunate enough, however, to be assigned to a teacher who knew me; my mother made her dresses. She was one of the ladies who used to pat me on the head and kiss me. She had the tact to address a few words directly to me; this gave me a certain sort of standing in the class and put me somewhat at ease.

Within a few days I had made one staunch friend and was on fairly good terms with most of the boys. I was shy of the girls, and remained so; even now a word or look from a pretty woman sets me all a-tremble. This friend I bound to me with hooks of steel in a very simple way. He was a big awkward boy with a face full of freckles and a head full of very red hair. He was perhaps fourteen years of age; that is, four or five years older than any other boy in the class. This seniority was due to the fact that he had spent twice the required amount of time in several of the preceding classes. I had not been at school many hours before I felt that "Red Head"—as I involuntarily called him—and I were to be friends. I do not doubt that this feeling was strengthened by the fact that I had been quick enough to see that a big, strong boy was a friend to be desired at a public school; and, perhaps, in spite of his dullness, "Red Head" had been able to discern that I could be of service to him. At any rate there was a simultaneous mutual attraction.

The teacher had strung the class promiscuously round the walls of the room for a sort of trial heat for places of rank; when the line was straightened out, I found that by skilful manœuvring I had placed myself third and had piloted "Red Head" to the place next to me. The teacher began by giving us to spell the words corresponding to our order in the line. "Spell *first.*" "Spell *second.*" "Spell *third.*" I rattled off: "T-h-i-r-d, third," in a way which said: "Why don't you give us something hard?" As the words went down the line, I could see how lucky I had been to get a good place together with an easy word. As young as I was, I felt impressed with the unfairness of the whole proceeding when I saw the tailenders going down before *twelfth* and *twentieth,* and I felt sorry for those who had to spell such words in order to hold a low position. "Spell *fourth.*" "Red Head," with his hands clutched tightly behind his back, began bravely: "F-o-r-t-h." Like a flash a score of hands went up, and the teacher began saying: "No snapping of fingers, no snapping of fingers." This was the first word missed, and it seemed to me that some of the scholars were about to lose their senses; some were dancing up and down on one foot with a hand above their heads, the fingers working furiously, and joy beaming all over their faces; others stood still, their hands raised not so high, their fingers working less rapidly, and their faces expressing not quite so much happiness; there were still others who did not move or raise their hands, but stood with great wrinkles on their foreheads, looking very thoughtful.

The whole thing was new to me, and I did not raise my hand, but slyly whispered the letter "u" to "Red Head" several times. "Second chance," said the teacher. The hands went down and the class became quiet. "Red Head," his face now red, after looking beseechingly at the ceiling, then pitiably at the floor, began very haltingly: "F-u——" Immediately an impulse to raise hands went through the class, but the teacher checked it, and poor "Red Head," though he knew that each letter he added only took him farther out of the way, went doggedly on and finished: "—r-t-h." The handraising was now repeated with more hubbub and excitement than at first. Those who before had not moved a finger were now waving their hands above their heads. "Red Head" felt that he was lost. He looked very big and foolish, and some of the scholars began to snicker. His helpless condition went straight to my heart, and gripped my sympathies. I felt that if he failed, it would in some way be my failure. I raised my hand, and, under cover of the excitement and the teacher's attempts to regain order, I hurriedly shot up into his ear twice, quite distinctly: "F-o-u-r-t-h, f-o-u-r-t-h." The teacher tapped on her desk and said: "Third and last chance." The hands came down, the silence became oppressive. "Red Head" began: "F——" Since that day I have waited anxiously for many a turn of the wheel of fortune, but never under greater tension than when I watched for the order in which those letters would fall from "Red's" lips—"o-u-r-t-h." A sigh of relief and disappointment went up from the class. Afterwards, through all our school-days, "Red Head" shared my wit and quickness and I benefited by his strength and dogged faithfulness.

There were some black and brown boys and girls in the school, and several of them were in my class. One of the boys strongly attracted my attention from the first day I saw him. His face was as black as night, but shone as though it were polished; he had sparkling eyes, and when he opened his mouth, he displayed glistening white teeth. It struck me at once as appropriate to call him "Shiny Face," or "Shiny Eyes," or "Shiny Teeth," and I spoke of him often by one of these names to the other boys. These terms were finally merged into "Shiny," and to that name he answered goodnaturedly during the balance of his public school days.

"Shiny" was considered without question to be the best speller, the best reader, the best penman—in a word, the best scholar, in the class. He was very quick to catch anything, but, nevertheless, studied hard; thus he possessed two powers very rarely combined in one boy. I saw him year after year, on up into the high school, win the majority of the prizes for punctuality, deportment, essay writing, and declamation. Yet it did not take me long to discover that, in spite of his standing as a scholar, he was in some way looked down upon.

The other black boys and girls were still more looked down upon. Some of the boys often spoke of them as "niggers." Sometimes on the way home from school a crowd would walk behind them repeating:

"Nigger, nigger, never die,
Black face and shiny eye."

On one such afternoon one of the black boys turned suddenly on his tormentors and hurled a slate; it struck one of the white boys in the mouth, cutting a slight gash in his lip. At sight of the blood the boy who had thrown the slate ran, and his companions quickly followed.

We ran after them pelting them with stones until they separated in several directions. I was very much wrought up over the affair, and went home and told my mother how one of the "niggers" had struck a boy with a slate. I shall never forget how she turned on me. "Don't you ever use that word again," she said, "and don't you ever bother the coloured children at school. You ought to be ashamed of yourself." I did hang my head in shame, not because she had convinced me that I had done wrong, but because I was hurt by the first sharp word she had ever given me.

My school-days ran along very pleasantly. I stood well in my studies, not always so well with regard to my behaviour. I was never guilty of any serious misconduct, but my love of fun sometimes got me into trouble. I remember, however, that my sense of humour was so sly that most of the trouble usually fell on the head of the other fellow. My ability to play on the piano at school exercises was looked upon as little short of marvellous in a boy of my age. I was not chummy with many of my mates, but, on the whole, was about as popular as it is good for a boy to be.

One day near the end of my second term at school the principal came into our room and, after talking to the teacher, for some reason said: "I wish all of the white scholars to stand for a moment." I rose with the others. The teacher looked at me and, calling my name, said: "You sit down for the present, and rise with the others." I did not quite understand her, and questioned: "Ma'm?" She repeated, with a softer tone in her voice: "You sit down now, and rise with the others." I sat down dazed. I saw and heard nothing. When the others were asked to rise, I did not know it. When school was dismissed, I went out in a kind of stupor. A few of the white boys jeered me, saying: "Oh, you're a nigger too." I heard some black children say: "We knew he was coloured." "Shiny" said to them: "Come along, don't tease him," and thereby won my undying gratitude.

I hurried on as fast as I could, and had gone some distance before I perceived that "Red Head" was walking by my side. After a while he said to me: "Le' me carry your books." I gave him my strap without being able to answer. When we got to my gate, he said as he handed me my books: "Say, you know my big red agate? I can't shoot with it any more. I'm going to bring it to school for you tomorrow." I took my books and ran into the house. As I passed through the hallway, I saw that my mother was busy with one of her customers; I rushed up into my own little room, shut the door, and went quickly to where my looking-glass hung on the wall. For an instant I was afraid to look, but when I did, I looked long and earnestly. I had often heard people say to my mother: "What a pretty boy you have!" I was accustomed to hear remarks about my beauty; but now, for the first time, I became conscious of it and recognized it. I noticed the ivory whiteness of my skin, the beauty of my mouth, the size and liquid darkness of my eyes, and how the long, black lashes that fringed and shaded them produced an effect that was strangely fascinating even to me. I noticed the softness and glossiness of my dark hair that fell in waves over my temples, making my forehead appear whiter than it really was. How long I stood there gazing at my image I do not know. When I came out and reached the head of the stairs, I heard the lady who had been with my mother going out. I ran downstairs and rushed to where my mother was sitting, with a piece of work in her hands. I buried my head in her lap and blurted out: "Mother, mother, tell me, am I a nigger?" I could not see her face, but I knew the piece of work dropped to the floor and I felt her hands on my head. I looked up into her face and repeated: "Tell me, mother, am I a nigger?" There were tears in her eyes and I could see that she was suffering for me. And then it was that I looked at her critically for the first time. I had thought of her in a childish way only as the most beautiful woman in the world; now I looked at her searching for defects. I could see that her skin was almost brown, that her hair was not so soft as mine, and that she did differ in some way from the other ladies who came to the house; yet, even so, I could see that she was very beautiful, more beautiful than any of them. She must have felt that I was examining her, for she hid her face in my hair and said with difficulty: "No, my darling, you are not a nigger." She went on: "You are as good as anybody; if anyone calls you a nigger, don't notice them." But the more she talked, the less was I reassured, and I stopped her by asking: "Well, mother, am I white? Are you white?" She answered tremblingly: "No, I am not white, but you—your father is one of the greatest men in the country—the best blood of the South is in you——" This suddenly opened up in my heart a fresh chasm of misgiving and fear, and I almost fiercely demanded: "Who is my father? Where is he?" She stroked my hair and said: "I'll tell you about him some day." I sobbed: "I want to know now." She answered: "No, not now."

Perhaps it had to be done, but I have never forgiven the woman who did it so cruelly. It may be that she never knew that she gave me a sword-thrust that day in school which was years in healing.

CHAPTER II

Since I have grown older I have often gone back and tried to analyse the change that came into my life after that fateful day in school. There did come a radical change, and, young as I was, I felt fully conscious of it, though I did not fully comprehend it. Like my first spanking, it is one of the few incidents in my life that I can remember clearly. In the life of everyone there is a limited number of unhappy experiences which are not written upon the memory, but stamped there with a die; and in long years after, they can be called up in detail, and every emotion that was stirred by them can be lived through anew; these are the tragedies of life. We may grow to include some of them among the trivial incidents of childhood—a broken toy, a promise made to us which was not kept, a harsh, heart-piercing word—but these, too, as well as the bitter experiences and disappointments of mature years, are the tragedies of life.

And so I have often lived through that hour, that day, that week, in which was wrought the miracle of my transition from one world into another; for I did indeed pass into another world. From that time I looked out through other eyes, my thoughts were coloured, my words dictated, my actions limited by one dominating, all-pervading idea which constantly increased in force and weight until I finally realized in it a great, tangible fact.

And this is the dwarfing, warping, distorting influence which operates upon each and every coloured man in the United States. He is forced to take his outlook on all things, not from the view-point of a citizen, or a man, or even a human being, but from the view-point of a *coloured* man. It is wonderful to me that the race has progressed so broadly as it has, since most of its thought and all of its activity must run through the narrow neck of this one funnel.

And it is this, too, which makes the coloured people of this country, in reality, a mystery to the whites. It is a difficult thing for a white man to learn what a coloured man really thinks; because, generally, with the latter an additional and different light must be brought to bear on what he thinks; and his thoughts are often influenced by considerations so delicate and subtle that it would be impossible for him to confess or explain them to one of the opposite race. This gives to every coloured man, in proportion to his intellectuality, a sort of dual personality; there is one phase of him which is disclosed only in the freemasonry of his own race. I have often watched with interest and sometimes with amazement even ignorant coloured men under cover of broad grins and minstrel antics maintain this dualism in the presence of white men.

I believe it to be a fact that the coloured people of this country know and understand the white people better than the white people know and understand them.

I now think that this change which came into my life was at first more subjective than objective. I do not think my friends at school changed so much toward me as I did toward them. I grew reserved, I might say suspicious. I grew constantly more and more afraid of laying myself open to some injury to my feelings or my pride. I frequently saw or fancied some slight where, I am sure, none was intended. On the other hand, my friends and teachers were, if anything different, more considerate of me; but I can remember that it was against this very attitude in particular that my sensitiveness revolted. "Red" was the only one who did not so wound me; up to this day I recall with a swelling heart his clumsy efforts to make me understand that nothing could change his love for me.

I am sure that at this time the majority of my white school-mates did not understand or appreciate any differences between me and themselves; but there were a few who had evidently received instructions at home on the matter, and more than once they displayed their knowledge in word and action. As the years passed, I noticed that the most innocent and ignorant among the others grew in wisdom.

I myself would not have so clearly understood this difference had it not been for the presence of the other coloured children at school; I had learned what their status was, and now I learned that theirs was mine. I had had no particular like or dislike for these black and brown boys and girls; in fact, with the exception of "Shiny," they had occupied very little of my thought; but I do know that when the blow fell, I had a very strong aversion to being classed with them. So I became something of a solitary. "Red" and I remained inseparable, and there was between "Shiny" and me a sort of sympathetic bond, but my intercourse with the others was never entirely free from a feeling of constraint. I must add, however, that this feeling was confined almost entirely to my intercourse with boys and girls of about my own age; I did not experience it with my seniors. And when I grew to manhood, I found myself freer with elderly white people than with those near my own age.

I was now about eleven years old, but these emotions and impressions which I have just described could not have been stronger or more distinct at an older age. There were two immediate results of my forced loneliness: I began to find company in books, and greater pleasure in music. I made the former discovery through a big, gilt-bound, illustrated copy of the Bible, which used to lie in splendid neglect on the centre table in our little parlour. On top of the Bible lay a photograph album. I had often looked at the pictures in the album, and one day, after taking the larger book down and opening it on the floor, I was overjoyed to find that it contained what seemed to be an inexhaustible supply of pictures. I looked at these pictures many times; in fact, so often that I knew the story of each one without having to read the subject, and then, somehow, I picked up the thread of history on which are strung the trials and tribulations of the Hebrew children; this I followed with feverish interest and excitement. For a long time King David, with Samson a close second, stood at the head of my list of heroes; he was not displaced until I came to know Robert the Bruce. I read a good portion of the Old Testament, all that part treating of wars and rumours of wars, and then started in on the New. I became interested in the life of Christ, but became impatient and disappointed when I found that, notwithstanding the great power he possessed, he did not make use of it when, in my judgment, he most needed to do so. And so my first general impression of the Bible was what my later impression has been of a number of modern books, that the authors put their best work in the first part, and grew either exhausted or careless toward the end.

After reading the Bible, or those parts which held my attention, I began to explore the glass-doored bookcase which I have already mentioned. I found there *Pilgrim's Progress,* Peter Parley's *History of the United States,* Grimm's *Household Stories, Tales of a Grandfather,* a bound volume of an old English publication (I think it was called *The*

Mirror), a little volume called *Familiar Science,* and somebody's *Natural Theology,* which last, of course, I could not read, but which, nevertheless, I tackled, with the result of gaining a permanent dislike for all kinds of theology. There were several other books of no particular name or merit, such as agents sell to people who know nothing of buying books. How my mother came by this little library which, considering all things, was so well suited to me I never sought to know. But she was far from being an ignorant woman and had herself, very likely, read the majority of these books, though I do not remember ever seeing her with a book in her hand, with the exception of the Episcopal Prayer-book. At any rate she encouraged in me the habit of reading, and when I had about exhausted those books in the little library which interested me, she began to buy books for me. She also regularly gave me money to buy a weekly paper which was then very popular for boys.

At this time I went in for music with an earnestness worthy of maturer years; a change of teachers was largely responsible for this. I began now to take lessons of the organist of the church which I attended with my mother; he was a good teacher and quite a thorough musician. He was so skilful in his instruction and filled me with such enthusiasm that my progress—these are his words—was marvellous. I remember that when I was barely twelve years old I appeared on a program with a number of adults at an entertainment given for some charitable purpose, and carried off the honours. I did more, I brought upon myself through the local newspapers the handicapping title of "infant prodigy."

I can believe that I did astonish my audience, for I never played the piano like a child; that is, in the "one-two-three" style with accelerated motion. Neither did I depend upon mere brilliancy of technique, a trick by which children often surprise their listeners; but I always tried to interpret a piece of music; I always played with feeling. Very early I acquired that knack of using the pedals, which makes the piano a sympathetic, singing instrument, quite a different thing from the source of hard or blurred sounds it so generally is. I think this was due not entirely to natural artistic temperament, but largely to the fact that I did not begin to learn the piano by counting out exercises, but by trying to reproduce the quaint songs which my mother used to sing, with all their pathetic turns and cadences.

Even at a tender age, in playing I helped to express what I felt by some of the mannerisms which I afterwards observed in great performers; I had not copied them. I have often heard people speak of the mannerisms of musicians as affectations adopted for mere effect; in some cases they may be so; but a true artist can no more play upon the piano or violin without putting his whole body in accord with the emotions he is striving to express than a swallow can fly without being graceful. Often when playing I could not keep the tears which formed in my eyes from rolling down my cheeks. Sometimes at the end or even in the midst of a composition, as big a boy as I was, I would jump from the piano, and throw myself sobbing into my mother's arms. She, by her caresses and often her tears, only encouraged these fits of sentimental hysteria. Of course, to counteract this tendency to temperamental excesses I should have been out playing ball or in swimming with other boys of my age; but my mother didn't know that. There was only once when she was really firm with me, making me do what she considered was best; I did not want to return to school after the unpleasant episode which I have related, and she was inflexible.

I began my third term, and the days ran along as I have already indicated. I had been promoted twice, and had managed each time to pull "Red" along with me. I think the teachers came to consider me the only hope of his ever getting through school, and I believe they secretly conspired with me to bring about the desired end. At any rate, I know it became easier in each succeeding examination for me not only to assist "Red," but absolutely to do his work. It is strange how in some things honest people can be dishonest without the slightest compunction. I knew boys at school who were too honourable to tell a fib even when one would have been just the right thing, but could not resist the temptation to assist or receive assistance in an examination. I have long considered it the highest proof of honesty in a man to hand his street-car fare to the conductor who had overlooked it.

One afternoon after school, during my third term, I rushed home in a great hurry to get my dinner and go to my music teacher's. I was never reluctant about going there, but on this particular afternoon I was impetuous. The reason of this was I had been asked to play the accompaniment for a young lady who was to play a violin solo at a concert given by the young people of the church, and on this afternoon we were to have our first rehearsal. At that time playing accompaniments was the only thing in music I did not enjoy; later this feeling grew into positive dislike. I have never been a really good accompanist because my ideas of interpretation were always too strongly individual. I constantly forced my *accelerandos* and *rubatos* upon the soloist, often throwing the duet entirely out of gear.

Perhaps the reader has already guessed why I was so willing and anxious to play the accompaniment to this violin solo; if not—the violinist was a girl of seventeen or eighteen whom I had first heard play a short time before on a Sunday afternoon at a special service of some kind, and who had moved me to a degree which now I can hardly think of as possible. At present I do not think it was due to her wonderful playing, though I judge she must have been a very fair performer, but there was just the proper setting to produce the effect upon a boy such as I was; the half-dim church, the air of devotion on the part of the listeners, the heaving tremor of the organ under the clear wail of the violin, and she, her eyes almost closing, the escaping strands of her dark hair wildly framing her pale face, and her slender body swaying to the tones she called forth, all combined to fire my imagination and my heart with a passion, though boyish, yet strong and, somehow, lasting. I have tried to describe the scene; if I have succeeded, it is only half success, for words can only partially express what I wish to convey. Always in recalling that Sunday afternoon I am subconscious of a faint but distinct fragrance which, like some old memory-awakening perfume, rises and suffuses my whole imagination, inducing a state of reverie so airy as just to evade the powers of expression.

She was my first love, and I loved her as only a boy loves. I dreamed of her, I built air castles for her, she was the incarnation of each beautiful heroine I knew; when I played the piano, it was to her, not even music furnished an adequate outlet for my passion; I bought a new notebook and, to sing her praises, made my first and last attempts at poetry. I remember one day at school, after we had given in our notebooks to have some exercises corrected, the teacher called me to her desk and said: "I couldn't correct your exercises because I found nothing in your book but a rhapsody on somebody's brown eyes." I had passed in the wrong note-book. I don't think I have felt greater embarrassment in my whole life than I did at that moment. I was ashamed not only that my teacher should see this nakedness of my heart, but that she should find out that I had any knowledge of such affairs. It did not then occur to me to be ashamed of the kind of poetry I had written.

Of course, the reader must know that all of this adoration was in secret; next to my great love for this young lady was the dread that in some way she would find it out. I did not know what some men never find out, that the woman who cannot discern when she is loved has never lived. It makes me laugh to think how successful I was in concealing it all; within a short time after our duet all of the friends of my dear one were referring to me as her "little sweetheart," or her "little beau," and she laughingly encouraged it. This did not entirely satisfy me; I wanted to be taken seriously. I had definitely made up my mind that I should never love another woman, and that if she deceived me I should do something desperate—the great difficulty was to think of something sufficiently desperate—and the heartless jade, how she led me on!

So I hurried home that afternoon, humming snatches of the violin part of the duet, my heart beating with pleasurable excitement over the fact that I was going to be near her, to have her attention placed directly upon me; that I was going to be of service to her, and in a way in which I could show myself to advantage—this last consideration has much to do with cheerful service.—The anticipation produced in me a sensation somewhat between bliss and fear. I rushed through the gate, took the three steps to the house at one bound, threw open the door, and was about to hang my cap on its accustomed peg of the hall rack when I noticed that that particular peg was occupied by a black derby hat. I stopped suddenly and gazed at this hat as though I had never seen an object of its description. I was still looking at it in open-eyed wonder when my mother, coming out of the parlour into the hallway, called me and said there was someone inside who wanted to see me. Feeling that I was being made a party to some kind of mystery, I went in with her, and there I saw a man standing leaning with one elbow on the mantel, his back partly turned toward the door. As I entered, he turned and I saw a tall, handsome, well-dressed gentleman of perhaps thirty-five; he advanced a step toward me with a smile on his face. I stopped and looked at him with the same feelings with which I had looked at the derby hat, except that they were greatly magnified. I looked at him from head to foot, but he was an absolute blank to me until my eyes rested on his slender, elegant polished shoes; then it seemed that indistinct and partly obliterated films of memory began, at first slowly, then rapidly, to unroll, forming a vague panorama of my childhood days in Georgia.

My mother broke the spell by calling me by name and saying: "This is your father."

"Father, father," that was the word which had been to me a source of doubt and perplexity ever since the interview with my mother on the subject. How often I had wondered about my father, who he was, what he was like, whether alive or dead, and, above all, why she would not tell me about him. More than once I had been on the point of recalling to her the promise she had made me, but I instinctively felt that she was happier for not telling me and that I was happier for not being told; yet I had not the slightest idea what the real truth was. And here he stood before me, just the kind of looking father I had wishfully pictured him to be; but I made no advance toward him; I stood there feeling embarrassed and foolish, not knowing what to say or do. I am not sure but that he felt pretty much the same. My mother stood at my side with one hand on my shoulder, almost pushing me forward, but I did not move. I can well remember the look of disappointment, even pain, on her face; and I can now understand that she could expect nothing else but that at the name "father" I should throw myself into his arms. But I could not rise to this dramatic, or, better, melodramatic, climax. Somehow I could not arouse any considerable feeling of need for a father. He broke the awkward tableau by saying: "Well, boy, aren't you glad to see me?" He evidently meant the words kindly enough, but I don't know what he could have said that would have had a worse effect; however, my good breeding came to my rescue, and I answered: "Yes, sir," and went to him and offered him my hand. He took my hand into one of his, and, with the other, stroked my head, saying that I had grown into a fine youngster. He asked me how old I was; which, of course, he must have done merely to say something more, or perhaps he did so as a test of my intelligence. I replied: "Twelve, sir." He then made the trite observation about the flight of time, and we lapsed into another awkward pause.

My mother was all in smiles; I believe that was one of the happiest moments of her life. Either to put me more at ease or to show me off, she asked me to play something for my father. There is only one thing in the world that can make music, at all times and under all circumstances, up to its general standard; that is a hand-organ, or one of its variations. I went to the piano and played something in a listless, half-hearted way. I simply was not in the mood. I was wondering, while playing, when my mother would dismiss me and let me go; but my father was so enthusiastic in his praise that he touched my vanity—which was great—and more than that; he displayed that sincere appreciation which always arouses an artist to his best effort, and, too, in an unexplainable manner, makes him feel like shedding tears. I showed my gratitude by playing for him a Chopin waltz with all the feeling that was in me. When I had finished, my mother's eyes were glistening with tears; my father stepped across the room, seized me in his arms, and squeezed me to his breast. I am certain that for that moment he was proud to be my father. He sat and held me standing between his knees while he talked to my mother. I, in the mean time, examined him with more curiosity, perhaps, than politeness. I interrupted the conversation by asking: "Mother, is he going to stay with us now?" I found it impossible to frame the word "father"; it was too new to me; so I asked the question through my mother. Without waiting for her to speak, my father answered: "I've got to go back to New York this afternoon, but I'm coming to see you again." I turned abruptly and went over to my mother, and almost in a whisper reminded her that I had an appointment which I should not miss; to my pleasant surprise she said that she would give me something to eat at once so that I might go. She went out of the room and I began to gather from off the piano the music I needed. When I had finished, my father, who had been watching me, asked: "Are you going?" I replied: "Yes, sir, I've got to go to practise for a concert." He spoke some words of advice to me about being a good boy and taking care of my mother when I grew up, and added that he was going to send me something nice from New York. My mother called, and I said good-bye to him and went out. I saw him only once after that.

I quickly swallowed down what my mother had put on the table for me, seized my cap and music, and hurried off to my teacher's house. On the way I could think of nothing but this new father, where he came from, where he had been, why he was here, and why he would not stay. In my mind I ran over the whole list of fathers I had become acquainted with in my reading, but I could not classify him. The thought did not cross my mind that he was different from me, and even if it had, the mystery would not thereby have been explained; for, notwithstanding my changed relations with most of my school-mates, I had only a faint knowledge of prejudice and no idea at all how it ramified and affected our entire social organism. I felt, however, that there was something about the whole affair which had to be hid.

When I arrived, I found that she of the brown eyes had been rehearsing with my teacher and was on the point of leaving. My teacher, with some expressions of surprise, asked why I was late, and I stammered out the first deliberate lie of which I have any recollection. I told him that when I reached home from school, I found my mother quite sick, and that I had stayed with her awhile before coming. Then unnecessarily and gratuitously—to give my words force of conviction, I suppose—I added: "I don't think she'll be with us very long." In speaking these words I must have been comical; for I noticed that my teacher, instead of showing signs of anxiety or sorrow, half hid a smile. But how little did I know that in that lie I was speaking a prophecy!

She of the brown eyes unpacked her violin, and we went through the duet several times. I was soon lost to all other thoughts in the delights of music and love. I saw delights of love without reservation; for at no time of life is love so pure, so delicious, so poetic, so romantic, as it is in boyhood. A great deal has been said about the heart of a girl when she stands "where the brook and river meet," but what she feels is negative; more interesting is the heart of a boy when just at the budding dawn of manhood he stands looking wide-eyed into the long vistas opening before him; when he first becomes conscious of the awakening and quickening of strange desires and unknown powers; when what he sees and feels is still shadowy and mystical enough to be intangible, and, so, more beautiful; when his imagination is unsullied, and his faith new and whole—then it is that love wears a halo. The man who has not loved before he was fourteen has missed a foretaste of Elysium.

When I reached home, it was quite dark and I found my mother without a light, sitting rocking in a chair, as she so often used to do in my childhood days, looking into the fire and singing softly to herself. I nestled close to her, and, with her arms round me, she haltingly told me who my father was—a great man, a fine gentleman—he loved me and loved her very much; he was going to make a great man of me. All she said was so limited by reserve and so coloured by her feelings that it was but half truth; and so I did not yet fully understand.

CHAPTER III

Perhaps I ought not pass on in this narrative without mentioning that the duet was a great success, so great that we were obliged to respond with two encores. It seemed to me that life could hold no greater joy than it contained when I took her hand and we stepped down to the front of the stage bowing to our enthusiastic audience. When we reached the little dressing-room, where the other performers were applauding as wildly as the audience, she impulsively threw both her arms round me and kissed me, while I struggled to get away.

One day a couple of weeks after my father had been to see us, a wagon drove up to our cottage loaded with a big box. I was about to tell the men on the wagon that they had made a mistake, when my mother, acting darkly wise, told them to bring their load in; she had them unpack the box, and quickly there was evolved from the boards, paper, and other packing-material a beautiful, brand-new, upright piano. Then she informed me that it was a present to me from my father. I at once sat down and ran my fingers over the keys; the full, mellow tone of the instrument was ravishing. I thought, almost remorsefully, of how I had left my father; but, even so, there momentarily crossed my mind a feeling of disappointment that the piano was not a grand. The new instrument greatly increased the pleasure of my hours of study and practice at home.

Shortly after this I was made a member of the boys' choir, it being found that I possessed a clear, strong soprano voice. I enjoyed the singing very much. About a year later I began the study of the pipe organ and the theory of music; and before I finished the grammar-school, I had written out several simple preludes for organ which won the admiration of my teacher, and which he did me the honour to play at services.

The older I grew, the more thought I gave to the question of my mother's and my position, and what was our exact relation to the world in general. My idea of the whole matter was rather hazy. My study of United States history had been confined to those periods which were designated in my book as "Discovery," "Colonial," "Revolutionary," and "Constitutional." I now began to study about the Civil War, but the story was told in such a condensed and skipping style that I gained from it very little real information. It is a marvel how children ever learn any history out of books of that sort. And, too, I began now to read the newspapers; I often saw articles which aroused my curiosity, but did not enlighten me. But one day I drew from the circulating library a book that cleared the whole mystery, a book that I read with the same feverish intensity with which I had read the old Bible stories, a book that gave me my first perspective of the life I was entering; that book was *Uncle Tom's Cabin.*

This work of Harriet Beecher Stowe has been the object of much unfavourable criticism. It has been assailed, not only as fiction of the most imaginative sort, but as being a direct misrepresentation. Several successful attempts have lately been made to displace the book from Northern school libraries. Its critics would brush it aside with the remark that there never was a Negro as good as Uncle Tom, nor a slave-holder as bad as Legree. For my part, I was never an admirer of Uncle Tom, nor of his type of goodness; but I believe that there were lots of old Negroes as foolishly good as he; the proof of which is that they knowingly stayed and worked the plantations that furnished sinews for the army which was fighting to keep them enslaved. But in these later years several cases have come to my personal knowledge in which old Negroes have died and left what was a considerable fortune to the descendants of their former masters. I do not think it takes any great stretch of the imagination to believe there was a fairly large class of slave-holders typified in Legree. And we must also remember that the author depicted a number of worthless if not vicious Negroes, and a slave-holder who was as much of a Christian and a gentleman as it was possible for one in his position to be; that she pictured the happy, singing, shuffling "darky" as well as the mother wailing for her child sold "down river."

I do not think it is claiming too much to say that *Uncle Tom's Cabin* was a fair and truthful panorama of slavery; however that may be, it opened my eyes as to who and what I was and what my country considered me; in fact, it gave me my bearing. But there was no shock; I took the whole revelation in a kind of stoical way. One of the greatest benefits I derived from reading the book was that I could afterwards talk frankly with my mother on all the questions which had been vaguely troubling my mind. As a result, she was entirely freed from reserve, and often herself brought up the subject, talking of things directly touching her life and mine and of things which had come down to her through the "old folks." What she told me interested and even fascinated me, and, what may seem strange, kindled in me a strong desire to see the South. She spoke to me quite frankly about herself, my father, and myself: she, the sewing girl of my father's mother; he, an impetuous young man home from college; I, the child of this unsanctioned love. She told me even the principal reason for our coming north. My father was about to be married to a young lady of another great Southern family. She did not neglect to add that another reason for our being in Connecticut was that he intended to give me an education and make a man of me. In none of her talks did she ever utter one word of complaint against my father. She always endeavoured to impress upon me how good he had been and still was, and that he was all to us that custom and the law would allow. She loved him; more, she worshipped him, and she died firmly believing that he loved her more than any other woman in the world. Perhaps she was right. Who knows?

All of these newly-awakened ideas and thoughts took the form of a definite aspiration on the day I graduated from the grammar-school. And what a day that was! The girls in white dresses, with fresh ribbons in their hair; the boys in new suits and creaky shoes; the great crowd of parents and friends; the flowers, the prizes and congratulations, made the day seem to me one of the greatest importance. I was on the program, and played a piano solo which was received by the audience with that amount of applause which I had come to look upon as being only the just due of my talent.

But the real enthusiasm was aroused by "Shiny." He was the principal speaker of the day, and well did he measure up to the honour. He made a striking picture, that thin little black boy standing on the platform, dressed in clothes that did not fit him any too well, his eyes burning with excitement, his shrill, musical voice vibrating in tones of appealing defiance, and his black face alight with such great intelligence and earnestness as to be positively handsome. What were his thoughts when he stepped forward and looked into that crowd of faces, all white with the exception of a score or so that were lost to view? I do not know, but I fancy he felt his loneliness. I think there must have rushed over him a feeling akin to that of a gladiator tossed into the arena and bade to fight for his life. I think that solitary little black figure standing there felt that for the particular time and place he bore the weight and responsibility of his race; that for him to fail meant general defeat; but he won, and nobly. His oration was Wendell Phillips's "Toussaint L'Ouverture," a speech which may now be classed as rhetorical—even, perhaps, bombastic; but as the words fell from "Shiny's" lips their effect was magical. How so young an orator could stir so great enthusiasm was to be wondered at. When, in the famous peroration, his voice, trembling with suppressed emotion, rose higher and higher and then rested on the name "Toussaint L'Ouverture," it was like touching an electric button which loosed the pent-up feelings of his listeners. They actually rose to him.

I have since known of coloured men who have been chosen as class orators in our leading universities, of others who have played on the varsity football and baseball teams, of coloured speakers who have addressed great white audiences. In each of these instances I believe the men were stirred by the same emotions which actuated "Shiny" on the day of his graduation; and, too, in each case where the efforts have reached any high standard of excellence they have been followed by the same phenomenon of enthusiasm. I think the explanation of the latter lies in what is a basic, though often dormant, principle of the Anglo-Saxon heart, love of fair play. "Shiny," it is true, was what is so common in his race, a natural orator; but I doubt that any white boy of equal talent could have wrought the same effect. The sight of that boy gallantly waging with puny, black arms so unequal a battle touched the deep springs in the hearts of his audience, and they were swept by a wave of sympathy and admiration.

But the effect upon me of "Shiny's" speech was double; I not only shared the enthusiasm of his audience, but he imparted to me some of his own enthusiasm. I felt leap within me pride that I was coloured; and I began to form wild dreams of bringing glory and honour to the Negro race. For days I could talk of nothing else with my mother except my ambitions to be a great man, a great coloured man, to reflect credit on the race and gain fame for myself. It was not until years after that I formulated a definite and feasible plan for realizing my dreams.

I entered the high school with my class, and still continued my study of the piano, the pipe organ, and the theory of music. I had to drop out of the boys' choir on account of a changing voice; this I regretted very much. As I grew older, my love for reading grew stronger. I read with studious interest everything I could find relating to coloured men who had gained prominence. My heroes had been King David, then Robert the Bruce; now Frederick Douglass was enshrined in the place of honour. When I learned that Alexandre Dumas was a coloured man, I re-read *Monte Cristo* and *The Three Guardsmen* with magnified pleasure. I lived between my music and books, on the whole a rather unwholesome life for a boy to lead. I dwelt in a world of imagination, of dreams and air castles—the kind of atmosphere that sometimes nourishes a genius, more often men unfitted for the practical struggles of life. I never played a game of ball, never went fishing or learned to swim; in fact, the only outdoor exercise in which I took any interest was skating. Nevertheless, though slender, I grew well formed and in perfect health. After I entered the high school, I began to notice the change in my mother's health, which I suppose had been going on for some years. She began to complain a little and to cough a great deal; she tried several remedies, and finally went to see a doctor; but though she was failing in health, she kept her spirits up. She still did a great deal of sewing, and in the busy seasons hired two women to help her. The purpose she had formed of having me go through college without financial worries kept her at work when she was not fit for it. I was so fortunate as to be able to organize a class of eight or ten beginners on the piano, and so start a separate little fund of my own. As the time for my graduation from the high school grew nearer, the plans for my college career became the chief subject of our talks. I sent for catalogues of all the prominent schools in the East and eagerly gathered all the information I could concerning them from different sources. My mother told me that my father wanted me to go to Harvard or Yale; she herself had a half desire for me to go to Atlanta University, and even had me write for a catalogue of that school. There were two reasons, however, that inclined her to my father's choice; the first, that at Harvard or Yale I should be near her; the second, that my father had promised to pay for a part of my college education.

Both "Shiny" and "Red" came to my house quite often of evenings, and we used to talk over our plans and prospects for the future. Sometimes I would play for them, and they seemed to enjoy the music very much. My mother often prepared sundry Southern dishes for them, which I am not sure but that they enjoyed more. "Shiny" had an uncle in Amherst, Mass., and he expected to live with him and work his way through Amherst College. "Red" declared that he had enough of school and that after he got his high school diploma, he would get a position in a bank. It was his ambition to become a banker and he felt sure of getting the opportunity through certain members of his family.

My mother barely had strength to attend the closing exercises of the high school when I graduated, and after that day she was seldom out of bed. She could no longer direct her work, and under the expense of medicines, doctors, and someone to look after her our college fund began to diminish rapidly. Many of her customers and some of the neighbours were very kind, and frequently brought her nourishment of one kind or another. My mother realized what I did not, that she was mortally ill, and she had me write a long letter to my father. For some time past she had heard from him only at irregular intervals; we never received an answer. In those last days I often sat at her bed-side and read to her until she fell asleep. Sometimes I would leave the parlour door open and play on the piano, just loud enough for the music to reach her. This she always enjoyed.

One night, near the end of July, after I had been watching beside her for some hours, I went into the parlour and, throwing myself into the big arm-chair, dozed off into a fitful sleep. I was suddenly aroused by one of the neighbours, who had come in to sit with her that night. She said: "Come to your mother at once." I hurried upstairs, and at the bedroom door met the woman who was acting as nurse. I noted with a dissolving heart the strange look of awe on her face. From my first glance at my mother I discerned the light of death upon her countenance. I fell upon my knees beside the bed and, burying my face in the sheets, sobbed convulsively. She died with the fingers of her left hand entwined in my hair.

I will not rake over this, one of the two sacred sorrows of my life; nor could I describe the feeling of unutterable loneliness that fell upon me. After the funeral I went to the house of my music teacher; he had kindly offered me the hospitality of his home for so long as I might need it. A few days later I moved my trunk, piano, my music, and most of my books to his home; the rest of my books I divided between "Shiny" and "Red." Some of the household effects I gave to "Shiny's" mother and to two or three of the neighbours who had been kind to us during my mother's illness; the others I sold. After settling up my little estate I found that, besides a good supply of clothes, a piano, some books and trinkets, I had about two hundred dollars in cash.

The question of what I was to do now confronted me. My teacher suggested a concert tour; but both of us realized that I was too old to be exploited as an infant prodigy and too young and inexperienced to go before the public as a finished artist. He, however, insisted that the people of the town would generously patronize a benefit concert; so he took up the matter and made arrangements for such an entertainment. A more than sufficient number of people with musical and elocutionary talent volunteered their services to make a program. Among these was my brown-eyed violinist. But our relations were not the same as they were when we had played our first duet together. A year or so after that time she had dealt me a crushing blow by getting married. I was partially avenged, however, by the fact that, though she was growing more beautiful, she was losing her ability to play the violin.

I was down on the program for one number. My selection might have appeared at that particular time as a bit of affectation, but I considered it deeply appropriate; I played Beethoven's "Sonata Pathétique." When I sat down at the piano and glanced into the faces of the several hundreds of people who were there solely on account of love or sympathy for me, emotions swelled in my heart which enabled me to play the "Pathétique" as I could never again play it. When the last tone died away, the few who began to applaud were hushed by the silence of the others; and for once I played without receiving an encore.

The benefit yielded me a little more than two hundred dollars, thus raising my cash capital to about four hundred dollars. I still held to my determination of going to college; so it was now a question of trying to squeeze through a year at Harvard or going to Atlanta, where the money I had would pay my actual expenses for at least two years. The peculiar fascination which the South held over my imagination and my limited capital decided me in favour of Atlanta University; so about the last of September I bade farewell to the friends and scenes of my boyhood and boarded a train for the south.

CHAPTER IV

The farther I got below Washington, the more disappointed I became in the appearance of the country. I peered through the car windows, looking in vain for the luxuriant semi-tropical scenery which I had pictured in my mind. I did not find the grass so green, nor the woods so beautiful, nor the flowers so plentiful, as they were in Connecticut. Instead, the red earth partly covered by tough, scrawny grass, the muddy, straggling roads, the cottages of unpainted pine boards, and the clay-daubed huts imparted a "burnt up" impression. Occasionally we ran through a little white and green village that was like an oasis in a desert.

When I reached Atlanta, my steadily increasing disappointment was not lessened. I found it a big, dull, red town. This dull red colour of that part of the South I was then seeing had much, I think, to do with the extreme depression of my spirits—no public squares, no fountains, dingy streetcars, and, with the exception of three or four principal thoroughfares, unpaved streets. It was raining when I arrived and some of these unpaved streets were absolutely impassable. Wheels sank to the hubs in red mire, and I actually stood for an hour and watched four or five men work to save a mule, which had stepped into a deep sink, from drowning, or, rather, suffocating in the mud. The Atlanta of today is a new city.

On the train I had talked with one of the Pullman-car porters, a bright young fellow who was himself a student, and told him that I was going to Atlanta to attend school. I had also asked him to tell me where I might stop for a day or two until the University opened. He said I might go with him to the place where he stopped during his "layovers" in Atlanta. I gladly accepted his offer and went with him along one of those muddy streets until we came to a rather rickety-looking frame-house, which we entered. The proprietor of the house was a big, fat, greasy-looking brown-skin man. When I asked him if he could give me accommodation, he wanted to know how long I would stay. I told him perhaps two days, not more than three. In reply he said: "Oh, dat's all right den," at the same time leading the way up a pair of creaky stairs. I followed him and the porter to a room, the door of which the proprietor opened while continuing, it seemed, his remark, "Oh, dat's all right den," by adding: "You kin sleep in dat cot in de corner der. Fifty cents, please." The porter interrupted by saying: "You needn't collect from him now, he's got a trunk." This seemed to satisfy the man, and he went down, leaving me and my porter friend in the room. I glanced round the apartment and saw that it contained a double bed and two cots, two wash-stands, three chairs, and a time-worn bureau, with a looking-glass that would have made Adonis appear hideous. I looked at the cot in which I was to sleep and suspected, not without good reasons, that I should not be the first to use the sheets and pillow-case since they had last come from the wash. When I thought of the clean, tidy, comfortable surroundings in which I had been reared, a wave of homesickness swept over me that made me feel faint. Had it not been for the presence of my companion, and that I knew this much of his history—that he was not yet quite twenty, just three years older than myself, and that he had been fighting his own way in the world, earning his own living and providing for his own education since he was fourteen—I should not have been able to stop the tears that were welling up in my eyes.

I asked him why it was that the proprietor of the house seemed unwilling to accommodate me for more than a couple of days. He informed me that the man ran a lodging-house especially for Pullman porters, and, as their stays in town were not longer than one or two nights, it would interfere with his arrangements to have anyone stay longer. He went on to say: "You see this room is fixed up to accommodate four men at a time. Well, by keeping a sort of table of trips, in and out, of the men, and working them like checkers, he can accommodate fifteen or sixteen in each week and generally avoid having an empty bed. You happen to catch a bed that would have been empty for a couple of nights." I asked him where he was going to sleep. He answered: "I sleep in that other cot tonight; tomorrow night I go out." He went on to tell me that the man who kept the house did not serve meals, and that if I was hungry, we would go out and get something to eat.

We went into the street, and in passing the railroad station I hired a wagon to take my trunk to my lodging-place. We passed along until, finally, we turned into a street that stretched away, up and down hill, for a mile or two; and here I caught my first sight of coloured people in large numbers. I had seen little squads around the railroad stations on my way south, but here I saw a street crowded with them. They filled the shops and thronged the sidewalks and lined the curb. I asked my companion if all the coloured people in Atlanta lived in this street. He said they did not and assured me that the ones I saw were of the lower class. I felt relieved, in spite of the size of the lower class. The unkempt appearance, the shambling, slouching gait and loud talk and laughter of these people aroused in me a feeling of almost repulsion. Only one thing about them awoke a feeling of interest; that was their dialect. I had read some Negro dialect and had heard snatches of it on my journey down from Washington; but here I heard it in all of its fullness and freedom. I was particularly struck by the way in which it was punctuated by such exclamatory phrases as "Lawd a mussy!" "G'wan, man!" "Bless ma soul!" "Look heah, chile!" These people talked and laughed without restraint. In fact, they talked straight from their lungs and laughed from the pits of their stomachs. And this hearty laughter was often justified by the droll humour of some remark. I paused long enough to hear one man say to another: "W'at's de mattah wid you an' yo' fr'en' Sam?" and the other came back like a flash: "Ma fr'en'? He ma fr'en'? Man! I'd go to his funeral jes' de same as I'd go to a minstrel show." I have since learned that this ability to laugh heartily is, in part, the salvation of the American Negro; it does much to keep him from going the way of the Indian.

The business places of the street along which we were passing consisted chiefly of low bars, cheap dry-goods and notion stores, barber shops, and fish and bread restaurants. We, at length, turned down a pair of stairs that led to a basement and I found myself in an eating-house somewhat better than those I had seen in passing; but that did not mean much for its excellence. The place was smoky, the tables were covered with oilcloth, the floor with sawdust, and from the kitchen came a rancid odour of fish fried over several times, which almost nauseated me. I asked my companion if this was the place where we were to eat. He informed me that it was the best place in town where a coloured man could get a meal. I then wanted to know why somebody didn't open a place where respectable coloured people who had money could be accommodated. He answered: "It wouldn't pay; all the respectable coloured people eat at home, and the few who travel generally have friends in the towns to which they go, who entertain them." He added: "Of course, you could go in any place in the city; they wouldn't know you from white."

I sat down with the porter at one of the tables, but was not hungry enough to eat with any relish what was put before me. The food was not badly cooked; but the iron knives and forks needed to be scrubbed, the plates and dishes and glasses needed to be washed and well dried. I minced over what I took on my plate while my companion ate. When we finished, we paid the waiter twenty cents each and went out. We walked round until the lights of the city were lit. Then the porter said that he must get to bed and have some rest, as he had not had six hours' sleep since he left Jersey City. I went back to our lodging-house with him.

When I awoke in the morning, there were, besides my new-found friend, two other men in the room, asleep in the double bed. I got up and dressed myself very quietly, so as not to awake anyone. I then drew from under the pillow my precious roll of greenbacks, took out a ten-dollar bill, and, very softly unlocking my trunk, put the remainder, about three hundred dollars, in the inside pocket of a coat near the bottom, glad of the opportunity to put it unobserved in a place of safety. When I had carefully locked my trunk, I tiptoed toward the door with the intention of going out to look for a decent restaurant where I might get something fit to eat. As I was easing the door open, my porter friend said with a yawn: "Hello! You're going out?" I answered him: "Yes." "Oh!" he yawned again, "I guess I've had enough sleep; wait a minute, I'll go with you." For the instant his friendship bored and embarrassed me. I had visions of another meal in the greasy restaurant of the day before. He must have divined my thoughts, for he went on to say: "I know a woman across town who takes a few boarders; I think we can go over there and get a good breakfast." With a feeling of mingled fears and doubts regarding what the breakfast might be, I waited until he had dressed himself.

When I saw the neat appearance of the cottage we entered, my fears vanished, and when I saw the woman who kept it, my doubts followed the same course. Scrupulously clean, in a spotless white apron and coloured head-handkerchief, her round face beaming with motherly kindness, she was picturesquely beautiful. She impressed me as one broad expanse of happiness and good nature. In a few minutes she was addressing me as "chile" and "honey." She made me feel as though I should like to lay my head on her capacious bosom and go to sleep.

And the breakfast, simple as it was, I could not have had at any restaurant in Atlanta at any price. There was fried chicken, as it is fried only in the South, hominy boiled to the consistency where it could be eaten with a fork, and biscuits so light and flaky that a fellow with any appetite at all would have no difficulty in disposing of eight or ten. When I had finished, I felt that I had experienced the realization of, at least, one of my dreams of Southern life.

During the meal we found out from our hostess, who had two boys in school, that Atlanta University opened on that very day. I had somehow mixed my dates. My friend the porter suggested that I go out to the University at once and offered to walk over and show me the way. We had to walk because, although the University was not more than twenty minutes' distance from the centre of the city, there were no street-cars running in that direction. My first sight of the school-grounds made me feel that I was not far from home; here the red hills had been terraced and covered with green grass; clean gravel walks, well shaded, led up to the buildings; indeed, it was a bit of New England transplanted. At the gate my companion said he would bid me good-bye, because it was likely that he would not see me again before his car went out. He told me that he would make two more trips to Atlanta and that he would come out and see me; that after his second trip he would leave the Pullman service for the winter and return to school in Nashville. We shook hands, I thanked him for all his kindness, and we said good-bye.

I walked up to a group of students and made some inquiries. They directed me to the president's office in the main building. The president gave me a cordial welcome; it was more than cordial; he talked to me, not as the official head of a college, but as though he were adopting me into what was his large family, personally to look after my general welfare as well as my education. He seemed especially pleased with the fact that I had come to them all the way from the North. He told me that I could have come to the school as soon as I had reached the city and that I had better move my trunk out at once. I gladly promised him that I would do so. He then called a boy and directed him to take me to the matron, and to show me round afterwards. I found the matron even more motherly than the president was fatherly. She had me register, which was in effect to sign a pledge to abstain from the use of intoxicating beverages, tobacco, and profane language while I was a student in the school. This act caused me no sacrifice, as, up to that time, I was free from all three habits. The boy who was with me then showed me about the grounds. I was especially interested in the industrial building.

The sounding of a bell, he told me, was the signal for the students to gather in the general assembly hall, and he asked me if I would go. Of course I would. There were between three and four hundred students and perhaps all of the teachers gathered in the room. I noticed that several of the latter were coloured. The president gave a talk addressed principally to new-comers; but I scarcely heard what he said, I was so much occupied in looking at those around me. They were of all types and colours, the more intelligent types predominating. The colours ranged from jet black to pure white, with light hair and eyes. Among the girls especially there were many so fair that it was difficult to believe that they had Negro blood in them. And, too, I could not help noticing that many of the girls, particularly those of the delicate brown shades, with black eyes and wavy dark hair, were decidedly pretty. Among the boys many of the blackest were fine specimens of young manhood, tall, straight, and muscular, with magnificent heads; these were the kind of boys who developed into the patriarchal "uncles" of the old slave regime.

When I left the University, it was with the determination to get my trunk and move out to the school before night. I walked back across the city with a light step and a light heart. I felt perfectly satisfied with life for the first time since my mother's death. In passing the railroad station I hired a wagon and rode with the driver as far as my stopping-place. I settled with my landlord and went upstairs to put away several articles I had left out. As soon as I opened my trunk, a dart of suspicion shot through my heart; the arrangement of things did not look familiar. I began to dig down excitedly to the bottom till I reached the coat in which I had concealed my treasure. My money was gone! Every single bill of it. I knew it was useless to do so, but I searched through every other coat, every pair of trousers, every vest, and even each pair of socks. When I had finished my fruitless search, I sat down dazed and heart-sick. I called the landlord up and informed him of my loss; he comforted me by saying that I ought to have better sense than to keep money in a trunk and that he was not responsible for his lodgers' personal effects. His cooling words brought me enough to my senses to cause me to look and see if anything else was missing. Several small articles were gone, among them a black and grey necktie of odd design upon which my heart was set; almost as much as the loss of my money I felt the loss of my tie.

After thinking for a while as best I could, I wisely decided to go at once back to the University and lay my troubles before the president. I rushed breathlessly back to the school. As I neared the grounds, the thought came across me, would not my story sound fishy? Would it not place me in the position of an impostor or beggar? What right had I to worry these busy people with the results of my carelessness? If the money could not be recovered, and I doubted that it could, what good would it do to tell them about it? The shame and embarrassment which the whole situation gave me caused me to stop at the gate. I paused, undecided, for a moment; then turned and slowly retraced my steps, and so changed the whole course of my life.

If the reader has never been in a strange city without money or friends, it is useless to try to describe what my feelings were; he could not understand. If he has been, it is equally useless, for he understands more than words could convey. When I reached my lodgings, I found in the room one of the porters who had slept there the night before. When he heard what misfortune had befallen me, he offered many words of sympathy and advice. He asked me how much money I had left. I told him that I had ten or twelve dollars in my pocket. He said: "That won't last you very long here, and you will hardly be able to find anything to do in Atlanta. I'll tell you what you do, go down to Jacksonville and you won't have any trouble to get a job in one of the big hotels there, or in St. Augustine." I thanked him, but intimated my doubts of being able to get to Jacksonville on the money I had. He reassured me by saying: "Oh, that's all right. You express your trunk on through, and I'll take you down in my closet." I thanked him again, not knowing then what it was to travel in a Pullman porter's closet. He put me under a deeper debt of gratitude by lending me fifteen dollars, which he said I could pay back after I had secured work. His generosity brought tears to my eyes, and I concluded that, after all, there were some kind hearts in the world.

I now forgot my troubles in the hurry and excitement of getting my trunk off in time to catch the train, which went out at seven o'clock. I even forgot that I hadn't eaten anything since morning. We got a wagon—the porter went with me—and took my trunk to the express office. My new friend then told me to come to the station at about a quarter of seven and walk straight to the car where I should see him standing, and not to lose my nerve. I found my role not so difficult to play as I thought it would be, because the train did not leave from the central station, but from a smaller one, where there were no gates and guards to pass. I followed directions, and the porter took me on his car and locked me in his closet. In a few minutes the train pulled out for Jacksonville.

I may live to be a hundred years old, but I shall never forget the agonies I suffered that night. I spent twelve hours doubled up in the porter's basket for soiled linen, not being able to straighten up on account of the shelves for clean linen just over my head. The air was hot and suffocating and the smell of damp towels and used linen was sickening. At each lurch of the car over the none too smooth track I was bumped and bruised against the narrow walls of my narrow compartment. I became acutely conscious of the fact that I had not eaten for hours. Then nausea took possession of me, and at one time I had grave doubts about reaching my destination alive. If I had the trip to make again, I should prefer to walk.

CHAPTER V

The next morning I got out of the car at Jacksonville with a stiff and aching body. I determined to ask no more porters, not even my benefactor, about stopping-places; so I found myself on the street not knowing where to go. I walked along listlessly until I met a coloured man who had the appearance of a preacher. I asked him if he could direct me to a respectable boarding-house for coloured people. He said that if I walked along with him in the direction he was going, he would show me such a place: I turned and walked at his side. He proved to be a minister, and asked me a great many direct questions about myself. I answered as many as I saw fit to answer; the others I evaded or ignored. At length we stopped in front of a frame-house, and my guide informed me that it was the place. A woman was standing in the doorway, and he called to her saying that he had brought her a new boarder. I thanked him for his trouble, and after he had urged upon me to attend his church while I was in the city, he went on his way.

I went in and found the house neat and not uncomfortable. The parlour was furnished with cane-bottomed chairs, each of which was adorned with a white crocheted tidy. The mantel over the fireplace had a white crocheted cover; a marble-topped centre table held a lamp, a photograph album and several trinkets, each of which was set upon a white crocheted mat. There was a cottage organ in a corner of the room, and I noted that the lamp-racks upon it were covered with white crocheted mats. There was a matting on the floor, but a white crocheted carpet would not have been out of keeping. I made arrangements with the landlady for my board and lodging; the amount was, I think, three dollars and a half a week. She was a rather fine-looking, stout, brown-skin woman of about forty years of age. Her husband was a light-coloured Cuban, a man about one half her size, and one whose age could not be guessed from his appearance. He was small in size, but a handsome black moustache and typical Spanish eyes redeemed him from insignificance.

I was in time for breakfast, and at the table I had the opportunity to see my fellow boarders. There were eight or ten of them. Two, as I afterwards learned, were coloured Americans. All of them were cigar-makers and worked in one of the large factories—cigar-making is one trade in which the colour line is not drawn. The conversation was carried on entirely in Spanish, and my ignorance of the language subjected me more to alarm than embarrassment. I had never heard such uproarious conversation; everybody talked at once, loud exclamations, rolling "*carambas*," menacing gesticulations with knives, forks, and spoons. I looked every moment for the clash of blows. One man was emphasizing his remarks by flourishing a cup in his hand, seemingly forgetful of the fact that it was nearly full of hot coffee. He ended by emptying it over what was, relatively, the only quiet man at the table excepting myself, bringing from him a volley of language which made the others appear dumb by comparison. I soon learned that in all of this clatter of voices and table utensils they were discussing purely ordinary affairs and arguing about mere trifles, and that not the least ill feeling was aroused. It was not long before I enjoyed the spirited chatter and *badinage* at the table as much as I did my meals—and the meals were not bad.

I spent the afternoon in looking round the town. The streets were sandy, but were well shaded by fine oak-trees and far preferable to the clay roads of Atlanta. One or two public squares with green grass and trees gave the city a touch of freshness. That night after supper I spoke to my landlady and her husband about my intentions. They told me that the big winter hotels would not open within two months. It can easily be imagined what effect this news had on me. I spoke to them frankly about my financial condition and related the main fact of my misfortune in Atlanta. I modestly mentioned my ability to teach music and asked if there was any likelihood of my being able to get some scholars. My landlady suggested that I speak to the preacher who had shown me her house; she felt sure that through his influence I should be able to get up a class in piano. She added, however, that the coloured people were poor, and that the general price for music lessons was only twenty-five cents. I noticed that the thought of my teaching white pupils did not even remotely enter her mind. None of this information made my prospects look much brighter.

The husband, who up to this time had allowed the woman to do most of the talking, gave me the first bit of tangible hope; he said that he could get me a job as a "stripper" in the factory where he worked, and that if I succeeded in getting some music pupils, I could teach a couple of them every night, and so make a living until something better turned up. He went on to say that it would not be a bad thing for me to stay at the factory and learn my trade as a cigar-maker, and impressed on me that, for a young man knocking about the country, a trade was a handy thing to have. I determined to accept his offer and thanked him heartily. In fact, I became enthusiastic, not only because I saw a way out of my financial troubles, but also because I was eager and curious over the new experience I was about to enter. I wanted to know all about the cigar-making business. This narrowed the conversation down to the husband and myself, so the wife went in and left us talking.

He was what is called a *regalía* workman, and earned from thirty-five to forty dollars a week. He generally worked a sixty-dollar job;

that is, he made cigars for which he was paid at the rate of sixty dollars per thousand. It was impossible for him to make a thousand in a week because he had to work very carefully and slowly. Each cigar was made entirely by hand. Each piece of filler and each wrapper had to be selected with care. He was able to make a bundle of one hundred cigars in a day, not one of which could be told from the others by any difference in size or shape, or even by any appreciable difference in weight. This was the acme of artistic skill in cigar-making. Workmen of this class were rare, never more than three or four in one factory, and it was never necessary for them to remain out of work. There were men who made two, three, and four hundred cigars of the cheaper grades in a day; they had to be very fast in order to make decent week's wages. Cigar-making was a rather independent trade; the men went to work when they pleased and knocked off when they felt like doing so. As a class the workmen were careless and improvident; some very rapid makers would not work more than three or four days out of the week, and there were others who never showed up at the factory on Mondays. "Strippers" were the boys who pulled the long stems from the tobacco leaves. After they had served at that work for a certain time they were given tables as apprentices.

All of this was interesting to me; and we drifted along in conversation until my companion struck the subject nearest his heart, the independence of Cuba. He was an exile from the island, and a prominent member of the Jacksonville Junta. Every week sums of money were collected from juntas all over the country. This money went to buy arms and ammunition for the insurgents. As the man sat there nervously smoking his long, "green" cigar, and telling me of the Gómezes, both the white one and the black one, of Macéo and Bandera, he grew positively eloquent. He also showed that he was a man of considerable education and reading. He spoke English excellently, and frequently surprised me by using words one would hardly expect from a foreigner. The first one of this class of words he employed almost shocked me, and I never forgot it; 'twas "ramify." We sat on the piazza until after ten o'clock. When we arose to go in to bed, it was with the understanding that I should start in the factory on the next day.

I began work the next morning seated at a barrel with another boy, who showed me how to strip the stems from the leaves, to smooth out each half leaf, and to put the "rights" together in one pile, and the "lefts" together in another pile on the edge of the barrel. My fingers, strong and sensitive from their long training, were well adapted to this kind of work, and within two weeks I was accounted the fastest "stripper" in the factory. At first the heavy odour of the tobacco almost sickened me, but when I became accustomed to it, I liked the smell. I was now earning four dollars a week, and was soon able to pick up a couple more by teaching a few scholars at night, whom I had secured through the good offices of the preacher I had met on my first morning in Jacksonville.

At the end of about three months, through my skill as a "stripper" and the influence of my landlord, I was advanced to a table and began to learn my trade; in fact, more than my trade; for I learned not only to make cigars, but also to smoke, to swear, and to speak Spanish. I discovered that I had a talent for languages as well as for music. The rapidity and ease with which I acquired Spanish astonished my associates. In a short time I was able not only to understand most of what was said at the table during meals, but to join in the conversation. I bought a method for learning the Spanish language, and with the aid of my landlord as a teacher, by constant practice with my fellow workmen, and by regularly reading the Cuban newspapers and finally some books of standard Spanish literature which were at the house, I was able in less than a year to speak like a native. In fact, it was my pride that I spoke better Spanish than many of the Cuban workmen at the factory.

After I had been in the factory a little over a year, I was repaid for all the effort I had put forth to learn Spanish by being selected as "reader." The "reader" is quite an institution in all cigar factories which employ Spanish-speaking workmen. He sits in the centre of the large room in which the cigar-makers work and reads to them for a certain number of hours each day all the important news from the papers and whatever else he may consider would be interesting. He often selects an exciting novel and reads it in daily instalments. He must, of course, have a good voice, but he must also have a reputation among the men for intelligence, for being well posted and having in his head a stock of varied information. He is generally the final authority on all arguments which arise, and in a cigar factory these arguments are many and frequent, ranging from the respective and relative merits of rival baseball clubs to the duration of the sun's light and energy—cigar-making is a trade in which talk does not interfere with work. My position as "reader" not only released me from the rather monotonous work of rolling cigars, and gave me something more in accord with my tastes, but also added considerably to my income. I was now earning about twenty-five dollars a week, and was able to give up my peripatetic method of giving music lessons. I hired a piano and taught only those who could arrange to take their lessons where I lived. I finally gave up teaching entirely, as what I made scarcely paid for my time and trouble. I kept the piano, however, in order to keep up my own studies, and occasionally I played at some church concert or other charitable entertainment.

Through my music teaching and my not absolutely irregular attendance at church I became acquainted with the best class of coloured people in Jacksonville. This was really my entrance into the race. It was my initiation into what I have termed the freemasonry of the race. I had formulated a theory of what it was to be coloured; now I was getting the practice. The novelty of my position caused me to observe and consider things which, I think, entirely escaped the young men I associated with; or, at least, were so commonplace to them as not to attract their attention. And of many of the impressions which came to me then I have realized the full import only within the past few years, since I have had a broader knowledge of men and history, and a fuller comprehension of the tremendous struggle which is going on between the races in the South.

It is a struggle; for though the black man fights passively, he nevertheless fights; and his passive resistance is more effective at present than active resistance could possibly be. He bears the fury of the storm as does the willow-tree.

It is a struggle; for though the white man of the South may be too proud to admit it, he is, nevertheless, using in the contest his best energies; he is devoting to it the greater part of his thought and much of his endeavour. The South today stands panting and almost breathless from its exertions.

And how the scene of the struggle has shifted! The battle was first waged over the right of the Negro to be classed as a human being with a soul; later, as to whether he had sufficient intellect to master even the rudiments of learning; and today it is being fought out over his social recognition.

I said somewhere in the early part of this narrative that because the coloured man looked at everything through the prism of his relationship to society as a *coloured* man, and because most of his mental efforts ran through the narrow channel bounded by his rights and his wrongs, it was to be wondered at that he has progressed so broadly as he has. The same thing may be said of the white man of the South; most of his mental efforts run through one narrow channel; his life as a man and a citizen, many of his financial activities, and all of his political activities are impassably limited by the ever present "Negro question." I am sure it would be safe to wager that no group of Southern white men could get together and talk for sixty minutes without bringing up the "race question." If a Northern white man happened to be in the group, the time could be safely cut to thirty minutes. In this respect I consider the conditions of the whites more to be deplored than that of the blacks. Here, a truly great people, a people that produced a majority of the great historic Americans from Washington to Lincoln, now forced to use up its energies in a conflict as lamentable as it is violent.

I shall give the observations I made in Jacksonville as seen through the light of after years; and they apply generally to every Southern community. The coloured people may be said to be roughly divided into three classes, not so much in respect to themselves as in respect to their relations with the whites. There are those constituting what might be called the desperate class—the men who work in the lumber and turpentine camps, the ex-convicts, the bar-room loafers are all in this class. These men conform to the requirements of civilization much as a trained lion with low muttered growls goes through his stunts under the crack of the trainer's whip. They cherish a sullen hatred for all white men, and they value life as cheap. I have heard more than one of them say: "I'll go to hell for the first white man that bothers me." Many who have expressed that sentiment have kept their word, and it is that fact which gives such prominence to this class; for in numbers it is only a small proportion of the coloured people, but it often dominates public opinion concerning the whole race. Happily, this class represents the black people of the South far below their normal physical and moral condition, but in its increase lies the possibility of grave dangers. I am sure there is no more urgent work before the white South, not only for its present happiness, but for its future safety, than the decreasing of this class of blacks. And it is not at all a hopeless class; for these men are but the creatures of conditions, as much so as the slum and criminal elements of all the great cities of the world are creatures of conditions. Decreasing their number by shooting and burning them off will not be successful; for these men are truly desperate, and thoughts of death, however terrible, have little effect in deterring them from acts the result of hatred or degeneracy. This class of blacks hate everything covered by a white skin, and in return they are loathed by the whites. The whites regard them just about as a man would a vicious mule, a thing to be worked, driven, and beaten, and killed for kicking.

The second class, as regards the relation between blacks and whites, comprises the servants, the washerwomen, the waiters, the cooks, the coachmen, and all who are connected with the whites by domestic service. These may be generally characterized as simple, kind-hearted, and faithful; not overfine in their moral deductions, but intensely religious, and relatively—such matters can be judged only relatively—about as honest and wholesome in their lives as any other grade of society. Any white person is "good" who treats them kindly, and they love him for that kindness. In return, the white people with whom they have to do regard them with indulgent affection. They come into close daily contact with the whites, and may be called the connecting link between whites and blacks; in fact, it is through them that the whites know the rest of their coloured neighbours. Between this class of the blacks and the whites there is little or no friction.

The third class is composed of the independent workmen and tradesmen, and of the well-to-do and educated coloured people; and, strange to say, for a directly opposite reason they are as far removed from the whites as the members of the first class I mentioned. These people live in a little world of their own; in fact, I concluded that if a coloured man wanted to separate himself from his white neighbours, he had but to acquire some money, education, and culture, and to live in accordance. For example, the proudest and fairest lady in the South could with propriety—and it is what she would most likely do—go to the cabin of Aunt Mary, her cook, if Aunt Mary was sick, and minister to her comfort with her own hands; but if Mary's daughter, Eliza, a girl who used to run round my lady's kitchen, but who has received an education and married a prosperous young coloured man, were at death's door, my lady would no more think of crossing the threshold of Eliza's cottage than she would of going into a bar-room for a drink.

I was walking down the street one day with a young man who was born in Jacksonville, but had been away to prepare himself for a professional life. We passed a young white man, and my companion said to me: "You see that young man? We grew up together; we have played, hunted, and fished together; we have even eaten and slept together; and now since I have come back home, he barely speaks to me." The fact that the whites of the South despise and ill-treat the desperate class of blacks is not only explainable according to the ancient laws of human nature, but it is not nearly so serious or important as the fact that as the progressive coloured people advance, they constantly widen the gulf between themselves and their white neighbours. I think that the white people somehow feel that coloured people who have education and money, who wear good clothes and live in comfortable houses, are "putting on airs," that they do these things for the sole purpose of "spiting the white folks," or are, at best, going through a sort of monkey-like imitation. Of course, such feelings can only cause irritation or breed disgust. It seems that the whites have not yet been able to realize and understand that these people in striving to better their physical and social surroundings in accordance with their financial and intellectual progress are simply obeying an impulse which is common to human nature the world over. I am in grave doubt as to whether the greater part of the friction in the South is caused by the whites' having a natural antipathy to Negroes as a race, or an acquired antipathy to Negroes in certain relations to themselves. However that may be, there is to my mind no more pathetic side of this many-sided question than the isolated position into which are forced the very coloured people who most need and who could best appreciate sympathetic co-operation; and their position grows tragic when the effort is made to couple them, whether or no, with the Negroes of the first class I mentioned.

This latter class of coloured people are well-disposed towards the whites, and always willing to meet them more than half-way. They, however, feel keenly any injustice or gross discrimination, and generally show their resentment. The effort is sometimes made to convey the impression that the better class of coloured people fight against riding in "Jim Crow" cars because they want to ride with white people or object to being with humbler members of their own race. The truth is they object to the humiliation of being forced to ride in a *par-*

ticular car, aside from the fact that that car is distinctly inferior, and that they are required to pay full first-class fare. To say that the whites are forced to ride in the superior car is less than a joke. And, too, odd as it may sound, refined coloured people get no more pleasure out of riding with offensive Negroes than anybody else would get.

I can realize more fully than I could years ago that the position of the advanced element of the coloured race is often very trying. They are the ones among the blacks who carry the entire weight of the race question; it worries the others very little, and I believe the only thing which at times sustains them is that they know that they are in the right. On the other hand, this class of coloured people get a good deal of pleasure out of life; their existence is far from being one long groan about their condition. Out of a chaos of ignorance and poverty they have evolved a social life of which they need not be ashamed. In cities where the professional and well-to-do class is large they have formed society—society as discriminating as the actual conditions will allow it to be; I should say, perhaps, society possessing discriminating tendencies which become rules as fast as actual conditions allow. This statement will, I know, sound preposterous, even ridiculous, to some persons; but as this class of coloured people is the least known of the race it is not surprising. These social circles are connected throughout the country, and a person in good standing in one city is readily accepted in another. One who is on the outside will often find it a difficult matter to get in. I know personally of one case in which money to the extent of thirty or forty thousand dollars and a fine house, not backed up by a good reputation, after several years of repeated effort, failed to gain entry for the possessor. These people have their dances and dinners and card parties, their musicals, and their literary societies. The women attend social affairs dressed in good taste, and the men in dress suits which they own; and the reader will make a mistake to confound these entertainments with the "Bellman's Balls" and "Whitewashers' Picnics" and "Lime-kiln Clubs" with which the humorous press of the country illustrates "Cullud Sassiety."

Jacksonville, when I was there, was a small town, and the number of educated and well-to-do coloured people was small; so this society phase of life did not equal what I have since seen in Boston, Washington, Richmond, and Nashville; and it is upon what I have more recently seen in these cities that I have made the observations just above. However, there were many comfortable and pleasant homes in Jacksonville to which I was often invited. I belonged to the literary society—at which we generally discussed the race question—and attended all of the church festivals and other charitable entertainments. In this way I passed three years which were not at all the least enjoyable of my life. In fact, my joy took such an exuberant turn that I fell in love with a young schoolteacher and began to have dreams of matrimonial bliss; but another turn in the course of my life brought these dreams to an end.

I do not wish to mislead my readers into thinking that I led a life in Jacksonville which would make copy for the hero of a Sunday-school library book. I was a hail fellow well met with all of the workmen at the factory, most of whom knew little and cared less about social distinctions. From their example I learned to be careless about money, and for that reason I constantly postponed and finally abandoned returning to Atlanta University. It seemed impossible for me to save as much as two hundred dollars. Several of the men at the factory were my intimate friends, and I frequently joined them in their pleasures. During the summer months we went almost every Monday on an excursion to a seaside resort called Pablo Beach. These excursions were always crowded. There was a dancing-pavilion, a great deal of drinking, and generally a fight or two to add to the excitement. I also contracted the cigar-maker's habit of riding round in a hack on Sunday afternoons. I sometimes went with my cigar-maker friends to public balls that were given at a large hall on one of the main streets. I learned to take a drink occasionally and paid for quite a number that my friends took; but strong liquors never appealed to my appetite. I drank them only when the company I was in required it, and suffered for it afterwards. On the whole, though I was a bit wild, I can't remember that I ever did anything disgraceful, or, as the usual standard for young men goes, anything to forfeit my claim to respectability.

At one of the first public balls I attended I saw the Pullman-car porter who had so kindly assisted me in getting to Jacksonville. I went immediately to one of my factory friends and borrowed fifteen dollars with which to repay the loan my benefactor had made me. After I had given him the money, and was thanking him, I noticed that he wore what was, at least, an exact duplicate of my lamented black and grey tie. It was somewhat worn, but distinct enough for me to trace the same odd design which had first attracted my eye. This was enough to arouse my strongest suspicions, but whether it was sufficient for the law to take cognizance of I did not consider. My astonishment and the ironical humour of the situation drove everything else out of my mind.

These balls were attended by a great variety of people. They were generally given by the waiters of some one of the big hotels, and were often patronized by a number of hotel guests who came to "see the sights." The crowd was always noisy, but good-natured; there was much quadrille-dancing, and a strong-lunged man called figures in a voice which did not confine itself to the limits of the hall. It is not worth the while for me to describe in detail how these people acted; they conducted themselves in about the same manner as I have seen other people at similar balls conduct themselves. When one has seen something of the world and human nature, one must conclude, after all, that between people in like stations of life there is very little difference the world over.

However, it was at one of these balls that I first saw the cake-walk. There was a contest for a gold watch, to be awarded to the hotel head-waiter receiving the greatest number of votes. There was some dancing while the votes were being counted. Then the floor was cleared for the cake-walk. A half-dozen guests from some of the hotels took seats on the stage to act as judges, and twelve or fourteen couples began to walk for a sure enough, highly decorated cake, which was in plain evidence. The spectators crowded about the space reserved for the contestants and watched them with interest and excitement. The couples did not walk round in a circle, but in a square, with the men on the inside. The fine points to be considered were the bearing of the men, the precision with which they turned the corners, the grace of the women, and the ease with which they swung round the pivots. The men walked with stately and soldierly step, and the women with considerable grace. The judges arrived at their decision by a process of elimination. The music and the walk continued for some minutes; then both were stopped while the judges conferred; when the walk began again, several couples were left out. In this way the contest was finally narrowed down to three or four couples. Then the excitement became intense; there was much partisan cheering as one couple or another would execute a turn in extra elegant style. When the cake was finally awarded, the spectators were about evenly divided between those who cheered the winners and those who muttered about the unfairness of the judges. This was the cake-walk in its original form, and it is what the coloured performers on the theatrical stage developed into the prancing movements now known all over the world, and which some Parisian critics pronounced the acme of poetic motion.

There are a great many coloured people who are ashamed of the cake-walk, but I think they ought to be proud of it. It is my opinion that the coloured people of this country have done four things which refute the oft-advanced theory that they are an absolutely inferior race, which demonstrate that they have originality and artistic conception, and, what is more, the power of creating that which can influence and appeal universally. The first two of these are the Uncle Remus stories, collected by Joel Chandler Harris, and the Jubilee songs, to which the Fisk singers made the public and the skilled musicians of both America and Europe listen. The other two are rag-time music and the cake-walk. No one who has travelled can question the world-conquering influence of rag-time, and I do not think it would be an exaggeration to say that in Europe the United States is popularly known better by rag-time than by anything else it has produced in a generation. In Paris they call it American music. The newspapers have already told how the practice of intricate cake-walk steps has taken up the time of European royalty and nobility. These are lower forms of art, but they give evidence of a power that will some day be applied to the higher forms. In this measure, at least, and aside from the number of prominent individuals the coloured people of the United States have produced, the race has been a world influence; and all of the Indians between Alaska and Patagonia haven't done as much.

Just when I was beginning to look upon Jacksonville as my permanent home and was beginning to plan about marrying the young school-teacher, raising a family, and working in a cigar factory the rest of my life, for some reason, which I do not now remember, the factory at which I worked was indefinitely shut down. Some of the men got work in other factories in town; some decided to go to Key West and Tampa, others made up their minds to go to New York for work. All at once a desire like a fever seized me to see the North again and I cast my lot with those bound for New York.

CHAPTER VI

We steamed up into New York harbour late one afternoon in spring. The last efforts of the sun were being put forth in turning the waters of the bay to glistening gold; the green islands on either side, in spite of their warlike mountings, looked calm and peaceful; the buildings of the town shone out in a reflected light which gave the city an air of enchantment; and, truly, it is an enchanted spot. New York City is the most fatally fascinating thing in America. She sits like a great witch at the gate of the country, showing her alluring white face and hiding her crooked hands and feet under the folds of her wide garments—constantly enticing thousands from far within, and tempting those who come from across the seas to go no farther. And all these become the victims of her caprice. Some she at once crushes beneath her cruel feet; others she condemns to a fate like that of galley-slaves; a few she favours and fondles, riding them high on the bubbles of fortune; then with a sudden breath she blows the bubbles out and laughs mockingly as she watches them fall.

Twice I had passed through it, but this was really my first visit to New York; and as I walked about that evening, I began to feel the dread power of the city; the crowds, the lights, the excitement, the gaiety, and all its subtler stimulating influences began to take effect upon me. My blood ran quicker and I felt that I was just beginning to live. To some natures this stimulant of life in a great city becomes a thing as binding and necessary as opium is to one addicted to the habit. It becomes their breath of life; they cannot exist outside of it; rather than be deprived of it they are content to suffer hunger, want, pain, and misery; they would not exchange even a ragged and wretched condition among the great crowd for any degree of comfort away from it.

As soon as we landed, four of us went directly to a lodging-house in Twenty-seventh Street, just west of Sixth Avenue. The house was run by a short, stout mulatto man, who was exceedingly talkative and inquisitive. In fifteen minutes he not only knew the history of the past life of each one of us, but had a clearer idea of what we intended to do in the future than we ourselves. He sought this information so much with an air of being very particular as to whom he admitted into his house that we tremblingly answered every question that he asked.

When we had become located, we went out and got supper, then walked round until about ten o'clock. At that hour we met a couple of young fellows who lived in New York and were known to one of the members of our party. It was suggested we go to a certain place which was known by the proprietor's name. We turned into one of the cross streets and mounted the stoop of a house in about the middle of a block between Sixth and Seventh Avenues. One of the young men whom we had met rang a bell, and a man on the inside cracked the door a couple of inches; then opened it and let us in. We found ourselves in the hallway of what had once been a residence. The front parlour had been converted into a bar, and a half-dozen or so well-dressed men were in the room. We went in and after a general introduction had several rounds of beer. In the back parlour a crowd was sitting and standing round the walls of the room watching an exciting and noisy game of pool. I walked back and joined this crowd to watch the game, and principally to get away from the drinking party. The game was really interesting, the players being quite expert, and the excitement was heightened by the bets which were being made on the result. At times the antics and remarks of both players and spectators were amusing. When, at a critical point, a player missed a shot, he was deluged, by those financially interested in his making it, with a flood of epithets synonymous with "chump"; while from the others he would be jeered by such remarks as "Nigger, dat cue ain't no hoe-handle." I noticed that among this class of coloured men the word "nigger" was freely used in about the same sense as the word "fellow," and sometimes as a term of almost endearment; but I soon learned that its use was positively and absolutely prohibited to white men.

I stood watching this pool game until I was called by my friends, who were still in the bar-room, to go upstairs. On the second floor there were two large rooms. From the hall I looked into the one on the front. There was a large, round table in the centre, at which five or six men were seated playing poker. The air and conduct here were greatly in contrast to what I had just seen in the pool-room; these men were evidently the aristocrats of the place; they were well, perhaps a bit flashily, dressed and spoke in low modulated voices, frequently using the word "gentlemen"; in fact, they seemed to be practising a sort of Chesterfieldian politeness towards each other. I was watching these men with a great deal of interest and some degree of admiration when

I was again called by the members of our party, and I followed them on to the back room. There was a door-keeper at this room, and we were admitted only after inspection. When we got inside, I saw a crowd of men of all ages and kinds grouped about an old billiard-table, regarding some of whom, in supposing them to be white, I made no mistake. At first I did not know what these men were doing; they were using terms that were strange to me. I could hear only a confusion of voices exclaiming: "Shoot the two!" "Shoot the four!" "Fate me! Fate me!" "I've got you fated!" "Twenty-five cents he don't turn!" This was the ancient and terribly fascinating game of dice, popularly known as "craps." I myself had played pool in Jacksonville—it is a favourite game among cigar-makers—and I had seen others play cards; but here was something new. I edged my way in to the table and stood between one of my new-found New York friends and a tall, slender, black fellow, who was making side bets while the dice were at the other end of the table. My companion explained to me the principles of the game; and they are so simple that they hardly need to be explained twice. The dice came round the table until they reached the man on the other side of the tall, black fellow. He lost, and the latter said: "Gimme the bones." He threw a dollar on the table and said: "Shoot the dollar." His style of play was so strenuous that he had to be allowed plenty of room. He shook the dice high above his head, and each time he threw them on the table, he emitted a grunt such as men give when they are putting forth physical exertion with a rhythmic regularity. He frequently whirled completely round on his heels, throwing the dice the entire length of the table, and talking to them as though they were trained animals. He appealed to them in short singsong phrases. "Come, dice," he would say. "Little Phœbe," "Little Joe," "'Way down yonder in the cornfield." Whether these mystic incantations were efficacious or not I could not say, but, at any rate, his luck was great, and he had what gamblers term "nerve." "Shoot the dollar!" "Shoot the two!" "Shoot the four!" "Shoot the eight!" came from his lips as quickly as the dice turned to his advantage. My companion asked me if I had ever played. I told him no. He said that I ought to try my luck: that everybody won at first. The tall man at my side was waving his arms in the air, exclaiming: "Shoot the sixteen!" "Shoot the sixteen!" "Fate me!" Whether it was my companion's suggestion or some latent dare-devil strain in my blood which suddenly sprang into activity I do not know; but with a thrill of excitement which went through my whole body I threw a twenty-dollar bill on the table and said in a trembling voice: "I fate you."

I could feel that I had gained the attention and respect of everybody in the room, every eye was fixed on me, and the widespread question, "Who is he?" went round. This was gratifying to a certain sense of vanity of which I have never been able to rid myself, and I felt that it was worth the money even if I lost. The tall man, with a whirl on his heels and a double grunt, threw the dice; four was the number which turned up. This is considered as a hard "point" to make. He redoubled his contortions and his grunts and his pleadings to the dice; but on his third or fourth throw the fateful seven turned up, and I had won. My companion and all my friends shouted to me to follow up my luck. The fever was on me. I seized the dice. My hands were so hot that the bits of bone felt like pieces of ice. I shouted as loudly as I could: "Shoot it all!" but the blood was tingling so about my ears that I could not hear my own voice. I was soon "fated." I threw the dice—seven—I had won. "Shoot it all!" I cried again. There was a pause; the stake was more than one man cared to or could cover. I was finally "fated" by several men taking each a part of it. I then threw the dice again. Seven. I had won. "Shoot it all!" I shouted excitedly. After a short delay I was "fated." Again I rolled the dice. Eleven. Again I won. My friends now surrounded me and, much against my inclination, forced me to take down all of the money except five dollars. I tried my luck once more, and threw some small "point" which I failed to make, and the dice passed on to the next man.

In less than three minutes I had won more than two hundred dollars, a sum which afterwards cost me dearly. I was the hero of the moment and was soon surrounded by a group of men who expressed admiration for my "nerve" and predicted for me a brilliant future as a gambler. Although at the time I had no thought of becoming a gambler, I felt proud of my success. I felt a bit ashamed, too, that I had allowed my friends to persuade me to take down my money so soon. Another set of men also got round me and begged me for twenty-five or fifty cents to put them back into the game. I gave each of them something. I saw that several of them had on linen dusters, and as I looked about, I noticed that there were perhaps a dozen men in the room similarly clad. I asked the fellow who had been my prompter at the dice table why they dressed in such a manner. He told me that men who had lost all the money and jewellery they possessed, frequently, in an effort to recoup their losses, would gamble away all their outer clothing and even their shoes; and that the proprietor kept on hand a supply of linen dusters for all who were so unfortunate. My informant went on to say that sometimes a fellow would become almost completely dressed and then, by a turn of the dice, would be thrown back into a state of semi-nakedness. Some of them were virtually prisoners and unable to get into the streets for days at a time. They ate at the lunch counter, where their credit was good so long as they were fair gamblers and did not attempt to jump their debts, and they slept round in chairs. They importuned friends and winners to put them back in the game, and kept at it until fortune again smiled on them. I laughed heartily at this, not thinking the day was coming which would find me in the same ludicrous predicament.

On passing downstairs I was told that the third and top floor of the house was occupied by the proprietor. When we passed through the bar, I treated everybody in the room—and that was no small number, for eight or ten had followed us down. Then our party went out. It was now about half past twelve, but my nerves were at such a tension that I could not endure the mere thought of going to bed. I asked if there was no other place to which we could go; our guides said yes, and suggested that we go to the "Club." We went to Sixth Avenue, walked two blocks, and turned to the west into another street. We stopped in front of a house with three stories and a basement. In the basement was a Chinese chop-suey restaurant. There was a red lantern at the iron gate to the areaway, inside of which the Chinaman's name was printed. We went up the steps of the stoop, rang the bell, and were admitted without any delay. From the outside the house bore a rather gloomy aspect, the windows being absolutely dark, but within, it was a veritable house of mirth. When we had passed through a small vestibule and reached the hallway, we heard mingled sounds of music and laughter, the clink of glasses, and the pop of bottles. We went into the main room and I was little prepared for what I saw. The brilliancy of the place, the display of diamond rings, scarf-pins, ear-rings, and breast-pins, the big rolls of money that were brought into evidence when drinks were paid for, and the air of gaiety that pervaded the place, all completely dazzled and dazed me. I felt positively giddy, and it was several minutes before I was able to make any clear and definite observations.

We at length secured places at a table in a corner of the room and, as soon as we could attract the attention of one of the busy waiters, ordered a round of drinks. When I had somewhat collected my senses, I realized that in a large back room into which the main room opened, there was a young fellow singing a song, accompanied on the piano by a short, thickset, dark man. After each verse he did some dance steps, which brought forth great applause and a shower of small coins at his feet. After the singer had responded to a rousing encore, the stout man at the piano began to run his fingers up and down the keyboard. This he did in a manner which indicated that he was master of a good deal of technique. Then he began to play; and such playing! I stopped talking to listen. It was music of a kind I had never heard before. It was music that demanded physical response, patting of the feet, drumming of the fingers, or nodding of the head in time with the beat. The barbaric harmonies, the audacious resolutions, often consisting of an abrupt jump from one key to another, the intricate rhythms in which the accents fell in the most unexpected places, but in which the beat was never lost, produced a most curious effect. And, too, the player—the dexterity of his left hand in making rapid octave runs and jumps was little short of marvellous; and with his right hand he frequently swept half the keyboard with clean-cut chromatics which he fitted in so nicely as never to fail to arouse in his listeners a sort of pleasant surprise at the accomplishment of the feat.

This was rag-time music, then a novelty in New York, and just growing to be a rage, which has not yet subsided. It was originated in the questionable resorts about Memphis and St. Louis by Negro piano-players who knew no more of the theory of music than they did of the theory of the universe, but were guided by natural musical instinct and talent. It made its way to Chicago, where it was popular some time before it reached New York. These players often improvised crude and, at times, vulgar words to fit the melodies. This was the beginning of the rag-time song. Several of these improvisations were taken down by white men, the words slightly altered, and published under the names of the arrangers. They sprang into immediate popularity and earned small fortunes, of which the Negro originators got only a few dollars. But I have learned that since that time a number of coloured men, of not only musical talent, but training, are writing out their own melodies and words and reaping the reward of their work. I have learned also that they have a large number of white imitators and adulterators.

American musicians, instead of investigating rag-time, attempt to ignore it, or dismiss it with a contemptuous word. But that has always been the course of scholasticism in every branch of art. Whatever new thing the *people* like is pooh-poohed; whatever is *popular* is spoken of as not worth the while. The fact is, nothing great or enduring, especially in music, has ever sprung full-fledged and unprecedented from the brain of any master; the best that he gives to the world he gathers from the hearts of the people, and runs it through the alembic of his genius. In spite of the bans which musicians and music teachers have placed upon it, the people still demand and enjoy rag-time. One thing cannot be denied; it is music which possesses at least one strong element of greatness: it appeals universally; not only the American, but the English, the French, and even the German people find delight in it. In fact, there is not a corner of the civilized world in which it is not known, and this proves its originality; for if it were an imitation, the people of Europe, anyhow, would not have found it a novelty. Anyone who doubts that there is a peculiar heel-tickling, smile-provoking, joy-awakening charm in rag-time needs only to hear a skilful performer play the genuine article to be convinced. I believe that it has its place as well as the music which draws from us sighs and tears.

I became so interested in both the music and the player that I left the table where I was sitting, and made my way through the hall into the back room, where I could see as well as hear. I talked to the piano-player between the musical numbers and found out that he was just a natural musician, never having taken a lesson in his life. Not only could he play almost anything he heard, but he could accompany singers in songs he had never heard. He had, by ear alone, composed some pieces, several of which he played over for me; each of them was properly proportioned and balanced. I began to wonder what this man with such a lavish natural endowment would have done had he been trained. Perhaps he wouldn't have done anything at all; he might have become, at best, a mediocre imitator of the great masters in what they have already done to a finish, or one of the modern innovators who strive after originality by seeing how cleverly they can dodge about through the rules of harmony and at the same time avoid melody. It is certain that he would not have been so delightful as he was in rag-time.

I sat by, watching and listening to this man until I was dragged away by my friends. The place was now almost deserted; only a few stragglers hung on, and they were all the worse for drink. My friends were well up in this class. We passed into the street; the lamps were pale against the sky; day was just breaking. We went home and got into bed. I fell into a fitful sort of sleep, with rag-time music ringing continually in my ears.

CHAPTER VII

I shall take advantage of this pause in my narrative to describe more closely the "Club" spoken of in the latter part of the preceding chapter—to describe it as I afterwards came to know it, as an habitué. I shall do this not only because of the direct influence it had on my life, but also because it was at that time the most famous place of its kind in New York, and was well known to both white and coloured people of certain classes.

I have already stated that in the basement of the house there was a Chinese restaurant. The Chinaman who kept it did an exceptionally good business; for chop-suey was a favourite dish among the frequenters of the place. It is a food that, somehow, has the power of absorbing alcoholic liquors that have been taken into the stomach. I have heard men claim that they could sober up on chop-suey. Perhaps that accounted, in some degree, for its popularity. On the main floor there were two large rooms: a parlour about thirty feet in length, and a large, square back room into which the parlour opened. The floor of the parlour was carpeted; small tables and chairs were arranged about the room; the windows were draped with lace curtains, and the walls were literally covered with photographs or lithographs of every coloured man in America who had ever "done anything." There were pictures of Frederick Douglass and of Peter Jackson, of all the lesser lights of the prize-fighting ring, of all the famous jockeys and the stage celebrities, down to the newest song and dance team. The most of these photographs were autographed and, in a sense, made a really valuable collection. In the back room there was a piano, and tables were placed round the wall. The floor was bare and the centre was left vacant for singers, dancers, and others who entertained the patrons. In a closet in this room which jutted out into the hall the proprietor kept his buffet. There was no open bar, because the place had no liquor licence. In this back room the tables were sometimes pushed aside, and the floor given over to general dancing. The front room on the next floor was a sort of private party room; a back room on the same floor contained no furniture and was devoted to the use of new and ambitious performers. In this room song and dance teams practised their steps, acrobatic teams practised their tumbles, and many other kinds of "acts" rehearsed their "turns." The other rooms of the house were used as sleeping-apartments.

No gambling was allowed, and the conduct of the place was surprisingly orderly. It was, in short, a centre of coloured Bohemians and sports. Here the great prize-fighters were wont to come, the famous jockeys, the noted minstrels, whose names and faces were familiar on every bill-board in the country; and these drew a multitude of those who love to dwell in the shadow of greatness. There were then no organizations giving performances of such order as are now given by several coloured companies; that was because no manager could imagine that audiences would pay to see Negro performers in any other role than that of Mississippi River roustabouts; but there was lots of talent and ambition. I often heard the younger and brighter men discussing the time when they would compel the public to recognize that they could do something more than grin and cut pigeon-wings.

Sometimes one or two of the visiting stage-professionals, after being sufficiently urged, would go into the back room and take the places of the regular amateur entertainers, but they were very sparing with these favours, and the patrons regarded them as special treats. There was one man, a minstrel, who, whenever he responded to a request to "do something," never essayed anything below a reading from Shakespeare. How well he read I do not know, but he greatly impressed me; and I can say that at least he had a voice which strangely stirred those who heard it. Here was a man who made people laugh at the size of his mouth, while he carried in his heart a burning ambition to be a tragedian; and so after all he did play a part in a tragedy.

These notables of the ring, the turf, and the stage, drew to the place crowds of admirers, both white and coloured. Whenever one of them came in, there were awe-inspired whispers from those who knew him by sight, in which they enlightened those round them as to his identity, and hinted darkly at their great intimacy with the noted one. Those who were on terms of approach immediately showed their privilege over others less fortunate by gathering round their divinity. I was, at first, among those who dwelt in darkness. Most of these celebrities I had never heard of. This made me an object of pity among many of my new associates. I soon learned, however, to fake a knowledge for the benefit of those who were greener than I; and, finally, I became personally acquainted with the majority of the famous personages who came to the "Club."

A great deal of money was spent here, so many of the patrons were men who earned large sums. I remember one night a dapper little brown-skin fellow was pointed out to me and I was told that he was the most popular jockey of the day, and that he earned $12,000 a year. This latter statement I couldn't doubt, for with my own eyes I saw him spending at about thirty times that rate. For his friends and those who were introduced to him he bought nothing but wine—in sporting circles, "wine" means champagne—and paid for it at five dollars a quart. He sent a quart to every table in the place with his compliments; and on the table at which he and his party were seated there were more than a dozen bottles. It was the custom at the "Club" for the waiter not to remove the bottles when champagne was being drunk until the party had finished. There were reasons for this; it advertised the brand of wine, it advertised that the party was drinking wine, and advertised how much they had bought. This jockey had won a great race that day, and he was rewarding his admirers for the homage they paid him, all of which he accepted with a fine air of condescension.

Besides the people I have just been describing, there was at the place almost every night one or two parties of white people, men and women, who were out sight-seeing, or slumming. They generally came in cabs; some of them would stay only for a few minutes, while others sometimes stayed until morning. There was also another set of white people who came frequently; it was made up of variety performers and others who delineated "darky characters"; they came to get their imitations firsthand from the Negro entertainers they saw there.

There was still another set of white patrons, composed of women; these were not occasional visitors, but five or six of them were regular habituées. When I first saw them, I was not sure that they were white. In the first place, among the many coloured women who came to the "Club" there were several just as fair; and, secondly, I always saw these women in company with coloured men. They were all good-looking and well dressed, and seemed to be women of some education. One of these in particular attracted my attention; she was an exceedingly beautiful woman of perhaps thirty-five; she had glistening copper-coloured hair, very white skin, and eyes very much like Du Maurier's conception of Trilby's "twin grey stars." When I came to know her, I found that she was a woman of considerable culture; she had travelled in Europe, spoke French, and played the piano well. She was always dressed elegantly, but in absolute good taste. She always came to the "Club" in a cab, and was soon joined by a well-set-up, very black young fellow. He was always faultlessly dressed; one of the most exclusive tailors in New York made his clothes, and he wore a number of diamonds in about as good taste as they could be worn in by a man. I learned that she paid for his clothes and his diamonds. I learned, too, that he was not the only one of his kind. More that I learned would be better suited to a book on social phenomena than to a narrative of my life.

This woman was known at the "Club" as the rich widow. She went by a very aristocratic-sounding name, which corresponded to her appearance. I shall never forget how hard it was for me to get over my feelings of surprise, perhaps more than surprise, at seeing her with her black companion; somehow I never exactly enjoyed the sight. I have devoted so much time to this pair, the "widow" and her companion, because it was through them that another decided turn was brought about in my life.

CHAPTER VIII

On the day following our night at the "club" we slept until late in the afternoon; so late that beginning search for work was entirely out of the question. This did not cause me much worry, for I had more than three hundred dollars, and New York had impressed me as a place where there was lots of money and not much difficulty in getting it. It is needless to inform my readers that I did not long hold this opinion. We got out of the house about dark, went to a restaurant on Sixth Avenue and ate something, then walked round for a couple of hours. I finally suggested that we visit the same places we had been in the night before. Following my suggestion, we started first to the gambling-house. The man on the door let us in without any question; I accredited this to my success of the night before. We went straight to the "crap" room, and I at once made my way to a table, where I was rather flattered by the murmur of recognition which went round. I played in up and down luck for three or four hours; then, worn with nervous excitement, quit, having lost about fifty dollars. But I was so strongly possessed with the thought that I would make up my losses the next time I played that I left the place with a light heart.

When we got into the street our party was divided against itself; two were for going home at once and getting to bed. They gave as a reason that we were to get up early and look for jobs. I think the real reason was that they had each lost several dollars in the game. I lived to learn that in the world of sport all men win alike, but lose differently; and so gamblers are rated, not by the way in which they win, but by the way in which they lose. Some men lose with a careless smile, recognizing that losing is a part of the game; others curse their luck and rail at fortune; and others, still, lose sadly; after each such experience they are swept by a wave of reform; they resolve to stop gambling and be good. When in this frame of mind it would take very little persuasion to lead them into a prayer-meeting. Those in the first class are looked upon with admiration; those in the second class are merely commonplace; while those in the third are regarded with contempt. I believe these distinctions hold good in all the ventures of life. After some minutes one of my friends and I succeeded in convincing the other two that a while at the "Club" would put us all in better spirits; and they consented to go, on our promise not to stay longer than an hour. We found the place crowded, and the same sort of thing going on which we had seen the night before. I took a seat at once by the side of the piano-player, and was soon lost to everything except the novel charm of the music. I watched the performer with the idea of catching the trick, and during one of his intermissions I took his place at the piano and made an attempt to imitate him, but even my quick ear and ready fingers were unequal to the task on first trial.

We did not stay at the "Club" very long, but went home to bed in order to be up early the next day. We had no difficulty in finding work, and my third morning in New York found me at a table rolling cigars. I worked steadily for some weeks, at the same time spending my earnings between the "crap" game and the "Club." Making cigars became more and more irksome to me; perhaps my more congenial work as a "reader" had unfitted me for work at the table. And, too, the late hours I was keeping made such a sedentary occupation almost beyond the powers of will and endurance. I often found it hard to keep my eyes open and sometimes had to get up and move round to keep from falling asleep. I began to miss whole days from the factory, days on which I was compelled to stay at home and sleep.

My luck at the gambling-table was varied; sometimes I was fifty to a hundred dollars ahead, and at other times I had to borrow money from my fellow workmen to settle my room rent and pay for my meals. Each night after leaving the dice game I went to the "Club" to hear the music and watch the gaiety. If I had won, this was in accord with my mood; if I had lost, it made me forget. I at last realized that making cigars for a living and gambling for a living could not both be carried on at the same time, and I resolved to give up the cigar-making. This resolution led me into a life which held me bound more than a year. During that period my regular time for going to bed was somewhere between four and six o'clock in the mornings. I got up late in the afternoons, walked about a little, then went to the gambling-house or the "Club." My New York was limited to ten blocks; the boundaries were Sixth Avenue from Twenty-third to Thirty-third Streets, with the cross streets one block to the west. Central Park was a distant forest, and the lower part of the city a foreign land. I look back upon the life I then led with a shudder when I think what would have been had I not escaped it. But had I not escaped it, I should have been no more unfortunate than are many young coloured men who come to New York. During that dark period I became acquainted with a score of bright, intelligent young fellows who had come up to the great city with high hopes and ambitions and who had fallen under the spell of this under life, a spell they could not throw off. There was one popularly known as "the doctor"; he had had two years in the Harvard

Medical School, but here he was, living this gas-light life, his will and moral sense so enervated and deadened that it was impossible for him to break away. I do not doubt that the same thing is going on now, but I have sympathy rather than censure for these victims, for I know how easy it is to slip into a slough from which it takes a herculean effort to leap.

I regret that I cannot contrast my views of life among coloured people of New York; but the truth is, during my entire stay in this city I did not become acquainted with a single respectable family. I knew that there were several coloured men worth a hundred or so thousand dollars each, and some families who proudly dated their free ancestry back a half-dozen generations. I also learned that in Brooklyn there lived quite a large colony in comfortable homes which they owned; but at no point did my life come in contact with theirs.

In my gambling-experiences I passed through all the states and conditions that a gambler is heir to. Some days found me able to peel ten- and twenty-dollar bills from a roll, and others found me clad in a linen duster and carpet slippers. I finally caught up another method of earning money, and so did not have to depend entirely upon the caprices of fortune at the gaming-table. Through continually listening to the music at the "Club," and through my own previous training, my natural talent and perseverance, I developed into a remarkable player of rag-time; indeed, I had the name at that time of being the best rag-time-player in New York. I brought all my knowledge of classic music to bear and, in so doing, achieved some novelties which pleased and even astonished my listeners. It was I who first made rag-time transcriptions of familiar classic selections. I used to play Mendelssohn's "Wedding March" in a manner that never failed to arouse enthusiasm among the patrons of the "Club." Very few nights passed during which I was not asked to play it. It was no secret that the great increase in slumming visitors was due to my playing. By mastering rag-time I gained several things: first of all, I gained the title of professor. I was known as "the professor" as long as I remained in that world. Then, too, I gained the means of earning a rather fair livelihood. This work took up much of my time and kept me almost entirely away from the gambling-table. Through it I also gained a friend who was the means by which I escaped from this lower world. And, finally, I secured a wedge which has opened to me more doors and made me a welcome guest than my playing of Beethoven and Chopin could ever have done.

The greater part of the money I now began to earn came through the friend to whom I alluded in the foregoing paragraph. Among the other white "slummers" there came into the "Club" one night a clean-cut, slender, but athletic-looking man, who would have been taken for a youth had it not been for the tinge of grey about his temples. He was cleanshaven and had regular features, and all of his movements bore the indefinable but unmistakable stamp of culture. He spoke to no one, but sat languidly puffing cigarettes and sipping a glass of beer. He was the centre of a great deal of attention; all of the old-timers were wondering who he was. When I had finished playing, he called a waiter and by him sent me a five-dollar bill. For about a month after that he was at the "Club" one or two nights each week, and each time after I had played, he gave me five dollars. One night he sent for me to come to his table; he asked me several questions about myself; then told me that he had an engagement which he wanted me to fill. He gave me a card containing his address and asked me to be there on a certain night.

I was on hand promptly and found that he was giving a dinner in his own apartments to a party of ladies and gentlemen and that I was expected to furnish the musical entertainment. When the grave, dignified man at the door let me in, the place struck me as being almost dark, my eyes had been so accustomed to the garish light of the "Club." He took my coat and hat, bade me take a seat, and went to tell his master that I had come. When my eyes were adjusted to the soft light, I saw that I was in the midst of elegance and luxury in a degree such as I had never seen; but not the elegance which makes one ill at ease. As I sank into a great chair, the subdued tone, the delicately sensuous harmony of my surroundings, drew from me a deep sigh of relief and comfort. How long the man was gone I do not know, but I was startled by a voice saying: "Come this way, if you please, sir," and I saw him standing by my chair. I had been asleep; and I awoke very much confused and a little ashamed, because I did not know how many times he may have called me. I followed him through into the dining-room, where the butler was putting the finishing touches to a table which already looked like a big jewel. The doorman turned me over to the butler, and I passed with the butler on back to where several waiters were busy polishing and assorting table utensils. Without being asked whether I was hungry or not, I was placed at a table and given something to eat. Before I had finished eating, I heard the laughter and talk of the guests who were arriving. Soon afterwards I was called in to begin my work.

I passed in to where the company was gathered and went directly to the piano. According to a suggestion from the host, I began with classic music. During the first number there was absolute quiet and appreciative attention, and when I had finished, I was given a round of generous applause. After that the talk and the laughter began to grow until the music was only an accompaniment to the chatter. This, however, did not disconcert me as it once would have done, for I had become accustomed to playing in the midst of uproarious noise. As the guests began to pay less attention to me, I was enabled to pay more to them. There were about a dozen of them. The men ranged in appearance from a girlish-looking youth to a big grizzled man whom everybody addressed as "Judge." None of the women appeared to be under thirty, but each of them struck me as being handsome. I was not long in finding out that they were all decidedly blasé. Several of the women smoked cigarettes, and with a careless grace which showed they were used to the habit. Occasionally a "Damn it!" escaped from the lips of some one of them, but in such a charming way as to rob it of all vulgarity. The most notable thing which I observed was that the reserve of the host increased in direct proportion with the hilarity of his guests. I thought that there was something going wrong which displeased him. I afterwards learned that it was his habitual manner on such occasions. He seemed to take cynical delight in watching and studying others indulging in excess. His guests were evidently accustomed to his rather non-participating attitude, for it did not seem in any degree to dampen their spirits.

When dinner was served, the piano was moved and the door left open, so that the company might hear the music while eating. At a word from the host I struck up one of my liveliest rag-time pieces. The effect was surprising, perhaps even to the host; the rag-time music came very near spoiling the party so far as eating the dinner was concerned. As soon as I began, the conversation suddenly stopped. It was a pleasure to me to watch the expression of astonishment and delight that grew on the faces of everybody. These were people—and they represented a large class—who were ever expecting to find happiness in novelty, each day restlessly exploring and exhausting every resource of this great city that might possibly furnish a new sensation or awaken a fresh emotion, and who were always grateful to anyone who aided them in their quest. Several of the women left the table and gathered about the piano. They watched my fingers and asked what kind of music it was that I was playing, where I had learned it, and a host of other questions. It was only by being repeatedly called back to the table that they were induced to finish their dinner. When the guests arose, I struck up my rag-time transcription of Mendelssohn's "Wedding March," playing it with terrific chromatic octave runs in the base. This raised everybody's spirits to the highest point of gaiety, and the whole company involuntarily and unconsciously did an impromptu cake-walk. From that time on until the time of leaving they kept me so busy that my arms ached. I obtained a little respite when the girlish-looking youth and one or two of the ladies sang several songs, but after each of these it was "back to rag-time."

In leaving, the guests were enthusiastic in telling the host that he had furnished them the most unusual entertainment they had ever enjoyed. When they had gone, my millionaire friend—for he was reported to be a millionaire—said to me with a smile: "Well, I have given them something they've never had before." After I had put on my coat and was ready to leave, he made me take a glass of wine; he then gave me a cigar and twenty dollars in bills. He told me that he would give me lots of work, his only stipulation being that I should not play any engagements such as I had just filled for him, except by his instructions. I readily accepted the proposition, for I was sure that I could not be the loser by such a contract.

I afterwards played for him at many dinners and parties of one kind or another. Occasionally he "loaned" me to some of his friends. And, too, I often played for him alone at his apartments. At such times he was quite a puzzle to me until I became accustomed to his manners. He would sometimes sit for three or four hours hearing me play, his eyes almost closed, making scarcely a motion except to light a fresh cigarette, and never commenting one way or another on the music. At first I sometimes thought he had fallen asleep and would pause in playing. The stopping of the music always aroused him enough to tell me to play this or that; and I soon learned that my task was not to be considered finished until he got up from his chair and said: "That will do." The man's powers of endurance in listening often exceeded mine in performing—yet I am not sure that he was always listening. At times I became so oppressed with fatigue and sleepiness that it took almost superhuman effort to keep my fingers going; in fact, I believe I sometimes did so while dozing. During such moments this man sitting there so mysteriously silent, almost hid in a cloud of heavy-scented smoke, filled me with a sort of unearthly terror. He seemed to be some grim, mute, but relentless tyrant, possessing over me a supernatural power which he used to drive me on mercilessly to exhaustion. But these feelings came very rarely; besides, he paid me so liberally I could forget much. There at length grew between us a familiar and warm relationship, and I am sure he had a decided personal liking for me. On my part, I looked upon him at that time as about all a man could wish to be.

The "Club" still remained my headquarters, and when I was not playing for my good patron, I was generally to be found there. However, I no longer depended on playing at the "Club" to earn my living; I rather took rank with the visiting celebrities and, occasionally, after being sufficiently urged, would favour my old and new admirers with a number or two. I say, without any egotistic pride, that among my admirers were several of the best-looking women who frequented the place, and who made no secret of the fact that they admired me as much as they did my playing. Among these was the "widow"; indeed, her attentions became so marked that one of my friends warned me to beware of her black companion, who was generally known as a "bad man." He said there was much more reason to be careful because the pair had lately quarrelled and had not been together at the "Club" for some nights. This warning greatly impressed me and I resolved to stop the affair before it should go any further; but the woman was so beautiful that my native gallantry and delicacy would not allow me to repulse her; my finer feelings entirely overcame my judgment. The warning also opened my eyes sufficiently to see that though my artistic temperament and skill made me interesting and attractive to the woman, she was, after all, using me only to excite the jealousy of her companion and revenge herself upon him. It was this surly, black despot who held sway over her deepest emotions.

One night, shortly afterwards, I went into the "Club" and saw the "widow" sitting at a table in company with another woman. She at once beckoned for me to come to her. I went, knowing that I was committing worse than folly. She ordered a quart of champagne and insisted that I sit down and drink with her. I took a chair on the opposite side of the table and began to sip a glass of the wine. Suddenly I noticed by an expression on the "widow's" face that something had occurred. I instinctively glanced round and saw that her companion had just entered. His ugly look completely frightened me. My back was turned to him, but by watching the "widow's" eyes I judged that he was pacing back and forth across the room. My feelings were far from being comfortable; I expected every moment to feel a blow on my head. She, too, was very nervous; she was trying hard to appear unconcerned, but could not succeed in hiding her real feelings. I decided that it was best to get out of such a predicament even at the expense of appearing cowardly, and I made a motion to rise. Just as I partly turned in my chair, I saw the black fellow approaching; he walked directly to our table and leaned over. The "widow" evidently feared he was going to strike her, and she threw back her head. Instead of striking her he whipped out a revolver and fired; the first shot went straight into her throat. There were other shots fired, but how many I do not know; for the first knowledge I had of my surroundings and actions was that I was rushing through the chop-suey restaurant into the street. Just which streets I followed when I got outside I do not know, but I think I must have gone towards Eighth Avenue, then down towards Twenty-third Street and across towards Fifth Avenue. I travelled, not by sight, but instinctively. I felt like one fleeing in a horrible nightmare.

How long and far I walked I cannot tell; but on Fifth Avenue, under a light, I passed a cab containing a solitary occupant, who called to me, and I recognized the voice and face of my millionaire friend. He stopped the cab and asked: "What on earth are you doing strolling in this part of the town?" For answer I got into the cab and related to him all that had happened. He reassured me by saying that no charge of any kind could be brought against me; then added: "But of course you don't want to be mixed up in such an affair." He directed the driver to turn round and go into the park, and then went on to say: "I decided last night that I'd go to Europe tomorrow. I think I'll take you along instead of Walter." Walter was his valet. It was settled that I should go to his apartments for the rest of the night and sail with him in the morning.

We drove round through the park, exchanging only an occasional word. The cool air somewhat calmed my nerves and I lay back and closed my eyes; but still I could see that beautiful white throat with the ugly wound. The jet of blood pulsing from it had placed an indelible red stain on my memory.

CHAPTER IX

I did not feel at ease until the ship was well out of New York harbour; and, notwithstanding the repeated reassurances of my millionaire friend and my own knowledge of the facts in the case, I somehow could not rid myself of the sentiment that I was, in a great degree, responsible for the "widow's" tragic end. We had brought most of the morning papers aboard with us, but my great fear of seeing my name in connexion with the killing would not permit me to read the accounts, although, in one of the papers, I did look at the picture of the victim, which did not in the least resemble her. This morbid state of mind, together with seasickness, kept me miserable for three or four days. At the end of that time my spirits began to revive, and I took an interest in the ship, my fellow passengers, and the voyage in general. On the second or third day out we passed several spouting whales, but I could not arouse myself to make the effort to go to the other side of the ship to see them. A little later we ran in close proximity to a large iceberg. I was curious enough to get up and look at it, and I was fully repaid for my pains. The sun was shining full upon it, and it glistened like a mammoth diamond, cut with a million facets. As we passed, it constantly changed its shape; at each different angle of vision it assumed new and astonishing forms of beauty. I watched it through a pair of glasses, seeking to verify my early conception of an iceberg—in the geographies of my grammar-school days the pictures of icebergs always included a stranded polar bear, standing desolately upon one of the snowy crags. I looked for the bear, but if he was there, he refused to put himself on exhibition.

It was not, however, until the morning that we entered the harbour of Havre that I was able to shake off my gloom. Then the strange sights, the chatter in an unfamiliar tongue, and the excitement of landing and passing the customs officials caused me to forget completely the events of a few days before. Indeed, I grew so lighthearted that when I caught my first sight of the train which was to take us to Paris, I enjoyed a hearty laugh. The toy-looking engine, the stuffy little compartment cars, with tiny, old-fashioned wheels, struck me as being extremely funny. But before we reached Paris my respect for our train rose considerably. I found that the "tiny" engine made remarkably fast time, and that the old-fashioned wheels ran very smoothly. I even began to appreciate the "stuffy" cars for their privacy. As I watched the passing scenery from the car window, it seemed too beautiful to be real. The bright-coloured houses against the green background impressed me as the work of some idealistic painter. Before we arrived in Paris, there was awakened in my heart a love for France which continued to grow stronger, a love which today makes that country for me the one above all others to be desired.

We rolled into the station Saint Lazare about four o'clock in the afternoon and drove immediately to the Hôtel Continental. My benefactor, humouring my curiosity and enthusiasm, which seemed to please him very much, suggested that we take a short walk before dinner. We stepped out of the hotel and turned to the right into the rue de Rivoli. When the vista of the Place de la Concorde and the Champs Élysées suddenly burst on me, I could hardly credit my own eyes. I shall attempt no such supererogatory task as a description of Paris. I wish only to give briefly the impressions which that wonderful city made upon me. It impressed me as the perfect and perfectly beautiful city; and even after I had been there for some time, and seen not only its avenues and palaces, but its most squalid alleys and hovels, this impression was not weakened. Paris became for me a charmed spot, and whenever I have returned there, I have fallen under the spell, a spell which compels admiration for all of its manners and customs and justification of even its follies and sins.

We walked a short distance up the Champs Élysées and sat for a while in chairs along the sidewalk, watching the passing crowds on foot and in carriages. It was with reluctance that I went back to the hotel for dinner. After dinner we went to one of the summer theatres, and after the performance my friend took me to a large café on one of the Grands Boulevards. Here it was that I had my first glimpse of the French life of popular literature, so different from real French life. There were several hundred people, men and women, in the place drinking, smoking, talking, and listening to the music. My millionaire friend and I took seats at a table, where we sat smoking and watching the crowd. It was not long before we were joined by two or three good-looking, well-dressed young women. My friend talked to them in French and bought drinks for the whole party. I tried to recall my high-school French, but the effort availed me little. I could stammer out a few phrases, but, very naturally, could not understand a word that was said to me. We stayed at the café a couple of hours, then went back to the hotel. The next day we spent several hours in the shops and at the tailor's. I had no clothes except what I had been able to gather together at my benefactor's apartments the night before we sailed. He bought me the same kind of clothes which he himself wore, and that was the best; and he treated me in every way as he dressed me, as an equal, not as a servant. In fact, I don't think anyone could have guessed that such a relation existed. My duties were light and few, and he was a man full of life and vigour, who rather enjoyed doing things for himself. He kept me supplied with money far beyond what ordinary wages would have amounted to. For the first two weeks we were together almost constantly, seeing the sights, sights old to him, but from which he seemed to get new pleasure in showing them to me. During the day we took in the places of interest, and at night the theatres and cafés. This sort of life appealed to me as ideal, and I asked him one day how long he intended to stay in Paris. He answered: "Oh, until I get tired of it." I could not understand how that could ever happen. As it was, including several short trips to the Mediterranean, to Spain, to Brussels, and to Ostend, we did remain there fourteen or fifteen months. We stayed at the Hôtel Continental about two months of this time. Then my millionaire took apartments, hired a piano, and lived almost the same life he lived in New York. He entertained a great deal, some of the parties being a good deal more blasé than the New York ones. I played for the guests at all of them with an effect which to relate would be but a tiresome repetition to the reader. I played not only for the guests, but continued, as I used to do in New York, to play often for the host when he was alone. This man of the world, who grew weary of everything and was always searching for something new, appeared never to grow tired of my music; he seemed to take it as a drug. He fell into a habit which caused me no little annoyance; sometimes he would come in during the early hours of the morning and, finding me in bed asleep, would wake me up and ask me to play something. This, so far as I can remember, was my only hardship during my whole stay with him in Europe.

After the first few weeks spent in sight-seeing I had a great deal of time left to myself; my friend was often I did not know where. When not with him, I spent the day nosing about the curious nooks and corners of Paris; of this I never grew tired. At night I usually went to some theatre, but always ended up at the big café on the Grands Boulevards. I wish the reader to know that it was not alone the gaiety which drew me there; aside from that I had a laudable purpose. I had purchased an English-French conversational dictionary, and I went there every night to take a language lesson. I used to get three or four of the young women who frequented the place at a table and buy beer and cigarettes for them. In return I received my lesson. I got more than my money's worth, for they actually compelled me to speak the language. This, together with reading the papers every day, enabled me within a few months to express myself fairly well, and, before I left Paris, to have more than an ordinary command of French. Of course, every person who goes to Paris could not dare to learn French in this manner, but I can think of no easier or quicker way of doing it. The acquiring of another foreign language awoke me to the fact that with a little effort I could secure an added accomplishment as fine and as valuable as music; so I determined to make myself as much of a linguist as possible. I bought a Spanish newspaper every day in order to freshen my memory of that language, and, for French, devised what was, so far as I knew, an original system of study. I compiled a list which I termed "Three hundred necessary words." These I thoroughly committed to memory, also the conjugation of the verbs which were included in the list. I studied these words over and over, much as children of a couple of generations ago studied the alphabet. I also practised a set of phrases like the following: "How?" "What did you say?" "What does the word——mean?" "I understand all you say except——." "Please repeat." "What do you call——?" "How do you say——?" These I called my working sentences. In an astonishingly short time I reached the point where the language taught itself—where I learned to speak merely by speaking. This point is the place which students taught foreign languages in our schools and colleges find great difficulty in reaching. I think the main trouble is that they learn too much of a language at a time. A French child with a vocabulary of two hundred words can express more spoken ideas than a student of French can with a knowledge of two thousand. A small vocabulary, the smaller the better, which embraces the common, everyday-used ideas, thoroughly mastered, is the key to a language. When that much is acquired the vocabulary can be increased simply by talking. And it is easy. Who cannot commit three hundred words to memory? Later I tried my method, if I may so term it, with German, and found that it worked in the same way.

I spent a good many evenings at the Opéra. The music there made me strangely reminiscent of my life in Connecticut; it was an atmosphere in which I caught a fresh breath of my boyhood days and early youth. Generally, in the morning after I had attended a performance, I would sit at the piano and for a couple of hours play the music which I used to play in my mother's little parlour.

One night I went to hear *Faust.* I got into my seat just as the lights went down for the first act. At the end of the act I noticed that my neighbour on the left was a young girl. I cannot describe her either as to feature, or colour of her hair, or of her eyes; she was so young, so fair, so ethereal, that I felt to stare at her would be a violation; yet I was distinctly conscious of her beauty. During the intermission she spoke English in a low voice to a gentleman and a lady who sat in the seats to her left, addressing them as father and mother. I held my program as though studying it, but listened to catch every sound of her voice. Her observations on the performance and the audience were so fresh and naïve as to be almost amusing. I gathered that she was just out of school, and that this was her first trip to Paris. I occasionally stole a glance at her, and each time I did so my heart leaped into my throat. Once I glanced beyond to the gentleman who sat next to her. My glance immediately turned into a stare. Yes, there he was, unmistakably, my father! looking hardly a day older than when I had seen him some ten years before. What a strange coincidence! What should I say to him? What would he say to me? Before I had recovered from my first surprise, there came another shock in the realization that the beautiful, tender girl at my side was my sister. Then all the springs of affection in my heart, stopped since my mother's death, burst out in fresh and terrible torrents, and I could have fallen at her feet and worshipped her. They were singing the second act, but I did not hear the music. Slowly the desolate loneliness of my position became clear to me. I knew that I could not speak, but I would have given a part of my life to touch her hand with mine and call her "sister." I sat through the opera until I could stand it no longer. I felt that I was suffocating. Valentine's love seemed like mockery, and I felt an almost uncontrollable impulse to rise up and scream to the audience: "Here, here in your very midst, is a tragedy, a real tragedy!" This impulse grew so strong that I became afraid of myself, and in the darkness of one of the scenes I stumbled out of the theatre. I walked aimlessly about for an hour or so, my feelings divided between a desire to weep and a desire to curse. I finally took a cab and went from café to café, and for one of the very few times in my life drank myself into a stupor.

It was unwelcome news for me when my benefactor—I could not think of him as employer—informed me that he was at last tired of Paris. This news gave me, I think, a passing doubt as to his sanity. I had enjoyed life in Paris, and, taking all things into consideration, enjoyed it wholesomely. One thing which greatly contributed to my enjoyment was the fact that I was an American. Americans are immensely popular in Paris; and this is not due solely to the fact that they spend lots of money there, for they spend just as much or more in London, and in the latter city they are merely tolerated because they do spend. The Londoner seems to think that Americans are people whose only claim to be classed as civilized is that they have money, and the regrettable thing about that is that the money is not English. But the French are more logical and freer from prejudices than the British; so the difference of attitude is easily explained. Only once in Paris did I have cause to blush for my American citizenship. I had become quite friendly with a young man from Luxemburg whom I had met at the big café. He was a stolid, slow-witted fellow, but, as we say, with a heart of gold. He and I grew attached to each other and were together frequently. He was a great admirer of the United States and never grew tired of talking to me about the country and asking for information. It was his intention to try his fortune there some day. One night he asked me in a tone of voice which indicated that he expected an authoritative denial of an ugly rumour: "Did they really burn a man alive in the United States?" I never knew what I stammered out to him as an answer. I should have felt relieved if I could even have said to him: "Well, only one."

When we arrived in London, my sadness at leaving Paris was turned into despair. After my long stay in the French capital, huge, ponderous, massive London seemed to me as ugly a thing as man could contrive to make. I thought of Paris as a beauty-spot on the face of the earth, and of London as a big freckle. But soon London's massiveness, I might say its very ugliness, began to impress me. I began to experience that sense of grandeur which one feels when he looks at a great mountain or a mighty river. Beside London Paris becomes a toy, a pretty plaything. And I must own that before I left the world's metropolis I discovered much there that was beautiful. The beauty in and about London is entirely different from that in and about Paris; and I could not but admit that the beauty of the French city seemed hand-made, artificial, as though set up for the photographer's camera, everything nicely adjusted so as not to spoil the picture; while that of the English city was rugged, natural, and fresh.

How these two cities typify the two peoples who built them! Even the sound of their names expresses a certain racial difference. Paris is the concrete expression of the gaiety, regard for symmetry, love of art, and, I might well add, of the morality of the French people. London stands for the conservatism, the solidarity, the utilitarianism, and, I might well add, the hypocrisy of the Anglo-Saxon. It may sound odd to speak of the morality of the French, if not of the hypocrisy of the English; but this seeming paradox impresses me as a deep truth. I saw many things in Paris which were immoral according to English standards, but the absence of hypocrisy, the absence of the spirit to do the thing if it might only be done in secret, robbed these very immoralities of the damning influence of the same evils in London. I have walked along the terrace cafés of Paris and seen hundreds of men and women sipping their wine and beer, without observing a sign of drunkenness. As they drank, they chatted and laughed and watched the passing crowds; the drinking seemed to be a secondary thing. This I have witnessed, not only in the cafés along the Grands Boulevards, but in the out-of-the-way places patronized by the working-classes. In London I have seen in the "pubs" men and women crowded in stuffy little compartments, drinking seemingly only for the pleasure of swallowing as much as they could hold. I have seen there women from eighteen to eighty, some in tatters, and some clutching babes in their arms, drinking the heavy English ales and whiskies served to them by women. In the whole scene, not one ray of brightness, not one flash of gaiety, only maudlin joviality or grim despair. And I have thought, if some men and women will drink—and it is certain that some will—is it not better that they do so under the open sky, in the fresh air, than huddled together in some close, smoky room? There is a sort of frankness about the evils of Paris which robs them of much of the seductiveness of things forbidden, and with that frankness goes a certain cleanliness of thought belonging to things not hidden. London will do whatever Paris does, provided exterior morals are not shocked. As a result, Paris has the appearance only of being the more immoral city. The difference may be summed up in this: Paris practises its sins as lightly as it does its religion, while London practises both very seriously.

I should not neglect to mention what impressed me most forcibly during my stay in London. It was not St. Paul's nor the British Museum nor Westminster Abbey. It was nothing more or less than the simple phrase "Thank you," or sometimes more elaborated, "Thank you very kindly, sir." I was continually surprised by the varied uses to which it was put; and, strange to say, its use as an expression of politeness seemed more limited than any other. One night I was in a cheap music-hall and accidentally bumped into a waiter who was carrying a tray-load of beer, almost bringing him to several shillings' worth of grief. To my amazement he righted himself and said: "Thank ye, sir," and left me wondering whether he meant that he thanked me for not completely spilling his beer, or that he would thank me for keeping out of his way.

I also found cause to wonder upon what ground the English accuse Americans of corrupting the language by introducing slang words. I think I heard more and more different kinds of slang during my few weeks' stay in London than in my whole "tenderloin" life in New York. But I suppose the English feel that the language is theirs, and that they may do with it as they please without at the same time allowing that privilege to others.

My millionaire was not so long in growing tired of London as of Paris. After a stay of six or eight weeks we went across into Holland.

Amsterdam was a great surprise to me. I had always thought of Venice as the city of canals; it had never entered my mind that I should find similar conditions in a Dutch town. I don't suppose the comparison goes far beyond the fact that there are canals in both cities—I have never seen Venice—but Amsterdam struck me as being extremely picturesque. From Holland we went to Germany, where we spent five or six months, most of the time in Berlin. I found Berlin more to my taste than London, and occasionally I had to admit that in some things it was superior to Paris.

In Berlin I especially enjoyed the orchestral concerts, and I attended a large number of them. I formed the acquaintance of a good many musicians, several of whom spoke of my playing in high terms. It was in Berlin that my inspiration was renewed. One night my millionaire entertained a party of men composed of artists, musicians, writers, and, for aught I know, a count or two. They drank and smoked a great deal, talked art and music, and discussed, it seemed to me, everything that ever entered man's mind. I could only follow the general drift of what they were saying. When they discussed music, it was more interesting to me; for then some fellow would run excitedly to the piano and give a demonstration of his opinions, and another would follow quickly, doing the same. In this way, I learned that, regardless of what his specialty might be, every man in the party was a musician. I was at the same time impressed with the falsity of the general idea that Frenchmen are excitable and emotional, and that Germans are calm and phlegmatic. Frenchmen are merely gay and never overwhelmed by their emotions. When they talk loud and fast, it is merely talk, while Germans get worked up and red in the face when sustaining an opinion, and in heated discussions are likely to allow their emotions to sweep them off their feet.

My millionaire planned, in the midst of the discussion on music, to have me play the "new American music" and astonish everybody present. The result was that I was more astonished than anyone else. I went to the piano and played the most intricate rag-time piece I knew. Before there was time for anybody to express an opinion on what I had done, a big bespectacled, bushy-headed man rushed over, and, shoving me out of the chair, exclaimed: "Get up! Get up!" He seated himself at the piano, and, taking the theme of my rag-time, played it through first in straight chords; then varied and developed it through every known musical form. I sat amazed. I had been turning classic music into rag-time, a comparatively easy task; and this man had taken rag-time and made it classic. The thought came across me like a flash—It can be done, why can't I do it? From that moment my mind was made up. I clearly saw the way of carrying out the ambition I had formed when a boy.

I now lost interest in our trip. I thought: "Here I am a man, no longer a boy, and what am I doing but wasting my time and abusing my talent? What use am I making of my gifts? What future have I before me following my present course?" These thoughts made me feel remorseful and put me in a fever to get to work, to begin to do something. Of course I know now that I was not wasting time; that there was nothing I could have done at that age which would have benefited me more than going to Europe as I did. The desire to begin work grew stronger each day. I could think of nothing else. I made up my mind to go back into the very heart of the South, to live among the people, and drink in my inspiration firsthand. I gloated over the immense amount of material I had to work with, not only modern rag-time, but also the old slave songs—material which no one had yet touched.

The more decided and anxious I became to return to the United States, the more I dreaded the ordeal of breaking with my millionaire. Between this peculiar man and me there had grown a very strong bond of affection, backed up by a debt which each owed to the other. He had taken me from a terrible life in New York and, by giving me the opportunity of travelling and of coming in contact with the people with whom he associated, had made me a polished man of the world. On the other hand, I was his chief means of disposing of the thing which seemed to sum up all in life that he dreaded—time. As I remember him now, I can see that time was what he was always endeavouring to escape, to bridge over, to blot out; and it is not strange that some years later he did escape it for ever, by leaping into eternity.

For some weeks I waited for just the right moment in which to tell my patron of my decision. Those weeks were a trying time to me. I felt that I was playing the part of a traitor to my best friend. At length, one day he said to me: "Well, get ready for a long trip; we are going to Egypt, and then to Japan." The temptation was for an instant almost overwhelming, but I summoned determination enough to say: "I don't think I want to go." "What!" he exclaimed, "you want to go back to your dear Paris? You still think that the only spot on earth? Wait until you see Cairo and Tokio, you may change your mind." "No," I stammered, "it is not because I want to go back to Paris. I want to go back to the United States." He wished to know my reason, and I told him, as best I could, my dreams, my ambition, and my decision. While I was talking, he watched me with a curious, almost cynical, smile growing on his lips. When I had finished he put his hand on my shoulder—this was the first physical expression of tender regard he had ever shown me—and looking at me in a big-brotherly way, said: "My boy, you are by blood, by appearance, by education, and by tastes a white man. Now, why do you want to throw your life away amidst the poverty and ignorance, in the hopeless struggle, of the black people of the United States? Then look at the terrible handicap you are placing on yourself by going home and working as a Negro composer; you can never be able to get the hearing for your work which it might deserve. I doubt that even a white musician of recognized ability could succeed there by working on the theory that American music should be based on Negro themes. Music is a universal art; anybody's music belongs to everybody; you can't limit it to race or country. Now, if you want to become a composer, why not stay right here in Europe? I will put you under the best teachers on the Continent. Then if you want to write music on Negro themes, why, go ahead and do it."

We talked for some time on music and the race question. On the latter subject I had never before heard him express any opinion. Between him and me no suggestion of racial differences had ever come up. I found that he was a man entirely free from prejudice, but he recognized that prejudice was a big stubborn entity which had to be taken into account. He went on to say: "This idea you have of making a Negro out of yourself is nothing more than a sentiment; and you do not realize the fearful import of what you intend to do. What kind of a Negro would you make now, especially in the South? If you had remained there, or perhaps even in your club in New York, you might have succeeded very well; but now you would be miserable. I can imagine no more dissatisfied human being than an educated, cultured, and refined coloured man in the United States. I have given more study to the race question in the United States than you may suppose, and I sympathize with the Negroes there; but what's the use? I can't right their wrongs, and neither can you; they must do that themselves.

They are unfortunate in having wrongs to right, and you would be foolish to take their wrongs unnecessarily on your shoulders. Perhaps some day, through study and observation, you will come to see that evil is a force, and, like the physical and chemical forces, we cannot annihilate it; we may only change its form. We light upon one evil and hit it with all the might of our civilization, but only succeed in scattering it into a dozen other forms. We hit slavery through a great civil war. Did we destroy it? No, we only changed it into hatred between sections of the country: in the South, into political corruption and chicanery, the degradation of the blacks through peonage, unjust laws, unfair and cruel treatment; and the degradation of the whites by their resorting to these practices, the paralysation of the public conscience, and the ever overhanging dread of what the future may bring. Modern civilization hit ignorance of the masses through the means of popular education. What has it done but turn ignorance into anarchy, socialism, strikes, hatred between poor and rich, and universal discontent? In like manner, modern philanthropy hit at suffering and disease through asylums and hospitals; it prolongs the sufferers' lives, it is true, but is, at the same time, sending down strains of insanity and weakness into future generations. My philosophy of life is this: make yourself as happy as possible, and try to make those happy whose lives come in touch with yours; but to attempt to right the wrongs and ease the sufferings of the world in general is a waste of effort. You had just as well try to bale the Atlantic by pouring the water into the Pacific."

This tremendous flow of serious talk from a man I was accustomed to see either gay or taciturn so surprised and overwhelmed me that I could not frame a reply. He left me thinking over what he had said. Whatever was the soundness of his logic or the moral tone of his philosophy, his argument greatly impressed me. I could see, in spite of the absolute selfishness upon which it was based, that there was reason and common sense in it. I began to analyse my own motives, and found that they, too, were very largely mixed with selfishness. Was it more a desire to help those I considered my people, or more a desire to distinguish myself, which was leading me back to the United States? That is a question I have never definitely answered.

For several weeks longer I was in a troubled state of mind. Added to the fact that I was loath to leave my good friend was the weight of the question he had aroused in my mind, whether I was not making a fatal mistake. I suffered more than one sleepless night during that time. Finally, I settled the question on purely selfish grounds, in accordance with my millionaire's philosophy. I argued that music offered me a better future than anything else I had any knowledge of, and, in opposition to my friend's opinion, that I should have greater chances of attracting attention as a coloured composer than as a white one. But I must own that I also felt stirred by an unselfish desire to voice all the joys and sorrows, the hopes and ambitions, of the American Negro, in classic musical form.

When my mind was fully made up, I told my friend. He asked me when I intended to start. I replied that I would do so at once. He then asked me how much money I had. I told him that I had saved several hundred dollars out of sums he had given me. He gave me a cheque for five hundred dollars, told me to write to him in care of his Paris bankers if I ever needed his help, wished me good luck, and bade me good-bye. All this he did almost coldly; and I often wondered whether he was in a hurry to get rid of what he considered a fool, or whether he was striving to hide deeper feelings.

And so I separated from the man who was, all in all, the best friend I ever had, except my mother, the man who exerted the greatest influence ever brought into my life, except that exerted by my mother. My affection for him was so strong, my recollections of him are so distinct, he was such a peculiar and striking character, that I could easily fill several chapters with reminiscences of him; but for fear of tiring the reader I shall go on with my narration.

I decided to go to Liverpool and take ship for Boston. I still had an uneasy feeling about returning to New York; and in a few days I found myself aboard ship headed for home.

CHAPTER X

Among the first of my fellow-passengers of whom I took any particular notice was a tall, broad-shouldered, almost gigantic, coloured man. His dark-brown face was clean-shaven; he was well-dressed and bore a decidedly distinguished air. In fact, if he was not handsome, he at least compelled admiration for his fine physical proportions. He attracted general attention as he strode the deck in a sort of majestic loneliness. I became curious to know who he was and determined to strike up an acquaintance with him at the first opportune moment. The chance came a day or two later. He was sitting in the smoking-room, with a cigar, which had gone out, in his mouth, reading a novel. I sat down beside him and, offering him a fresh cigar, said: "You don't mind my telling you something unpleasant, do you?" He looked at me with a smile, accepted the proffered cigar, and replied in a voice which comported perfectly with his size and appearance: "I think my curiosity overcomes any objections I might have." "Well," I said, "have you noticed that the man who sat at your right in the saloon during the first meal has not sat there since?" He frowned slightly without answering my question. "Well," I continued, "he asked the steward to remove him; and not only that, he attempted to persuade a number of the passengers to protest against your presence in the dining-saloon." The big man at my side took a long draw from his cigar, threw his head back, and slowly blew a great cloud of smoke toward the ceiling. Then turning to me he said: "Do you know, I don't object to anyone's having prejudices so long as those prejudices don't interfere with my personal liberty. Now, the man you are speaking of had a perfect right to change his seat if I in any way interfered with his appetite or his digestion. I should have no reason to complain if he removed to the farthest corner of the saloon, or even if he got off the ship; but when his prejudice attempts to move *me* one foot, one inch, out of the place where I am comfortably located, then I object." On the word "object" he brought his great fist down on the table in front of us with such a crash that everyone in the room turned to look. We both covered up the slight embarrassment with a laugh and strolled out on the deck.

We walked the deck for an hour or more, discussing different phases of the Negro question. In referring to the race I used the personal pronoun "we"; my companion made no comment about it, nor evinced any surprise, except to raise his eyebrows slightly the first time he caught the significance of the word. He was the broadest-minded coloured man I have ever talked with on the Negro question. He even went so far as to sympathize with and offer excuses for some white Southern points of view. I asked him what were his main reasons for being so hopeful. He replied: "In spite of all that is written, said, and done, this great, big, incontrovertible fact stands out—the Negro is progressing, and that disproves all the arguments in the world that he is incapable of progress. I was born in slavery, and at emancipation was set adrift a ragged, penniless bit of humanity. I have seen the Negro in every grade, and I know what I am talking about. Our detractors point to the increase of crime as evidence against us; certainly we have progressed in crime as in other things; what less could be expected? And yet, in this respect, we are far from the point which has been reached by the more highly civilized white race. As we continue to progress, crime among us will gradually lose much of its brutal, vulgar, I might say healthy, aspect, and become more delicate, refined, and subtile. Then it will be less shocking and noticeable, although more dangerous to society." Then dropping his tone of irony, he continued with some show of eloquence: "But, above all, when I am discouraged and disheartened, I have this to fall back on: if there is a principle of right in the world, which finally prevails, and I believe that there is; if there is a merciful but justice-loving God in heaven, and I believe that there is, we shall win; for we have right on our side, while those who oppose us can defend themselves by nothing in the moral law, nor even by anything in the enlightened thought of the present age."

For several days, together with other topics, we discussed the race problem, not only of the United States, but as it affected native Africans and Jews. Finally, before we reached Boston, our conversation had grown familiar and personal. I had told him something of my past and much about my intentions for the future. I learned that he was a physician, a graduate of Howard University, Washington, and had done post-graduate work in Philadelphia; and this was his second trip abroad to attend professional courses. He had practised for some years in the city of Washington, and though he did not say so, I gathered that his practice was a lucrative one. Before we left the ship, he had made me promise that I would stop two or three days in Washington before going on south.

We put up at a hotel in Boston for a couple of days and visited several of my new friend's acquaintances; they were all people of education and culture and, apparently, of means. I could not help being struck by the great difference between them and the same class of coloured people in the South. In speech and thought they were genuine Yankees. The difference was especially noticeable in their speech. There was none of that heavy-tongued enunciation which characterizes even the best-educated coloured people of the South. It is remarkable, after all, what an adaptable creature the Negro is. I have seen the black West Indian gentleman in London, and he is in speech and manners a perfect Englishman. I have seen natives of Haiti and Martinique in Paris, and they are more Frenchy than a Frenchman. I have no doubt that the Negro would make a good Chinaman, with exception of the pigtail.

My stay in Washington, instead of being two or three days, was two or three weeks. This was my first visit to the national capital, and I was, of course, interested in seeing the public buildings and something of the working of the government; but most of my time I spent with the doctor among his friends and acquaintances. The social phase of life among coloured people is more developed in Washington than in any other city in the country. This is on account of the large number of individuals earning good salaries and having a reasonable amount of leisure time to draw from. There are dozens of physicians and lawyers, scores of schoolteachers, and hundreds of clerks in the departments. As to the coloured department clerks, I think it fair to say that in educational equipment they average above the white clerks of the same grade; for, whereas a coloured college-graduate will seek such a job, the white university-man goes into one of the many higher vocations which are open to him.

In a previous chapter I spoke of social life among coloured people; so there is no need to take it up again here. But there is one thing I did not mention: among Negroes themselves there is the peculiar inconsistency of a colour question. Its existence is rarely admitted and hardly ever mentioned; it may not be too strong a statement to say that the greater portion of the race is unconscious of its influence; yet this influence, though silent, is constant. It is evidenced most plainly in marriage selection; thus the black men generally marry women fairer than themselves; while, on the other hand, the dark women of stronger mental endowment are very often married to light-complexioned men; the effect is a tendency toward lighter complexions, especially among the more active elements in the race. Some might claim that this is a tacit admission of coloured people among themselves of their own inferiority judged by the colour line. I do not think so. What I have termed an inconsistency is, after all, most natural; it is, in fact, a tendency in accordance with what might be called an economic necessity. So far as racial differences go, the United States puts a greater premium on colour, or, better, lack of colour, than upon anything else in the world. To paraphrase, "Have a white skin, and all things else may be added unto you." I have seen advertisements in newspapers for waiters, bell-boys, or elevator men, which read: "Light coloured man wanted." It is this tremendous pressure which the sentiment of the country exerts that is operating on the race. There is involved not only the question of higher opportunity, but often the question of earning a livelihood; and so I say it is not strange, but a natural tendency. Nor is it any more a sacrifice of self-respect that a black man should give to his children every advantage he can which complexion of the skin carries than that the new or vulgar rich should purchase for their children the advantages which ancestry, aristocracy, and social position carry. I once heard a coloured man sum it up in these words: "It's no disgrace to be black, but it's often very inconvenient."

Washington shows the Negro not only at his best, but also at his worst. As I drove round with the doctor, he commented rather harshly on those of the latter class which we saw. He remarked: "You see those lazy, loafing, good-for-nothing darkies; they're not worth digging graves for; yet they are the ones who create impressions of the race for the casual observer. It's because they are always in evidence on the street corners, while the rest of us are hard at work, and you know a dozen loafing darkies make a bigger crowd and a worse impression in this country than fifty white men of the same class. But they ought not to represent the race. We are the race, and the race ought to be judged by us, not by them. Every race and every nation should be judged by the best it has been able to produce, not by the worst."

The recollection of my stay in Washington is a pleasure to me now. In company with the doctor I visited Howard University, the public schools, the excellent coloured hospital, with which he was in some way connected, if I remember correctly, and many comfortable and even elegant homes. It was with some reluctance that I continued my journey south. The doctor was very kind in giving me letters to people in Richmond and Nashville when I told him that I intended to stop in both of these cities. In Richmond a man who was then editing a very creditable coloured newspaper gave me a great deal of his time and made my stay there of three or four days very pleasant. In

Nashville I spent a whole day at Fisk University, the home of the "Jubilee Singers," and was more than repaid for my time. Among my letters of introduction was one to a very prosperous physician. He drove me about the city and introduced me to a number of people. From Nashville I went to Atlanta, where I stayed long enough to gratify an old desire to see Atlanta University again. I then continued my journey to Macon.

During the trip from Nashville to Atlanta I went into the smoking-compartment of the car to smoke a cigar. I was travelling in a Pullman, not because of an abundance of funds, but because through my experience with my millionaire a certain amount of comfort and luxury had become a necessity to me whenever it was obtainable. When I entered the car, I found only a couple of men there; but in a half-hour there were half a dozen or more. From the general conversation I learned that a fat Jewish-looking man was a cigar-manufacturer, and was experimenting in growing Havana tobacco in Florida; that a slender bespectacled young man was from Ohio and a professor in some State institution in Alabama; that a white-moustached, well-dressed man was an old Union soldier who had fought through the Civil War; and that a tall, raw-boned, red-faced man, who seemed bent on leaving nobody in ignorance of the fact that he was from Texas, was a cotton-planter.

In the North men may ride together for hours in a "smoker" and unless they are acquainted with each other never exchange a word; in the South men thrown together in such manner are friends in fifteen minutes. There is always present a warm-hearted cordiality which will melt down the most frigid reserve. It may be because Southerners are very much like Frenchmen in that they must talk; and not only must they talk, but they must express their opinions.

The talk in the car was for a while miscellaneous—on the weather, crops, business prospects; the old Union soldier had invested capital in Atlanta, and he predicted that that city would soon be one of the greatest in the country. Finally the conversation drifted to politics; then, as a natural sequence, turned upon the Negro question.

In the discussion of the race question the diplomacy of the Jew was something to be admired; he had the faculty of agreeing with everybody without losing his allegiance to any side. He knew that to sanction Negro oppression would be to sanction Jewish oppression and would expose him to a shot along that line from the old soldier, who stood firmly on the ground of equal rights and opportunity to all men; long traditions and business instincts told him when in Rome to act as a Roman. Altogether his position was a delicate one, and I gave him credit for the skill he displayed in maintaining it. The young professor was apologetic. He had had the same views as the G. A. R. man; but a year in the South had opened his eyes, and he had to confess that the problem could hardly be handled any better than it was being handled by the Southern whites. To which the G. A. R. man responded somewhat rudely that he had spent ten times as many years in the South as his young friend and that he could easily understand how holding a position in a State institution in Alabama would bring about a change of views. The professor turned very red and had very little more to say. The Texan was fierce, eloquent, and profane in his argument, and, in a lower sense, there was a direct logic in what he said, which was convincing; it was only by taking higher ground, by dealing in what Southerners call "theories," that he could be combated. Occasionally some one of the several other men in the "smoker" would throw in a remark to reinforce what he said, but he really didn't need any help; he was sufficient in himself.

In the course of a short time the controversy narrowed itself down to an argument between the old soldier and the Texan. The latter maintained hotly that the Civil War was a criminal mistake on the part of the North and that the humiliation which the South suffered during Reconstruction could never be forgotten. The Union man retorted just as hotly that the South was responsible for the war and that the spirit of unforgetfulness on its part was the greatest cause of present friction; that it seemed to be the one great aim of the South to convince the North that the latter made a mistake in fighting to preserve the Union and liberate the slaves. "Can you imagine," he went on to say, "what would have been the condition of things eventually if there had been no war, and the South had been allowed to follow its course? Instead of one great, prosperous country with nothing before it but the conquests of peace, a score of petty republics, as in Central and South America, wasting their energies in war with each other or in revolutions."

"Well," replied the Texan, "anything—no country at all—is better than having niggers over you. But anyhow, the war was fought and the niggers were freed; for it's no use beating around the bush, the niggers, and not the Union, was the cause of it; and now do you believe that all the niggers on earth are worth the good white blood that was spilt? You freed the nigger and you gave him the ballot, but you couldn't make a citizen out of him. He don't know what he's voting for, and we buy 'em like so many hogs. You're giving 'em education, but that only makes slick rascals out of 'em."

"Don't fancy for a moment," said the Northern man, "that you have any monopoly in buying ignorant votes. The same thing is done on a larger scale in New York and Boston, and in Chicago and San Francisco; and they are not black votes either. As to education's making the Negro worse, you might just as well tell me that religion does the same thing. And, by the way, how many educated coloured men do you know personally?"

The Texan admitted that he knew only one, and added that he was in the penitentiary. "But," he said, "do you mean to claim, ballot or no ballot, education or no education, that niggers are the equals of white men?"

"That's not the question," answered the other, "but if the Negro is so distinctly inferior, it is a strange thing to me that it takes such tremendous effort on the part of the white man to make him realize it, and to keep him in the same place into which inferior men naturally fall. However, let us grant for sake of argument that the Negro is inferior in every respect to the white man; that fact only increases our moral responsibility in regard to our actions toward him. Inequalities of numbers, wealth, and power, even of intelligence and morals, should make no difference in the essential rights of men."

"If he's inferior and weaker, and is shoved to the wall, that's his own look-out," said the Texan. "That's the law of nature; and he's bound to go to the wall; for no race in the world has ever been able to stand competition with the Anglo-Saxon. The Anglo-Saxon race has always been and always will be the masters of the world, and the niggers in the South ain't going to change all the records of history."

"My friend," said the old soldier slowly, "if you have studied history, will you tell me, as confidentially between white men, what the Anglo-Saxon has ever done?"

The Texan was too much astonished by the question to venture any reply.

His opponent continued: "Can you name a single one of the great fundamental and original intellectual achievements which have raised man in the scale of civilization that may be credited to the Anglo-Saxon? The art of letters, of poetry, of music, of sculpture, of painting, of the drama, of architecture; the science of mathematics, of astronomy, of philosophy, of logic, of physics, of chemistry, the use of the metals, and the principles of mechanics, were all invented or discovered by darker and what we now call inferior races and nations. We have carried many of these to their highest point of perfection, but the foundation was laid by others. Do you know the only original contribution to civilization we can claim is what we have done in steam and electricity and in making implements of war more deadly? And there we worked largely on principles which we did not discover. Why, we didn't even originate the religion we use. We are a great race, the greatest in the world today, but we ought to remember that we are standing on a pile of past races, and enjoy our position with a little less show of arrogance. We are simply having our turn at the game, and we were a long time getting to it. After all, racial supremacy is merely a matter of dates in history. The man here who belongs to what is, all in all, the greatest race the world ever produced, is almost ashamed to own it. If the Anglo-Saxon is the source of everything good and great in the human race from the beginning, why wasn't the German forest the birthplace of civilization, rather than the valley of the Nile?"

The Texan was somewhat disconcerted, for the argument had passed a little beyond his limits, but he swung it back to where he was sure of his ground by saying: "All that may be true, but it hasn't got much to do with us and the niggers here in the South. We've got 'em here, and we've got 'em to live with, and it's a question of white man or nigger, no middle ground. You want us to treat niggers as equals. Do you want to see 'em sitting around in our parlours? Do you want to see a mulatto South? To bring it right home to you, would you let your daughter marry a nigger?"

"No, I wouldn't consent to my daughter's marrying a nigger, but that doesn't prevent my treating a black man fairly. And I don't see what fair treatment has to do with niggers sitting round in your parlours; they can't come there unless they're invited. Out of all the white men I know, only a hundred or so have the privilege of sitting round in my parlour. As to the mulatto South, if you Southerners have one boast that is stronger than another, it is your women; you put them on a pinnacle of purity and virtue and bow down in a chivalric worship before them; yet you talk and act as though, should you treat the Negro fairly and take the anti-intermarriage laws off your statute books, these same women would rush into the arms of black lovers and husbands. It's a wonder to me that they don't rise up and resent the insult."

"Colonel," said the Texan, as he reached into his handbag and brought out a large flask of whisky, "you might argue from now until hell freezes over, and you might convince me that you're right, but you'll never convince me that I'm wrong. All you say sounds very good, but it's got nothing to do with facts. You can say what men ought to be, but they ain't that; so there you are. Down here in the South we're up against facts, and we're meeting 'em like facts. We don't believe the nigger is or ever will be the equal of the white man, and we ain't going to treat him as an equal; I'll be damned if we will. Have a drink." Everybody except the professor partook of the generous Texan's flask, and the argument closed in a general laugh and good feeling.

I went back into the main part of the car with the conversation on my mind. Here I had before me the bald, raw, naked aspects of the race question in the South; and, in consideration of the step I was just taking, it was far from encouraging. The sentiments of the Texan—and he expressed the sentiments of the South—fell upon me like a chill. I was sick at heart. Yet I must confess that underneath it all I felt a certain sort of admiration for the man who could not be swayed from what he held as his principles. Contrasted with him, the young Ohio professor was indeed a pitiable character. And all along, in spite of myself, I have been compelled to accord the same kind of admiration to the Southern white man for the manner in which he defends not only his virtues, but his vices. He knows that, judged by a high standard, he is narrow and prejudiced, that he is guilty of unfairness, oppression, and cruelty, but this he defends as stoutly as he would his better qualities. This same spirit obtains in a great degree among the blacks; they, too, defend their faults and failings. This they generally do whenever white people are concerned. And yet among themselves they are their own most merciless critics. I have never heard the race so terribly arraigned as I have by coloured speakers to strictly coloured audiences. It is the spirit of the South to defend everything belonging to it. The North is too cosmopolitan and tolerant for such a spirit. If you should say to an Easterner that Paris is a gayer city than New York, he would be likely to agree with you, or at least to let you have your own way; but to suggest to a South Carolinian that Boston is a nicer city to live in than Charleston would be to stir his greatest depths of argument and eloquence.

But today, as I think over that smoking-car argument, I can see it in a different light. The Texan's position does not render things so hopeless, for it indicates that the main difficulty of the race question does not lie so much in the actual condition of the blacks as it does in the mental attitude of the whites; and a mental attitude, especially one not based on truth, can be changed more easily than actual conditions. That is to say, the burden of the question is not that the whites are struggling to save ten million despondent and moribund people from sinking into a hopeless slough of ignorance, poverty, and barbarity in their very midst, but that they are unwilling to open certain doors of opportunity and to accord certain treatment to ten million aspiring, education-and-property-acquiring people. In a word, the difficulty of the problem is not so much due to the facts presented as to the hypothesis assumed for its solution. In this it is similar to the problem of the solar system. By a complex, confusing, and almost contradictory mathematical process, by the use of zigzags instead of straight lines, the earth can be proved to be the centre of things celestial; but by an operation so simple that it can be comprehended by a schoolboy, its position can be verified among the other worlds which revolve about the sun, and its movements harmonized with the laws of the universe. So, when the white race assumes as a hypothesis that it is the main object of creation and that all things else are merely subsidiary to its well-being, sophism, subterfuge, perversion of conscience, arrogance, injustice, oppression, cruelty, sacrifice of human blood, all are required to maintain the position, and its dealings with other races become indeed a problem, a problem which, if based on a hypothesis of common humanity, could be solved by the simple rules of justice.

When I reached Macon, I decided to leave my trunk and all my surplus belongings, to pack my bag, and strike out into the interior. This I did; and by train, by mule and ox-cart, I travelled through many counties. This was my first real experience among rural coloured people, and all that I saw was interesting to me; but there was a great deal which does not require description at my hands; for log-cabins and plantations and dialect-speaking "darkies" are perhaps better known in American literature than any other single picture of our national life. Indeed, they form an ideal and exclusive literary concept of the American Negro to such an extent that it is almost impossible to get the reading public to recognize him in any other setting; so I shall endeavour to avoid giving the reader any already overworked and hackneyed descriptions. This generally accepted literary ideal of the American Negro constitutes what is really an obstacle in the way of the thoughtful and progressive element of the race. His character has been established as a happy-go-lucky, laughing, shuffling, banjo-picking being, and the reading public has not yet been prevailed upon to take him seriously. His efforts to elevate himself socially are looked upon as a sort of absurd caricature of "white civilization." A novel dealing with coloured people who lived in respectable homes and amidst a fair degree of culture and who naturally acted "just like white folks" would be taken in a comic-opera sense. In this respect the Negro is much in the position of a great comedian who gives up the lighter roles to play tragedy. No matter how well he may portray the deeper passions, the public is loath to give him up in his old character; they even conspire to make him a failure in serious work, in order to force him back into comedy. In the same respect, the public is not too much to be blamed, for great comedians are far more scarce than mediocre tragedians; every amateur actor is a tragedian. However, this very fact constitutes the opportunity of the future Negro novelist and poet to give the country something new and unknown, in depicting the life, the ambitions, the struggles, and the passions of those of their race who are striving to break the narrow limits of traditions. A beginning has already been made in that remarkable book by Dr. Du Bois, *The Souls of Black Folk.*

Much, too, that I saw while on this trip, in spite of my enthusiasm, was disheartening. Often I thought of what my millionaire had said to me, and wished myself back in Europe. The houses in which I had to stay were generally uncomfortable, sometimes worse. I often had to sleep in a division or compartment with several other people. Once or twice I was not so fortunate as to find divisions; everybody slept on pallets on the floor. Frequently I was able to lie down and contemplate the stars which were in their zenith. The food was at times so distasteful and poorly cooked that I could not eat it. I remember that once I lived for a week or more on buttermilk, on account of not being able to stomach the fat bacon, the rank turnip-tops, and the heavy damp mixture of meal, salt, and water which was called corn bread. It was only my ambition to do the work which I had planned that kept me steadfast to my purpose. Occasionally I would meet with some signs of progress and uplift in even one of these backwood settlements—houses built of boards, with windows, and divided into rooms; decent food, and a fair standard of living. This condition was due to the fact that there was in the community some exceptionally capable Negro farmer whose thrift served as an example. As I went about among these dull, simple people—the great majority of them hard working, in their relations with the whites submissive, faithful, and often affectionate, negatively content with their lot—and contrasted them with those of the race who had been quickened by the forces of thought, I could not but appreciate the logic of the position held by those Southern leaders who have been bold enough to proclaim against the education of the Negro. They are consistent in their public speech with Southern sentiment and desires. Those public men of the South who have not been daring or heedless enough to defy the ideals of twentieth-century civilization and of modern humanitarianism and philanthropy, find themselves in the embarrassing situation of preaching one thing and praying for another. They are in the position of the fashionable woman who is compelled by the laws of polite society to say to her dearest enemy: "How happy I am to see you!"

And yet in this respect how perplexing is Southern character; for, in opposition to the above, it may be said that the claim of the Southern whites that they love the Negro better than the Northern whites do is in a manner true. Northern white people love the Negro in a sort of abstract way, as a race; through a sense of justice, charity, and philanthropy, they will liberally assist in his elevation. A number of them have heroically spent their lives in this effort (and just here I wish to say that when the coloured people reach the monument-building stage, they should not forget the men and women who went South after the war and founded schools for them). Yet, generally speaking, they have no particular liking for individuals of the race. Southern white people despise the Negro as a race, and will do nothing to aid in his elevation as such; but for certain individuals they have a strong affection, and are helpful to them in many ways. With these individual members of the race they live on terms of the greatest intimacy; they entrust to them their children, their family treasures, and their family secrets; in trouble they often go to them for comfort and counsel; in sickness they often rely upon their care. This affectionate relation between the Southern whites and those blacks who come into close touch with them has not been overdrawn even in fiction.

This perplexity of Southern character extends even to the intermixture of the races. That is spoken of as though it were dreaded worse than smallpox, leprosy, or the plague. Yet, when I was in Jacksonville, I knew several prominent families there with large coloured branches, which went by the same name and were known and acknowledged as blood relatives. And what is more, there seemed to exist between these black brothers and sisters and uncles and aunts a decidedly friendly feeling.

I said above that Southern whites would do nothing for the Negro as a race. I know the South claims that it has spent millions for the education of the blacks, and that it has of its own free will shouldered this awful burden. It seems to be forgetful of the fact that these millions have been taken from the public tax funds for education, and that the law of political economy which recognizes the land-owner as the one who really pays the taxes is not tenable. It would be just as reasonable for the relatively few land-owners of Manhattan to complain that they had to stand the financial burden of the education of the thousands and thousands of children whose parents pay rent for tenements and flats. Let the millions of producing and consuming Negroes be taken out of the South, and it would be quickly seen how much less of public funds there would be to appropriate for education or any other purpose.

In thus travelling about through the country I was sometimes amused on arriving at some little railroad-station town to be taken for and treated as a white man, and six hours later, when it was learned that I was stopping at the house of the coloured preacher or schoolteacher, to note the attitude of the whole town change. At times this led even to embarrassment. Yet it cannot be so embarrassing for a coloured man to be taken for white as for a white man to be taken for coloured; and I have heard of several cases of the latter kind.

All this while I was gathering material for work, jotting down in my note-book themes and melodies, and trying to catch the spirit of the Negro in his relatively primitive state. I began to feel the necessity of hurrying so that I might get back to some city like Nashville to begin my compositions and at the same time earn at least a living by teaching and performing before my funds gave out. At the last settlement in which I stopped I found a mine of material. This was due to the fact that "big meeting" was in progress. "Big meeting" is an institution something like camp-meeting, the difference being that it is held in a permanent church, and not in a temporary structure. All the churches of some one denomination—of course, either Methodist or Baptist—in a county, or, perhaps, in several adjoining counties, are closed, and the congregations unite at some centrally located church for a series of meetings lasting a week. It is really a social as well as a religious function. The people come in great numbers, making the trip, according to their financial status, in buggies drawn by sleek, fleet-footed mules, in ox-carts, or on foot. It was amusing to see some of the latter class trudging down the hot and dusty road, with their shoes, which were brand-new, strung across their shoulders. When they got near the church, they sat on the side of the road and, with many grimaces, tenderly packed their feet into those instruments of torture. This furnished, indeed, a trying test of their religion. The famous preachers come from near and far and take turns in warning sinners of the day of wrath. Food, in the form of those two Southern luxuries, fried chicken and roast pork, is plentiful, and no one need go hungry. On the opening Sunday the women are immaculate in starched stiff white dresses adorned with ribbons, either red or blue. Even a great many of the men wear streamers of vari-coloured ribbons in the buttonholes of their coats. A few of them carefully cultivate a forelock of hair by wrapping it in twine, and on such festive occasions decorate it with a narrow ribbon streamer. Big meetings afford a fine opportunity to the younger people to meet each other dressed in their Sunday clothes, and much rustic courting, which is as enjoyable as any other kind, is indulged in.

This big meeting which I was lucky enough to catch was particularly well attended; the extra large attendance was due principally to two attractions, a man by the name of John Brown, who was renowned as the most powerful preacher for miles around; and a wonderful leader of singing, who was known as "Singing Johnson." These two men were a study and a revelation to me. They caused me to reflect upon how great an influence their types have been in the development of the Negro in America. Both these types are now looked upon generally with condescension or contempt by the progressive element among the coloured people; but it should never be forgotten that it was they who led the race from paganism and kept it steadfast to Christianity through all the long, dark years of slavery.

John Brown was a jet-black man of medium size, with a strikingly intelligent head and face, and a voice like an organ peal. He preached each night after several lesser lights had successively held the pulpit during an hour or so. As far as subject-matter is concerned, all of the sermons were alike: each began with the fall of man, ran through various trials and tribulations of the Hebrew children, on to the redemption by Christ, and ended with a fervid picture of the judgment-day and the fate of the damned. But John Brown possessed magnetism and an imagination so free and daring that he was able to carry through what the other preachers would not attempt. He knew all the arts and tricks of oratory, the modulation of the voice to almost a whisper, the pause for effect, the rise through light, rapid-fire sentences to the terrific, thundering outburst of an electrifying climax. In addition, he had the intuition of a born theatrical manager. Night after night this man held me fascinated. He convinced me that, after all, eloquence consists more in the manner of saying than in what is said. It is largely a matter of tone pictures.

The most striking example of John Brown's magnetism and imagination was his "heavenly march"; I shall never forget how it impressed me when I heard it. He opened his sermon in the usual way; then, proclaiming to his listeners that he was going to take them on the heavenly march, he seized the Bible under his arm and began to pace up and down the pulpit platform. The congregation immediately began with their feet a tramp, tramp, tramp, in time with the preacher's march in the pulpit, all the while singing in an undertone a hymn about marching to Zion. Suddenly he cried: "Halt!" Every foot stopped with the precision of a company of well-drilled soldiers, and the singing ceased. The morning star had been reached. Here the preacher described the beauties of that celestial body. Then the march, the tramp, tramp, tramp, and the singing were again taken up. Another "Halt!" They had reached the evening star. And so on, past the sun and moon—the intensity of religious emotion all the time increasing—along the milky way, on up to the gates of heaven. Here the halt was longer, and the preacher described at length the gates and walls of the New Jerusalem. Then he took his hearers through the pearly gates, along the golden streets, pointing out the glories of the city, pausing occasionally to greet some patriarchal members of the church, well-known to most of his listeners in life, who had had "the tears wiped from their eyes, were clad in robes of spotless white, with crowns of gold upon their heads and harps within their hands," and ended his march before the great white throne. To the reader this may sound ridiculous, but listened to under the circumstances, it was highly and effectively dramatic. I was a more or less sophisticated and non-religious man of the world, but the torrent of the preacher's words, moving with the rhythm and glowing with the eloquence of primitive poetry, swept me along, and I, too, felt like joining in the shouts of "Amen! Hallelujah!"

John Brown's powers in describing the delights of heaven were no greater than those in depicting the horrors of hell. I saw great, strapping fellows trembling and weeping like children at the "mourners' bench." His warnings to sinners were truly terrible. I shall never forget one expression that he used, which for originality and aptness could not be excelled. In my opinion, it is more graphic and, for us, far more expressive than St. Paul's "It is hard to kick against the pricks." He struck the attitude of a pugilist and thundered out: "Young man, your arm's too short to box with God!"

Interesting as was John Brown to me, the other man, "Singing Johnson," was more so. He was a small, dark-brown, one-eyed man, with a clear, strong, high-pitched voice, a leader of singing, a maker of songs, a man who could improvise at the moment lines to fit the occasion. Not so striking a figure as John Brown, but, at "big meetings," equally important. It is indispensable to the success of the singing, when the congregation is a large one made up of people from different communities, to have someone with a strong voice who knows just what hymn to sing and when to sing it, who can pitch it in the right key, and who has all the leading lines committed to memory. Sometimes it devolves upon the leader to "sing down" a long-winded or uninteresting speaker. Committing to memory the leading lines of all the Negro spiritual songs is no easy task, for they run up into the hundreds. But the accomplished leader must know them all, because the congregation sings only the refrains and repeats; every ear in the church is fixed upon him, and if he becomes mixed in his lines or forgets them, the responsibility falls directly on his shoulders.

For example, most of these hymns are constructed to be sung in the following manner:

Leader. Swing low, sweet chariot.
Congregation. Coming for to carry me home.
Leader. Swing low, sweet chariot.
Congregation. Coming for to carry me home.
Leader. I look over yonder, what do I see?
Congregation. Coming for to carry me home.
Leader. Two little angels coming after me.
Congregation. Coming for to carry me home....

The solitary and plaintive voice of the leader is answered by a sound like the roll of the sea, producing a most curious effect.

In only a few of these songs do the leader and the congregation start off together. Such a song is the well-known "Steal away to Jesus."

The leader and the congregation begin with part-singing:

Steal away, steal away,
Steal away to Jesus;
Steal away, steal away home,
I ain't got long to stay here.

Then the leader alone or the congregation in unison:

My Lord he calls me,
He calls me by the thunder,
The trumpet sounds within-a my soul.

Then all together:

I ain't got long to stay here.

The leader and the congregation again take up the opening refrain; then the leader sings three more leading lines alone, and so on almost *ad infinitum.* It will be seen that even here most of the work falls upon the leader, for the congregation sings the same lines over and over, while his memory and ingenuity are taxed to keep the songs going.

Generally the parts taken up by the congregation are sung in a three-part harmony, the women singing the soprano and a transposed tenor, the men with high voices singing the melody, and those with low voices a thundering bass. In a few of these songs, however, the leading part is sung in unison by the whole congregation, down to the last line, which is harmonized. The effect of this is intensely thrilling. Such a hymn is "Go down, Moses." It stirs the heart like a trumpet-call.

"Singing Johnson" was an ideal leader, and his services were in great demand. He spent his time going about the country from one church to another. He received his support in much the same way as the preachers—part of a collection, food and lodging. All of his leisure time he devoted to originating new words and melodies and new lines for old songs. He always sang with his eyes—or, to be more exact, his eye—closed, indicating the *tempo* by swinging his head to and fro. He was a great judge of the proper hymn to sing at a particular moment; and I noticed several times, when the preacher reached a certain climax, or expressed a certain sentiment, that Johnson broke in with a line or two of some appropriate hymn. The speaker understood and would pause until the singing ceased.

As I listened to the singing of these songs, the wonder of their production grew upon me more and more. How did the men who originated them manage to do it? The sentiments are easily accounted for; they are mostly taken from the Bible; but the melodies, where did they come from? Some of them so weirdly sweet, and others so wonderfully strong. Take, for instance, "Go down, Moses." I doubt that there is a stronger theme in the whole musical literature of the world. And so many of these songs contain more than mere melody; there is sounded in them that elusive undertone, the note in music which is not heard with the ears. I sat often with the tears rolling down my cheeks and my heart melted within me. Any musical person who has never heard a Negro congregation under the spell of religious fervour sing these old songs has missed one of the most thrilling emotions which the human heart may experience. Anyone who without shedding tears can listen to Negroes sing "Nobody knows de trouble I see, Nobody knows but Jesus" must indeed have a heart of stone.

As yet, the Negroes themselves do not fully appreciate these old slave songs. The educated classes are rather ashamed of them and prefer to sing hymns from books. This feeling is natural; they are still too close to the conditions under which the songs were produced; but the day will come when this slave music will be the most treasured heritage of the American Negro.

At the close of the "big meeting" I left the settlement where it was being held, full of enthusiasm. I was in that frame of mind which, in the artistic temperament, amounts to inspiration. I was now ready and anxious to get to some place where I might settle down to work, and give expression to the ideas which were teeming in my head; but I strayed into another deviation from my path of life as I had it marked out, which led me upon an entirely different road. Instead of going to the nearest and most convenient railroad station, I accepted the invitation of a young man who had been present the closing Sunday at the meeting to drive with him some miles farther to the town in which he taught school, and there take the train. My conversation with this young man as we drove along through the country was extremely interesting. He had been a student in one of the Negro colleges—strange coincidence, in the very college, as I learned through him, in which "Shiny" was now a professor. I was, of course, curious to hear about my boyhood friend; and had it not been vacation time, and that I was not sure that I should find him, I should have gone out of my way to pay him a visit; but I determined to write to him as soon as the school opened. My companion talked to me about his work among the people, of his hopes and his discouragements. He was tremendously in earnest; I might say, too much so. In fact, it may be said that the majority of intelligent coloured people are, in some degree, too much in earnest over the race question. They assume and carry so much that their progress is at times impeded and they are unable to see things in their proper proportions. In many instances a slight exercise of the sense of humour would save much anxiety of soul. Anyone who marks the general tone of editorials in coloured newspapers is apt to be impressed with this idea. If the mass of Negroes took their present and future as seriously as do the most of their leaders, the race would be in no mental condition to sustain the terrible pressure which it undergoes; it would sink of its own weight. Yet it must be acknowledged that in the making of a race over-seriousness is a far lesser failing than its reverse, and even the faults resulting from it lean toward the right.

We drove into the town just before dark. As we passed a large, unpainted church, my companion pointed it out as the place where he held his school. I promised that I would go there with him the next morning and visit awhile. The town was of that kind which hardly requires or deserves description; a straggling line of brick and wooden stores on one side of the railroad track and some cottages of various sizes on the other side constituted about the whole of it. The young school-teacher boarded at the best house in the place owned by a coloured man. It was painted, had glass windows, contained "store bought" furniture, an organ, and lamps with chimneys. The owner held a job of some kind on the railroad. After supper it was not long before everybody was sleepy. I occupied the room with the school-teacher. In a few minutes after we got into the room he was in bed and asleep; but I took advantage of the unusual luxury of a lamp which gave light, and sat looking over my notes and jotting down some ideas which were still fresh in my mind. Suddenly I became conscious of that sense of alarm which is always aroused by the sound of hurrying footsteps on the silence of the night. I stopped work and looked at my watch. It was after eleven. I listened, straining every nerve to hear above the tumult of my quickening pulse. I caught the murmur of voices, then the gallop of a horse, then of another and another. Now thoroughly alarmed, I woke my companion, and together we both listened. After a moment he put out the light and softly opened the window-blind, and we cautiously peeped out. We saw men moving in one direction, and from the mutterings we vaguely caught the rumour that some terrible crime had been committed. I put on my coat and hat. My friend did all in his power to dissuade me from venturing out, but it was impossible for me to remain in the house under such tense excitement. My nerves would not have stood it. Perhaps what bravery I exercised in going out was due to the fact that I felt sure my identity as a coloured man had not yet become known in the town.

I went out and, following the drift, reached the railroad station. There was gathered there a crowd of men, all white, and others were steadily arriving, seemingly from all the surrounding country. How did the news spread so quickly? I watched these men moving under the yellow glare of the kerosene lamps about the station, stern, comparatively silent, all of them armed, some of them in boots and spurs; fierce, determined men. I had come to know the type well, blond, tall, and lean, with ragged moustache and beard, and glittering grey eyes. At the first suggestion of daylight they began to disperse in groups, going in several directions. There was no extra noise or excitement, no loud talking, only swift, sharp words of command given by those who seemed to be accepted as leaders by mutual understanding. In fact, the impression made upon me was that everything was being done in quite an orderly manner. In spite of so many leaving, the crowd around the station continued to grow; at sunrise there were a great many women and children. By this time I also noticed some coloured people; a few seemed to be going about customary tasks; several were standing on the outskirts of the crowd; but the gathering of Negroes usually seen in such towns was missing.

Before noon they brought him in. Two horsemen rode abreast; between them, half dragged, the poor wretch made his way through the dust. His hands were tied behind him, and ropes round his body were fastened to the saddle horns of his double guard. The men who at midnight had been stern and silent were now emitting that terror-instilling sound known as the "rebel yell." A space was quickly cleared in the crowd, and a rope placed about his neck, when from somewhere came the suggestion, "Burn him!" It ran like an electric current. Have you ever witnessed the transformation of human beings into savage beasts? Nothing can be more terrible. A railroad tie was sunk into the ground, the rope was removed, and a chain brought and securely coiled round the victim and the stake. There he stood, a man only in form and stature, every sign of degeneracy stamped upon his countenance. His eyes were dull and vacant, indicating not a single ray of thought. Evidently the realization of his fearful fate had robbed him of whatever reasoning power he had ever possessed. He was too stunned and stupefied even to tremble. Fuel was brought from everywhere, oil, the torch; the flames crouched for an instant as though to gather strength, then leaped up as high as their victim's head. He squirmed, he writhed, strained at his chains, then gave out cries and groans that I shall always hear. The cries and groans were choked off by the fire and smoke; but his eyes, bulging from their sockets, rolled from side to side, appealing in vain for help. Some of the crowd yelled and cheered, others seemed appalled at what they had done, and there were those who turned away sickened at the sight. I was fixed to the spot where I stood, powerless to take my eyes from what I did not want to see.

It was over before I realized that time had elapsed. Before I could make myself believe that what I saw was really happening, I was looking at a scorched post, a smouldering fire, blackened bones, charred fragments sifting down through coils of chain; and the smell of burnt flesh—human flesh—was in my nostrils.

I walked a short distance away and sat down in order to clear my dazed mind. A great wave of humiliation and shame swept over me. Shame that I belonged to a race that could be so dealt with; and shame for my country, that it, the great example of democracy to the world, should be the only civilized, if not the only state on earth, where a human being would be burned alive. My heart turned bitter within me. I could understand why Negroes are led to sympathize with even their worst criminals and to protect them when possible. By all the impulses of normal human nature they can and should do nothing less.

Whenever I hear protests from the South that it should be left alone to deal with the Negro question, my thoughts go back to that scene of brutality and savagery. I do not see how a people that can find in its conscience any excuse whatever for slowly burning to death a human being, or for tolerating such an act, can be entrusted with the salvation of a race. Of course, there are in the South men of liberal thought who do not approve lynching, but I wonder how long they will endure the limits which are placed upon free speech. They still cower and tremble before "Southern opinion." Even so late as the recent Atlanta riot those men who were brave enough to speak a word in behalf of justice and humanity felt called upon, by way of apology, to preface what they said with a glowing rhetorical tribute to the Anglo-Saxon's superiority and to refer to the "great and impassable gulf" between the races "fixed by the Creator at the foundation of the world." The question of the relative qualities of the two races is still an open one. The reference to the "great gulf" loses force in face of the fact that there are in this country perhaps three or four million people with the blood of both races in their veins; but I fail to see the pertinency of either statement subsequent to the beating and murdering of scores of innocent people in the streets of a civilized and Christian city.

The Southern whites are in many respects a great people. Looked at from a certain point of view, they are picturesque. If one will put oneself in a romantic frame of mind, one can admire their notions of chivalry and bravery and justice. In this same frame of mind an intelligent man can go to the theatre and applaud the impossible hero, who with his single sword slays everybody in the play except the equally impossible heroine. So can an ordinary peace-loving citizen sit by a comfortable fire and read with enjoyment of the bloody deeds of pirates and the fierce brutality of vikings. This is the way in which we gratify the old, underlying animal instincts and passions; but we should shudder with horror at the mere idea of such practices being realities in this day of enlightened and humanitarianized thought. The Southern whites are not yet living quite in the present age; many of their general ideas hark back to a former century, some of them to the Dark Ages. In the light of other days they are sometimes magnificent. Today they are often cruel and ludicrous.

How long I sat with bitter thoughts running through my mind I do not know; perhaps an hour or more. When I decided to get up and go back to the house, I found that I could hardly stand on my feet. I was as weak as a man who had lost blood. However, I dragged myself along, with the central idea of a general plan well fixed in my mind. I did not find my school-teacher friend at home, so I did not see him again. I swallowed a few mouthfuls of food, packed my bag, and caught the afternoon train.

When I reached Macon, I stopped only long enough to get the main part of my luggage and to buy a ticket for New York. All along the journey I was occupied in debating with myself the step which I had decided to take. I argued that to forsake one's race to better one's condition was no less worthy an action than to forsake one's country for the same purpose. I finally made up my mind that I would neither disclaim the black race nor claim the white race; but that I would change my name, raise a moustache, and let the world take me for what it would; that it was not necessary for me to go about with a label of inferiority pasted across my forehead. All the while I understood that it was not discouragement or fear or search for a larger field of action and opportunity that was driving me out of the Negro race. I knew that it was shame, unbearable shame. Shame at being identified with a people that could with impunity be treated worse than animals.

For certainly the law would restrain and punish the malicious burning alive of animals.

So once again I found myself gazing at the towers of New York and wondering what future that city held in store for me.

CHAPTER XI

I have now reached that part of my narrative where I must be brief and touch only on important facts; therefore the reader must make up his mind to pardon skips and jumps and meagre details.

When I reached New York, I was completely lost. I could not have felt more a stranger had I been suddenly dropped into Constantinople. I knew not where to turn or how to strike out. I was so oppressed by a feeling of loneliness that the temptation to visit my old home in Connecticut was well-nigh irresistible. I reasoned, however, that unless I found my old music teacher, I should be, after so many years of absence, as much of a stranger there as in New York; and, furthermore, that in view of the step which I had decided to take, such a visit would be injudicious. I remembered, too, that I had some property there in the shape of a piano and a few books, but decided that it would not be worth what it might cost me to take possession.

By reason of the fact that my living-expenses in the South had been very small, I still had nearly four hundred dollars of my capital left. In contemplation of this, my natural and acquired Bohemian tastes asserted themselves, and I decided to have a couple of weeks' good time before worrying seriously about the future. I went to Coney Island and the other resorts, took in the pre-season shows along Broadway, and ate at first-class restaurants; but I shunned the old Sixth Avenue district as though it were pest-infected. My few days of pleasure made appalling inroads upon what cash I had, and caused me to see that it required a good deal of money to live in New York as I wished to live and that I should have to find, very soon, some more or less profitable employment. I was sure that unknown, without friends or prestige, it would be useless to try to establish myself as a teacher of music; so I gave that means of earning a livelihood scarcely any consideration. And even had I considered it possible to secure pupils, as I then felt, I should have hesitated about taking up a work in which the chances for any considerable financial success are necessarily so small. I had made up my mind that since I was not going to be a Negro, I would avail myself of every possible opportunity to make a white man's success; and that, if it can be summed up in any one word, means "money."

I watched the "want" columns in the newspapers and answered a number of advertisements, but in each case found the positions were such as I could not fill or did not want. I also spent several dollars for "ads" which brought me no replies. In this way I came to know the hopes and disappointments of a large and pitiable class of humanity in this great city, the people who look for work through the newspapers. After some days of this sort of experience I concluded that the main difficulty with me was that I was not prepared for what I wanted to do. I then decided upon a course which, for an artist, showed an uncommon amount of practical sense and judgment. I made up my mind to enter a business college. I took a small room, ate at lunch counters, in order to economize, and pursued my studies with the zeal that I have always been able to put into any work upon which I set my heart. Yet, in spite of all my economy, when I had been at the school for several months, my funds gave out completely. I reached the point where I could not afford sufficient food for each day. In this plight I was glad to get, through one of the teachers, a job as an ordinary clerk in a downtown wholesale house. I did my work faithfully, and received a raise of salary before I expected it. I even managed to save a little money out of my modest earnings. In fact, I began then to contract the money fever, which later took strong possession of me. I kept my eyes open, watching for a chance to better my condition. It finally came in the form of a position with a house which was at the time establishing a South American department. My knowledge of Spanish was, of course, the principal cause of my good luck; and it did more for me: it placed me where the other clerks were practically put out of competition with me. I was not slow in taking advantage of the opportunity to make myself indispensable to the firm.

What an interesting and absorbing game is money-making! After each deposit at my savings-bank I used to sit and figure out, all over again, my principal and interest, and make calculations on what the increase would be in such and such time. Out of this I derived a great deal of pleasure. I denied myself as much as possible in order to swell my savings. As much as I enjoyed smoking, I limited myself to an occasional cigar, and that was generally of a variety which in my old days at the "Club" was known as a "Henry Mud." Drinking I cut out altogether, but that was no great sacrifice.

The day on which I was able to figure up a thousand dollars marked an epoch in my life. And this was not because I had never before had money. In my gambling days and while I was with my millionaire I handled sums running high up into the hundreds; but they had come to me like fairy godmother's gifts, and at a time when my conception of money was that it was made only to spend. Here, on the other hand, was a thousand dollars which I had earned by days of honest and patient work, a thousand dollars which I had carefully watched grow from the first dollar; and I experienced, in owning them, a pride and satisfaction which to me was an entirely new sensation. As my capital went over the thousand-dollar mark, I was puzzled to know what to do with it, how to put it to the most advantageous use. I turned down first one scheme and then another, as though they had been devised for the sole purpose of gobbling up my money. I finally listened to a friend who advised me to put all I had in New York real estate; and under his guidance I took equity in a piece of property on which stood a rickety old tenement-house. I did not regret following this friend's advice, for in something like six months I disposed of my equity for more than double my investment. From that time on I devoted myself to the study of New York real estate and watched for opportunities to make similar investments. In spite of two or three speculations which did not turn out well, I have been remarkably successful. Today I am the owner and part-owner of several flat-houses. I have changed my place of employment four times since returning to New York, and each change has been a decided advancement. Concerning the position which I now hold I shall say nothing except that it pays extremely well.

As my outlook on the world grew brighter, I began to mingle in the social circles of the men with whom I came in contact; and gradually, by a process of elimination, I reached a grade of society of no small degree of culture. My appearance was always good and my ability to play on the piano, especially rag-time, which was then at the height of its vogue, made me a welcome guest. The anomaly of my social position often appealed strongly to my sense of humour. I frequently smiled inwardly at some remark not altogether complimentary to people of colour; and more than once I felt like declaiming: "I am a coloured man. Do I not disprove the theory that one drop of Negro blood renders a man unfit?" Many a night when I returned to my room after an enjoyable evening, I laughed heartily over what struck me as the capital joke I was playing.

Then I met her, and what I had regarded as a joke was gradually changed into the most serious question of my life. I first saw her at a musical which was given one evening at a house to which I was frequently invited. I did not notice her among the other guests before she came forward and sang two sad little songs. When she began, I was out in the hallway, where many of the men were gathered; but with the first few notes I crowded with others into the doorway to see who the singer was. When I saw the girl, the surprise which I had felt at the first sound of her voice was heightened; she was almost tall and quite slender, with lustrous yellow hair and eyes so blue as to appear almost black. She was as white as a lily, and she was dressed in white. Indeed, she seemed to me the most dazzlingly white thing I had ever seen. But it was not her delicate beauty which attracted me most; it was her voice, a voice which made one wonder how tones of such passionate colour could come from so fragile a body.

I determined that when the program was over, I would seek an introduction to her; but at the moment, instead of being the easy man of the world, I became again the bashful boy of fourteen, and my courage failed me. I contented myself with hovering as near her as politeness would permit; near enough to hear her voice, which in conversation was low, yet thrilling, like the deeper middle tones of a flute. I watched the men gather round her talking and laughing in an easy manner, and wondered how it was possible for them to do it. But destiny, my special destiny, was at work. I was standing near, talking with affected gaiety to several young ladies, who, however, must have remarked my preoccupation; for my second sense of hearing was alert to what was being said by the group of which the girl in white was the centre, when I heard her say: "I think his playing of Chopin is exquisite." And one of my friends in the group replied: "You haven't met him? Allow me——" Then turning to me, "Old man, when you have a moment I wish you to meet Miss——." I don't know what she said to me or what I said to her. I can remember that I tried to be clever, and experienced a growing conviction that I was making myself appear more and more idiotic. I am certain, too, that, in spite of my Italian-like complexion, I was as red as a beet.

Instead of taking the car, I walked home. I needed the air and exercise as a sort of sedative. I am not sure whether my troubled condition of mind was due to the fact that I had been struck by love or to the feeling that I had made a bad impression upon her.

As the weeks went by, and when I had met her several more times, I came to know that I was seriously in love; and then began for me days of worry, for I had more than the usual doubts and fears of a young man in love to contend with.

Up to this time I had assumed and played my role as a white man with a certain degree of nonchalance, a carelessness as to the outcome, which made the whole thing more amusing to me than serious; but now I ceased to regard "being a white man" as a sort of practical joke. My acting had called for mere external effects. Now I began to doubt my ability to play the part. I watched her to see if she was scrutinizing me, to see if she was looking for anything in me which made me differ from the other men she knew. In place of an old inward feeling of superiority over many of my friends I began to doubt myself. I began even to wonder if I really was like the men I associated with; if there was not, after all, an indefinable something which marked a difference.

But, in spite of my doubts and timidity, my affair progressed, and I finally felt sufficiently encouraged to decide to ask her to marry me. Then began the hardest struggle of my life, whether to ask her to marry me under false colours or to tell her the whole truth. My sense of what was exigent made me feel there was no necessity of saying anything; but my inborn sense of honour rebelled at even indirect deception in this case. But however much I moralized on the question, I found it more and more difficult to reach the point of confession. The dread that I might lose her took possession of me each time I sought to speak, and rendered it impossible for me to do so. That moral courage requires more than physical courage is no mere poetic fancy. I am sure I should have found it easier to take the place of a gladiator, no matter how fierce the Numidian lion, than to tell that slender girl that I had Negro blood in my veins. The fact which I had at times wished to cry out, I now wished to hide for ever.

During this time we were drawn together a great deal by the mutual bond of music. She loved to hear me play Chopin and was herself far from being a poor performer of his compositions. I think I carried her every new song that was published which I thought suitable to her voice, and played the accompaniment for her. Over these songs we were like two innocent children with new toys. She had never been anything but innocent; but my innocence was a transformation wrought by my love for her, love which melted away my cynicism and whitened my sullied soul and gave me back the wholesome dreams of my boyhood.

My artistic temperament also underwent an awakening. I spent many hours at my piano, playing over old and new composers. I also wrote several little pieces in a more or less Chopinesque style, which I dedicated to her. And so the weeks and months went by. Often words of love trembled on my lips, but I dared not utter them, because I knew they would have to be followed by other words which I had not the courage to frame. There might have been some other woman in my set whom I could have fallen in love with and asked to marry me without a word of explanation; but the more I knew this girl, the less could I find it in my heart to deceive her. And yet, in spite of this spectre that was constantly looming up before me, I could never have believed that life held such happiness as was contained in those dream days of love.

One Saturday afternoon, in early June, I was coming up Fifth Avenue, and at the corner of Twenty-third Street I met her. She had been shopping. We stopped to chat for a moment, and I suggested that we spend half an hour at the Eden Musée. We were standing leaning on the rail in front of a group of figures, more interested in what we had to say to each other than in the group, when my attention became fixed upon a man who stood at my side studying his catalogue. It took me only an instant to recognize in him my old friend "Shiny." My first impulse was to change my position at once. As quick as a flash I considered all the risks I might run in speaking to him, and most especially the delicate question of introducing him to her. I confess that in my embarrassment and confusion I felt small and mean. But before I could decide what to do, he looked round at me and, after an instant, quietly asked: "Pardon me; but isn't this——?" The nobler part in me responded to the sound of his voice and I took his hand in a hearty clasp. Whatever fears I had felt were quickly banished, for he seemed, at a glance, to divine my situation, and let drop no word that would have aroused suspicion as to the truth. With a slight misgiving I presented him to her and was again relieved of fear. She received the introduction in her usual gracious manner, and without the least hesitancy or embarrassment joined in the conversation. An amusing part about the introduction was that I was upon the point of introducing him as "Shiny," and stammered a second or two before I could recall his name. We chatted for some fifteen minutes. He was spending his vacation north, with the intention of doing four or six weeks' work in one of the summer schools; he was also going to take a bride back with him in the fall. He asked me about myself, but in so diplomatic a way that I found no difficulty in answering him. The polish of his language and the unpedantic manner in which he revealed his culture greatly impressed her; and after we had left the Musée she showed it by questioning me about him. I was surprised at the amount of interest a refined black man could arouse. Even after changes in the conversation she reverted several times to the subject of "Shiny." Whether it was more than mere curiosity I could not tell, but I was convinced that she herself knew very little about prejudice.

Just why it should have done so I do not know, but somehow the "Shiny" incident gave me encouragement and confidence to cast the die of my fate. I reasoned, however, that since I wanted to marry her only, and since it concerned her alone, I would divulge my secret to no one else, not even her parents.

One evening, a few days afterwards, at her home we were going over some new songs and compositions when she asked me, as she often did, to play the Thirteenth Nocturne. When I began, she drew a chair near to my right and sat leaning with her elbow on the end of the piano, her chin resting on her hand, and her eyes reflecting the emotions which the music awoke in her. An impulse which I could not control rushed over me, a wave of exultation, the music under my fingers sank almost to a whisper, and calling her for the first time by her Christian name, but without daring to look at her, I said: "I love you, I love you, I love you." My fingers were trembling so that I ceased playing. I felt her hand creep to mine, and when I looked at her, her eyes were glistening with tears. I understood, and could scarcely resist the longing to take her in my arms; but I remembered, remembered that which has been the sacrificial altar of so much happiness—Duty; and bending over her hand in mine, I said: "Yes, I love you; but there is something more, too, that I must tell you." Then I told her, in what words I do not know, the truth. I felt her hand grow cold, and when I looked up, she was gazing at me with a wild, fixed stare as though I was some object she had never seen. Under the strange light in her eyes I felt that I was growing black and thick-featured and crimp-haired. She appeared not to have comprehended what I had said. Her lips trembled and she attempted to say something to me, but the words stuck in her throat. Then, dropping her head on the piano, she began to weep with great sobs that shook her frail body. I tried to console her, and blurted out incoherent words of love, but this seemed only to increase her distress, and when I left her, she was still weeping.

When I got into the street, I felt very much as I did the night after meeting my father and sister at the opera in Paris, even a similar desperate inclination to get drunk; but my self-control was stronger. This was the only time in my life that I ever felt absolute regret at being coloured, that I cursed the drops of African blood in my veins and wished that I were really white. When I reached my rooms, I sat and smoked several cigars while I tried to think out the significance of what had occurred. I reviewed the whole history of our acquaintance, recalled each smile she had given me, each word she had said to me that nourished my hope. I went over the scene we had just gone through, trying to draw from it what was in my favour and what was against me. I was rewarded by feeling confident that she loved me, but I could not estimate what was the effect upon her of my confession. At last, nervous and unhappy, I wrote her a letter, which I dropped into the mail-box before going to bed, in which I said:

> I understand, understand even better than you, and so I suffer even more than you. But why should either of us suffer for what neither of us is to blame for? If there is any blame, it belongs to me and I can only make the old, yet strongest plea that can be offered, I love you; and I know that my love, my great love, infinitely overbalances that blame and blots it out. What is it that stands in the way of our happiness? It is not what you feel or what I feel; it is not what you are or what I am. It is what others feel and are. But, oh! is that a fair price? In all the endeavours and struggles of life, in all our strivings and longings, there is only one thing worth seeking, only one thing worth winning, and that is love. It is not always found; but when it is, there is nothing in all the world for which it can be profitably exchanged.

The second morning after, I received a note from her which stated briefly that she was going up into New Hampshire to spend the summer with relatives there. She made no reference to what had passed between us; nor did she say exactly when she would leave the city. The note contained no single word that gave me any clue to her feelings. I could gather hope only from the fact that she had written at all. On the same evening, with a degree of trepidation which rendered me almost frightened, I went to her house.

I met her mother, who told me that she had left for the country that very afternoon. Her mother treated me in her usual pleasant manner, which fact greatly reassured me; and I left the house with a vague sense of hope stirring in my breast, which sprang from the conviction that she had not yet divulged my secret. But that hope did not remain with me long. I waited one, two, three weeks, nervously examining my mail every day, looking for some word from her. All of the letters received by me seemed so insignificant, so worthless, because there was none from her. The slight buoyancy of spirit which I had felt gradually dissolved into gloomy heart-sickness. I became preoccupied; I lost appetite, lost sleep, and lost ambition. Several of my friends intimated to me that perhaps I was working too hard.

She stayed away the whole summer. I did not go to the house, but saw her father at various times, and he was as friendly as ever. Even after I knew that she was back in town, I did not go to see her. I determined to wait for some word or sign. I had finally taken refuge and comfort in my pride, pride which, I suppose, I came by naturally enough.

The first time I saw her after her return was one night at the theatre. She and her mother sat in company with a young man whom I knew slightly, not many seats away from me. Never did she appear more beautiful; and yet, it may have been my fancy, she seemed a trifle paler, and there was a suggestion of haggardness in her countenance. But that only heightened her beauty; the very delicacy of her charm melted down the strength of my pride. My situation made me feel weak and powerless, like a man trying with his bare hands to break the iron bars of his prison cell. When the performance was over, I hurried out and placed myself where, unobserved, I could see her as she passed out. The haughtiness of spirit in which I had sought relief was all gone, and I was willing and ready to undergo any humiliation.

Shortly afterward we met at a progressive card party, and during the evening we were thrown together at one of the tables as partners. This was really our first meeting since the eventful night at her house. Strangely enough, in spite of our mutual nervousness, we won every trick of the game, and one of our opponents jokingly quoted the old saw: "Lucky at cards, unlucky in love." Our eyes met and I am sure that in the momentary glance my whole soul went out to her in one great plea. She lowered her eyes and uttered a nervous little laugh. During the rest of the game I fully merited the unexpressed and expressed abuse of my various partners; for my eyes followed her wherever she was and I played whatever card my fingers happened to touch.

Later in the evening she went to the piano and began to play very softly, as to herself, the opening bars of the Thirteenth Nocturne. I felt that the psychic moment of my life had come, a moment which, if lost, could never be called back; and, in as careless a manner as I could assume, I sauntered over to the piano and stood almost bending over her. She continued playing, but, in a voice that was almost a whisper, she called me by my Christian name and said: "I love you, I love you, I love you." I took her place at the piano and played the Nocturne in a manner that silenced the chatter of the company both in and out of the room, involuntarily closing it with the major triad.

We were married the following spring, and went to Europe for several months. It was a double joy for me to be in France again under such conditions.

First there came to us a little girl, with hair and eyes dark like mine, but who is growing to have ways like her mother. Two years later there came a boy, who has my temperament, but is fair like his mother, a little golden-headed god, with a face and head that would have delighted the heart of an old Italian master. And this boy, with his mother's eyes and features, occupies an inner sanctuary of my heart; for it was for him that she gave all; and that is the second sacred sorrow of my life.

The few years of our married life were supremely happy, and perhaps she was even happier than I; for after our marriage, in spite of all the wealth of her love which she lavished upon me, there came a new dread to haunt me, a dread which I cannot explain and which was unfounded, but one that never left me. I was in constant fear that she would discover in me some shortcoming which she would unconsciously attribute to my blood rather than to a failing of human nature. But no cloud ever came to mar our life together; her loss to me is irreparable. My children need a mother's care, but I shall never marry again. It is to my children that I have devoted my life. I no longer have the same fear for myself of my secret's being found out, for since my wife's death I have gradually dropped out of social life; but there is nothing I would not suffer to keep the brand from being placed upon them.

It is difficult for me to analyse my feelings concerning my present position in the world. Sometimes it seems to me that I have never really been a Negro, that I have been only a privileged spectator of their inner life; at other times I feel that I have been a coward, a deserter, and I am possessed by a strange longing for my mother's people.

Several years ago I attended a great meeting in the interest of Hampton Institute at Carnegie Hall. The Hampton students sang the old songs and awoke memories that left me sad. Among the speakers were R. C. Ogden, ex-Ambassador Choate, and Mark Twain; but the greatest interest of the audience was centred in Booker T. Washington, and not because he so much surpassed the others in eloquence, but because of what he represented with so much earnestness and faith. And it is this that all of that small but gallant band of coloured men who are publicly fighting the cause of their race have behind them. Even those who oppose them know that these men have the eternal principles of right on their side, and they will be victors even though they should go down in defeat. Beside them I feel small and selfish. I am an ordinarily successful white man who has made a little money. They are men who are making history and a race. I, too, might have taken part in a work so glorious.

My love for my children makes me glad that I am what I am and keeps me from desiring to be otherwise; and yet, when I sometimes open a little box in which I still keep my fast yellowing manuscripts, the only tangible remnants of a vanished dream, a dead ambition, a sacrificed talent, I cannot repress the thought that, after all, I have chosen the lesser part, that I have sold my birthright for a mess of pottage.

PART THREE

POETRY

POETRY

"I am glad," writes James Weldon Johnson to Joel E. Spingarn, "that you like 'The Creation.' I have been experimenting for some time to find a form which would hold all the character of 'Negro' poetry, and at the same time be capable of expressing deep emotion and lofty sentiment—something which I have not found possible in the 'dialect' form. I believe I have it in 'The Creation.'" In this letter of December 11, 1920, the first of many such letters to his friend Spingarn on the subject of the poems that would comprise *God's Trombones,* Johnson sketches in broad outline the aesthetic challenges and goals associated with this much celebrated volume of verse. "The Creation" and the other six folk sermons that comprise *God's Trombones* were born of Johnson's desire to "take the primitive stuff of the old-time Negro sermons and, through art-governed expression, make it into poetry."

Johnson wrote "The Creation" in 1919 after hearing a black preacher address a congregation in Kansas City. Johnson was impressed by the delivery and performance of this unnamed black preacher who, as he recalled in *Along This Way,* "excited my envy" through his mastery of language and the occasion and who, as a consequence, stirred "something primordial in me." A few weeks later Johnson completed "The Creation," which was subsequently published in *The Freeman.* While he was deeply committed to completing his volume of folk sermons, six years would pass before he "formulated the subject matter and chose the title of the second poem of the group" entitled "Go Down Death," a funeral sermon.

Johnson resumed his work on what would become *God's Trombones* after the publication in 1925 of the very successful *The Book of American Negro Spirituals,* a two-volume work he co-edited with his brother J. Rosamond Johnson. Johnson writes that the completion of this volume and its accompanying introduction had a similar effect on him as that of hearing the black evangelist in Kansas City in 1919. "This work tempered in me," recalls Johnson, "to just the right mood to go on with what I had started when I wrote 'The Creation.' I was in touch with the deepest revelation of the Negro's soul that has yet been made, and I felt myself attuned to it." On Thanksgiving day, 1926, Johnson wrote "Go Down Death." Remembering the exhilaration associated with writing this funeral sermon Johnson observes: "As I worked, my own spirit rose till it reached a degree almost of ecstasy. The poem shaped itself easily and before the hour for dinner I had written it as it stands published." Wishing to preserve the special mood born of writing the second sermon, Johnson left Manhattan and retired to Five Acres, his country residence in Great Barrington, Massachusetts, where he wrote the remaining five sermons. As he struggled to give voice to "the old-time Negro preacher," Johnson states that his "aim was to interpret what was in the mind, to express, if possible, the dream to which, despite limitations, he strove to give utterance." Within two weeks of the composition of "Go Down Death," he had completed his seven folk sermons in verse.

As the folk sermons were now finished, the next challenge for Johnson was selecting the right title for the collection. The title was not an insignificant matter for Johnson, who wrote again to Spingarn soliciting his advice. "I am still somewhat at sea," the Executive Secretary of the NAACP confided to his chairman. "I want a title that comprehends the poems but one which is also arresting... a bit daring—one with a slight touch of the fantastic in it, but which at the same time will bear no construction of comedy. A big order." Johnson sent to Spingarn a list of nine possible titles for his consideration: "Cloven Tongues"; "Halleluiah!"; "God's Trumpeters"; "Black Trumpeters of God"; "God's Trombones"; "Trombones of God"; "Brimstone and Glory"; "Sons of Thunder"; and "That Old Time Religion." In his letter Johnson expresses a preference for the title

"God's Trombones," but is cautious as the trombone's "connection with the modern jazz band" could very well "offend the religious sense of some people." In his reply a few days later, Spingarn ranked his preferences: 1) "That Old Time Religion"; 2) "Brimstone and Glory"; 3) "Halleluiah!" He also took the liberty of providing a fourth title for the volume, "The Creation and Other Poems," one which Johnson had mentioned but abandoned for lack of interest. A few days later, Johnson wrote to Spingarn to inform him of his decision regarding the bothersome matter of a title: "I have decided upon what perhaps you would consider a bizarre title—God's Trombones. There is a slight touch of the fantastic about it, but I feel that when the poems and the preface which I have done for the book are taken together the title will be found fitting."

Published in 1927 and dedicated to the NAACP's legal counsel Arthur B. Spingarn (the younger brother of Joel E. Spingarn), Johnson's prediction concerning the appropriateness of the title and the content of the volume were confirmed by his dear friend Carl Van Vechten, who wrote to express his admiration of *God's Trombones:* "It is a marvel to me how you have contrived to put down on paper the ecstasy, almost the personality, of the preachers. The preface is a little masterpiece of suave information.... I salute you!" As was the case with the reprint of *The Autobiography of an Ex-Coloured Man* in the same year, the artist Aaron Douglass created the drawings that grace Johnson's celebrated volume. Wishing to create an audience for Johnson's sermons that extended beyond the United States, in 1930 Amy Spingarn translated *God's Trombones* into German, but, notwithstanding the excellence of the translation, she had no success in securing a publisher in Germany.

Winner of the Harmon Award, *God's Trombones* was enormously popular among both the black cognoscenti as well as the masses of black Americans. The famed minister Francis Grimke captured the feelings of many readers when he wrote to Johnson in 1929 to express his admiration: "You have certainly rendered a lasting service in preserving in the splendid manner in which you have in these poems, the thoughts, sentiments, imagery, striking conceptions of the old time preachers of the race." In due time, Johnson's sermons were recited from memory by African Americans at oratorical contests across the country. In 1932 the young poet Owen Dodson wrote Johnson to inform him that Dodson and his younger brother had participated in oratorical contests in which they had recited "The Creation" and "Go Down Death" and "won first and second prizes respectively. I thought you might be interested in this. I am sending you the programs of those contests." Characteristically, Johnson penned a warm congratulatory note to Dodson: "I need not tell you how pleased I was to see that you won with two of my poems from *God's Trombones.* My only regret is that I did not have the pleasure of being present and witnessing your achievement.... I wish you and your brother the fullest success."

Johnson's reputation as a poet reposes upon not only the critical success of *God's Trombones* but also upon *Saint Peter Relates an Incident: Selected Poems.* Published in 1932, this collection is comprised of *Fifty Years and Other Poems,* Johnson's first volume of poems published in 1917, as well as others he composed and published between the years 1917 and 1932. *Saint Peter Relates an Incident* contains such landmark works as "Fifty Years" and "Saint Peter Relates an Incident of the Resurrection Day."

"Fifty Years" established Johnson as a national figure in American and African American poetry. Written to commemorate the fiftieth anniversary of Abraham Lincoln's "Emancipation Proclamation," Johnson composed the poem in six weeks while also meeting his responsibilities as Consul General of Nicaragua during a period of marked civil strife in that country's history. With the assistance of scholar Brander Matthews of Columbia University, "Fifty Years" was published in the *New York Times* on January 1, 1913. Johnson recalls that on the following day "*The Times* printed a fairly long and quite laudatory editorial comment on the poem." Shortly after the publication of "Fifty Years" the writer Charles Chesnutt wrote to Johnson to express his admiration for what he termed "your magnificent Emancipation Anniversary poem." Chesnutt asserted that the poem "is the finest thing I have ever read on the subject, which is saying a good deal, and the finest thing I have seen from the pen of a colored writer for a long time—which is not saying quite so much." Chesnutt's congratulatory letter ended thusly: "You have rendered a service to your race and to humanity by giving the world this beautiful poem, and I hope the appreciation it must have received has given you as much pleasure as the poem has given your readers." As an alumnus of

Atlanta University, Johnson was doubtless very pleased with the praise he received from Horace Bumstead, his former teacher and the former president of his alma mater: "The elevation of thought, the fidelity to history, the noble and dignified self-assertion, the confident faith in the future—all these are fine beyond the need of any praise from me, for they will be universally recognized."

While "Fifty Years" reveals Johnson's considerable powers at the beginning of his career as a poet, "Saint Peter Relates an Incident of the Resurrection Day" reveals Johnson at the height of his powers in verse. Published in 1930, the poem memorializes the heroic service and sacrifices of African American soldiers during World War I. Johnson writes that he "attempted an ironic poem about the unknown soldier. The poem was written 'while meditating upon Heaven and Hell and Democracy and War and America and the Negro Gold Star Mothers.' " The genesis of the poem arises from an insult to black mothers and their "soldier sons." Johnson read "one morning in the newspaper that the United States government was sending a contingent of gold-star mothers to France to visit the graves of their soldier sons buried there; and that the Negro gold-star mothers would not be allowed to sail on the same ship with the white gold-star mothers, but would be sent over on a second and second-class vessel. [Johnson] threw aside the manuscript on which he had been working and did not take it up again until he had finished . . . 'St. Peter Relates an Incident.' " The volume in which the poem first appeared was printed for private distribution in a limited edition of two hundred copies.

In a letter to Johnson, the artist Aaron Douglass described "Saint Peter Relates an Incident" as a "magnificent poem." Similarly, the journalist and writer George Schuyler also had high praise for Johnson's achievement: " 'St. Peter' is, to my way of thinking, propaganda literature at its best, so excellent that it will be enjoyed by the very people against whom its shafts of irony are aimed."

In many ways, the most incisive assessment of "Saint Peter Relates an Incident of the Resurrection Day" came from the poet Sterling A. Brown. In a fulsome letter to Johnson, the author of *Southern Road* (1930), for which volume Johnson had written a laudatory introduction, offers the following observations about the poem: "All that I can say of the poem is that you've done it again. . . . The whole poem keeps to its tone of high wit, and tempered irony. And it's not 'wise cracking'—it's the spirit best seen in Dryden and Pope, at their best. . . . The raillery may be gentle—but it is trenchant;—there's so much real social criticism compressed in such a small space. . . . But with all the raillery, the satire, the poem is moving, and saddening. I think you have put in final form what had to be said."

Sence You Went Away

Seems lak to me de stars don't shine so bright,
Seems lak to me de sun done loss his light,
Seems lak to me der's nothin' goin' right,
Sence you went away.

Seems lak to me de sky ain't half so blue,
Seems lak to me dat ev'ything wants you,
Seems lak to me I don't know what to do,
Sence you went away.

Seems lak to me dat ev'ything is wrong,
Seems lak to me de day's jes twice ez long,
Seems lak to me de bird's forgot his song,
Sence you went away.

Seems lak to me I jes can't he'p but sigh,
Seems lak to me ma th'oat keeps gittin' dry,
Seems lak to me a tear stays in ma eye,
Sence you went away.

Lift Every Voice and Sing

Lift every voice and sing
Till earth and heaven ring,
Ring with the harmonies of Liberty;
Let our rejoicing rise
High as the listening skies,
Let it resound loud as the rolling sea.
Sing a song full of the faith that the dark past has taught us,
Sing a song full of the hope that the present has brought us.
Facing the rising sun of our new day begun,
Let us march on till victory is won.

Stony the road we trod,
Bitter the chastening rod,
Felt in the days when hope unborn had died;
Yet with a steady beat,
Have not our weary feet
Come to the place for which our fathers sighed?
We have come over a way that with tears has been watered,
We have come, treading our path through the blood of the
slaughtered,
Out from the gloomy past,
Till now we stand at last
Where the white gleam of our bright star is cast.

God of our weary years,
God of our silent tears,
Thou who hast brought us thus far on the way;
Thou who hast by Thy might
Led us into the light,
Keep us forever in the path, we pray.
Lest our feet stray from the places, our God, where we met Thee,
Lest, our hearts drunk with the wine of the world, we forget Thee;
Shadowed beneath Thy hand,
May we forever stand.
True to our God,
True to our native land.

Fifty Years
(1863-1913)

O brothers mine, today we stand
    Where half a century sweeps our ken,
Since God, through Lincoln's ready hand,
    Struck off our bonds and made us men.

Just fifty years—a winter's day,
    As runs the history of a race;
Yet, as we look back o'er the way,
    How distant seems our starting place!

Look farther back! Three centuries!
    To where a naked, shivering score,
Snatched from their haunts across the seas,
    Stood, wide-eyed, on Virginia's shore.

Then let us here erect a stone,
    To mark the place, to mark the time;
As witness to God's purpose shown,
    A pledge to hold this day sublime.

A part of His unknown design,
    We've lived within a mighty age;

And we have helped to write a line
    On history's most wondrous page.

A few black bondmen strewn along
    The borders of our eastern coast,
Now grown a race, ten million strong,
    An upward, onward, marching host.

Far, far the way that we have trod,
    From slave and pagan denizens,
To freedmen, freemen, sons of God,
    Americans and Citizens.

For never let the thought arise
    That we are here on sufferance bare;
Outcasts asylumed 'neath these skies,
    And aliens without part or share.

This land is ours by right of birth,
    This land is ours by right of toil;
We helped to turn its virgin earth,
    Our sweat is in its fruitful soil.

Where once the tangled forest stood,
    Where flourished once rank weed and thorn,
Behold the path-traced, peaceful wood,
    The cotton white, the yellow corn.

To gain these fruits that have been earned,
    To hold these fields that have been won,
Our arms have strained, our backs have burned,
    Bent bare beneath a ruthless sun.

That Banner which is now the type
    Of victory on field and flood—
Remember, its first crimson stripe
    Was dyed by Attucks' willing blood.

And never yet has come the cry—
    When that fair flag has been assailed—
For men to do, for men to die,
    That we have faltered or have failed.

We've helped to bear it, rent and torn,
    Through many a hot-breath'd battle breeze;
Held in our hands, it has been borne
    And planted far across the seas.

And never yet—O haughty Land,
    Let us, at least, for this be praised—
Has one black, treason-guided hand
    Ever against that flag been raised.

Then should we speak but servile words,
    Or shall we hang our heads in shame?
Stand back of new-come foreign hordes,
    And fear our heritage to claim?

No! Stand erect and without fear,
    And for our foes let this suffice—
We've brought a rightful sonship here,
    And we have more than paid the price.

And yet, my brothers, well I know
    The tethered feet, the pinioned wings,
The spirit bowed beneath the blow,
    The heart grown faint from wounds and stings;

The staggering force of brutish might,
    That strikes and leaves us stunned and dazed;
The long, vain waiting through the night
    To hear some voice for justice raised.

Full well I know the hour when hope
    Sinks dead, and round us everywhere

Hangs stifling darkness, and we grope
  With hands uplifted in despair.

Courage! Look out, beyond, and see
  The far horizon's beckoning span!
Faith in your God-known destiny!
  We are a part of some great plan.

Because the tongues of Garrison
  And Phillips now are cold in death,
Think you their work can be undone?
  Or quenched the fires lit by their breath?

Think you that John Brown's spirit stops?
  That Lovejoy was but idly slain?
Or do you think those precious drops
  From Lincoln's heart were shed in vain?

That for which millions prayed and sighed,
  That for which tens of thousands fought,
For which so many freely died,
  God cannot let it come to naught.

The Creation

And God stepped out on space,
And he looked around and said:
I'm lonely—
I'll make me a world.

And far as the eye of God could see
Darkness covered everything,
Blacker than a hundred midnights
Down in a cypress swamp.

Then God smiled,
And the light broke,
And the darkness rolled up on one side,
And the light stood shining on the other,
And God said: That's good!

Then God reached out and took the light in his hands
And God rolled the light around in his hands
Until he made the sun;
And he set that sun a-blazing in the heavens.
And the light that was left from making the sun
God gathered it up in a shining ball

And flung it against the darkness,
Spangling the night with the moon and stars.
Then down between
The darkness and the light
He hurled the world;
And God said: That's good!

Then God himself stepped down—
And the sun was on his right hand,
And the moon was on his left;
The stars were clustered about his head,
And the earth was under his feet.
And God walked, and where he trod
His footsteps hollowed the valleys out
And bulged the mountains up.

Then he stopped and looked and saw
That the earth was hot and barren.
So God stepped over to the edge of the world
And he spat out the seven seas—
He batted his eyes, and the lightnings flashed—
He clapped his hands, and the thunders rolled—
And the waters above the earth came down,
The cooling waters came down.

Then the green grass sprouted,
And the little red flowers blossomed,
The pine tree pointed his finger to the sky,
And the oak spread out his arms,
The lakes cuddled down in the hollows of the ground,
And the rivers ran down to the sea;
And God smiled again,
And the rainbow appeared,
And curled itself around his shoulder.

Then God raised his arm and he waved his hand
Over the sea and over the land,

And he said: Bring forth! Bring forth!
And quicker than God could drop his hand,
Fishes and fowls
And beasts and birds
Swam the rivers and the seas,
Roamed the forests and the woods,
And split the air with their wings.
And God said: That's good!

Then God walked around,
And God looked around
On all that he had made.
He looked at his sun,
And he looked at his moon,
And he looked at his little stars;
He looked on his world
With all its living things,
And God said: I'm lonely still.

Then God sat down—
On the side of a hill where he could think;
By a deep, wide river he sat down;
With his head in his hands,
God thought and thought,
Till he thought: I'll make me a man!

Up from the bed of the river
God scooped the clay;
And by the bank of the river
He kneeled him down;
And there the great God Almighty
Who lit the sun and fixed it in the sky,
Who flung the stars to the most far corner of the night,
Who rounded the earth in the middle of his hand;
This Great God,
Like a mammy bending over her baby,
Kneeled down in the dust

Toiling over a lump of clay
Till he shaped it in his own image;

Then into it he blew the breath of life,
And man became a living soul.
Amen. Amen.

Noah Built the Ark

In the cool of the day—
God was walking—
Around in the Garden of Eden.
And except for the beasts, eating in the fields,
And except for the birds, flying through the trees,
The garden looked like it was deserted.
And God called out and said: Adam,
Adam, where art thou?
And Adam, with Eve behind his back,
Came out from where he was hiding.

And God said: Adam,
What hast thou done?
Thou hast eaten of the tree!
And Adam,
With his head hung down,
Blamed it on the woman.
For after God made the first man Adam,
He breathed a sleep upon him;
Then he took out of Adam one of his ribs,
And out of that rib made woman.
And God put the man and woman together
In the beautiful Garden of Eden,

With nothing to do the whole day long
But play all around in the garden.
And God called Adam before him,
And he said to him:
Listen now, Adam,
Of all the fruit in the garden you can eat,
Except of the tree of knowledge;
For the day thou eatest of that tree,
Thou shalt surely die.

Then pretty soon along came Satan.
Old Satan came like a snake in the grass
To try out his tricks on the woman.
I imagine I can see Old Satan now
A-sidling up to the woman.
I imagine the first word Satan said was:
Eve, you're surely good looking.
I imagine he brought her a present, too,—
And, if there was such a thing in those ancient days,
He brought her a looking-glass.

And Eve and Satan got friendly—
Then Eve got to walking on shaky ground;
Don't ever get friendly with Satan.—
And they started to talk about the garden,
And Satan said: Tell me, how do you like
The fruit on the nice, tall, blooming tree
Standing in the middle of the garden?
And Eve said:
That's the forbidden fruit,
Which if we eat we die.

And Satan laughed a devilish little laugh,
And he said to the woman: God's fooling you, Eve;
That's the sweetest fruit in the garden.
I know you can eat that forbidden fruit,
And I know that you will not die.

And Eve looked at the forbidden fruit,
And it was red and ripe and juicy.
And Eve took a taste, and she offered it to Adam,
And Adam wasn't able to refuse;
So he took a bite, and they both sat down
And ate the forbidden fruit.—
Back there, six thousand years ago,
Man first fell by woman—
Lord, and he's doing the same today.

And that's how sin got into this world.
And man, as he multiplied on the earth,
Increased in wickedness and sin.
He went on down from sin to sin,
From wickedness to wickedness,
Murder and lust and violence,
All kinds of fornications,
Till the earth was corrupt and rotten with flesh,
An abomination in God's sight.

And God was angry at the sins of men.
And God got sorry that he ever made man.
And he said: I will destroy him.
I'll bring down judgment on him with a flood.
I'll destroy ev'rything on the face of the earth,
Man, beasts and birds, and creeping things.
And he did—
Ev'rything but the fishes.

But Noah was a just and righteous man.
Noah walked and talked with God.
And, one day, God said to Noah,
He said: Noah, build thee an ark.
Build it out of gopher wood.
Build it good and strong.
Pitch it within and pitch it without.
And build it according to the measurements

That I will give to thee.
Build it for you and all your house,
And to save the seeds of life on earth;
For I'm going to send down a mighty flood
To destroy this wicked world.

And Noah commenced to work on the ark.
And he worked for about one hundred years.
And ev'ry day the crowd came round
To make fun of Old Man Noah.
And they laughed and they said: Tell us, old man,
Where do you expect to sail that boat
Up here amongst the hills?
But Noah kept on a-working.
And ev'ry once in a while Old Noah would stop,
He'd lay down his hammer and lay down his saw,
And take his staff in hand;
And with his long, white beard a-flying in the wind,
And the gospel light a-gleaming from his eye,
Old Noah would preach God's word:

Sinners, oh, sinners,
Repent, for the judgment is at hand.
Sinners, oh, sinners,
Repent, for the time is drawing nigh.
God's wrath is gathering in the sky.
God's a-going to rain down rain on rain.
God's a-going to loosen up the bottom of the deep,
And drown this wicked world.
Sinners, repent while yet there's time
For God to change his mind.

Some smart young fellow said: This old man's
Got water on the brain.
And the crowd all laughed—Lord, but didn't they laugh;
And they paid no mind to Noah,
But kept on sinning just the same.

One bright and sunny morning,
Not a cloud nowhere to be seen,
God said to Noah: Get in the ark!
And Noah and his folks all got in the ark,
And all the animals, two by two,
A he and a she marched in.
Then God said: Noah, Bar the door!
And Noah barred the door.

And a little black spot begun to spread,
Like a bottle of ink spilling over the sky;
And the thunder rolled like a rumbling drum;
And the lightning jumped from pole to pole;
And it rained down rain, rain, rain,
Great God, but didn't it rain!
For forty days and forty nights
Waters poured down and waters gushed up;
And the dry land turned to sea.
And the old ark-a she begun to ride;
The old ark-a she begun to rock;
Sinners came a-running down to the ark;
Sinners came a-swimming all round the ark;
Sinners pleaded and sinners prayed—
Sinners wept and sinners wailed—
But Noah'd done barred the door.

And the trees and the hills and the mountain tops
Slipped underneath the waters.
And the old ark sailed that lonely sea—
For twelve long months she sailed that sea,
A sea without a shore.

Then the waters begun to settle down,
And the ark touched bottom on the tallest peak
Of old Mount Ararat.
The dove brought Noah the olive leaf,
And Noah when he saw that the grass was green,
Opened up the ark, and they all climbed down,

The folks, and the animals, two by two,
Down from the mount to the valley.
And Noah wept and fell on his face
And hugged and kissed the dry ground.

And then—

God hung out his rainbow cross the sky,
And he said to Noah: That's my sign!
No more will I judge the world by flood—
Next time I'll rain down fire.

The Judgment Day

In that great day,
People, in that great day,
God's a-going to rain down fire.
God's a-going to sit in the middle of the air
To judge the quick and the dead.

Early one of these mornings,
God's a-going to call for Gabriel,
That tall, bright angel, Gabriel;
And God's a-going to say to him: Gabriel,
Blow your silver trumpet,
And wake the living nations.

And Gabriel's going to ask him: Lord,
How loud must I blow it?
And God's a-going to tell him: Gabriel,
Blow it calm and easy.
Then putting one foot on the mountain top,
And the other in the middle of the sea,
Gabriel's going to stand and blow his horn,
To wake the living nations.

Then God's a-going to say to him: Gabriel,
Once more blow your silver trumpet,
And wake the nations underground.

And Gabriel's going to ask him: Lord
How loud must I blow it?
And God's a-going to tell him: Gabriel,
Like seven peals of thunder.
Then the tall, bright angel, Gabriel,
Will put one foot on the battlements of heaven
And the other on the steps of hell,
And blow that silver trumpet
Till he shakes old hell's foundations.

And I feel Old Earth a-shuddering—
And I see the graves a-bursting—
And I hear a sound,
A blood-chilling sound.
What sound is that I hear?
It's the clicking together of the dry bones,
Bone to bone—the dry bones.
And I see coming out of the bursting graves,
And marching up from the valley of death,
The army of the dead.

And the living and the dead in the twinkling of an eye
Are caught up in the middle of the air,
Before God's judgment bar.

Oh-o-oh, sinner,
Where will you stand,
In that great day when God's a-going to rain down fire?
Oh, you gambling man—where will you stand?
You whore-mongering man—where will you stand?
Liars and backsliders—where will you stand,
In that great day when God's a-going to rain down fire?

And God will divide the sheep from the goats,
The one on the right, the other on the left.
And to them on the right God's a-going to say:
Enter into my kingdom.
And those who've come through great tribulations,
And washed their robes in the blood of the Lamb,
They will enter in—
Clothed in spotless white,
With starry crowns upon their heads,
And silver slippers on their feet,
And harps within their hands;—

And two by two they'll walk
Up and down the golden street,
Feasting on the milk and honey
Singing new songs of Zion,
Chattering with the angels
All around the Great White Throne.

And to them on the left God's a-going to say:
Depart from me into everlasting darkness,
Down into the bottomless pit.
And the wicked like lumps of lead will start to fall,
Headlong for seven days and nights they'll fall,
Plumb into the big, black, red-hot mouth of hell,
Belching out fire and brimstone.
And their cries like howling, yelping dogs,
Will go up with the fire and smoke from hell,
But God will stop his ears.

Too late, sinner! Too late!
Good-bye, sinner! Good-bye!
In hell, sinner! In hell!
Beyond the reach of the love of God.

And I hear a voice, crying, crying:
Time shall be no more!
Time shall be no more!

Time shall be no more!
And the sun will go out like a candle in the wind,
The moon will turn to dripping blood,
The stars will fall like cinders,
And the sea will burn like tar;
And the earth shall melt away and be dissolved,
And the sky will roll up like a scroll.
With a wave of his hand God will blot out time,
And start the wheel of eternity.

Sinner, oh, sinner,
Where will you stand
In that great day when God's a going to rain down fire?

Saint Peter Relates an Incident of the Resurrection Day

Eternities—now numbering six or seven—
Hung heavy on the hands of all in heaven.
Archangels tall and fair had reached the stage
Where they began to show some signs of age.

The faces of the flaming seraphim
Were slightly drawn, their eyes were slightly dim.
The cherubs, too, for now—oh, an infinite while
Had worn but a wistful shade of their dimpling smile.

The serried singers of the celestial choir
Disclosed a woeful want of pristine fire;
When they essayed to strike the glad refrain,
Their attack was weak, their tone revealed voice strain.

Their expression seemed to say, "We must! We must!" though
'Twas more than evident they lacked the gusto;
It could not be elsewise—that fact all can agree on—
Chanting the selfsame choral æon after æon.

Thus was it that Saint Peter at the gate
Began a brand new thing in heaven: to relate
Some reminiscences from heavenly history,
Which had till then been more or less a mystery.

So now and then, by turning back the pages,
Were whiled away some moments from the ages,
Was gained a respite from the monotony
That can't help settling on eternity.

II

Now, there had been a lapse of ages hoary,
And the angels clamored for another story.
"Tell us a tale, Saint Peter," they entreated;
And gathered close around where he was seated.

Saint Peter stroked his beard,
And "Yes," he said
By the twinkle in his eye
And the nodding of his head.

A moment brief he fumbled with his keys—
It seemed to help him call up memories—
Straightway there flashed across his mind the one
About the unknown soldier
Who came from Washington.

The hosts stood listening,
Breathlessly awake;
And thus Saint Peter spake:

III

'Twas Resurrection morn,
And Gabriel blew a blast upon his horn
That echoed through the arches high and vast
Of Time and Space—a long resounding blast

To wake the dead, dead for a million years;
A blast to reach and pierce their dust-stopped ears;
To quicken them, wherever they might be,
Deep in the earth or deeper in the sea.

A shudder shook the world, and gaping graves
Gave up their dead. Out from the parted waves
Came the prisoners of old ocean. The dead belonging
To every land and clime came thronging.

From the four corners of all the earth they drew,
Their faces radiant and their bodies new.
Creation pulsed and swayed beneath the tread
Of all the living, and all the risen dead.

Swift-winged heralds of heaven flew back and forth,
Out of the east, to the south, the west, the north,
Giving out quick commands, and yet benign,
Marshaling the swarming milliards into line.

The recording angel in words of thundering might,
At which the timid, doubting souls took fright,
Bade all to await the grand roll-call; to wit,
To see if in the Book their names were writ.

The multitudinous business of the day
Progressed, but naturally, not without delay.
Meanwhile, within the great American border
There was the issuance of a special order.

IV

The word went forth, spoke by some grand panjandrum,
Perhaps, by some high potentate of Klandom,
That all the trusty patriotic mentors,
And duly qualified Hundred-Percenters

Should forthwith gather together upon the banks
Of the Potomac, there to form their ranks,
March to the tomb, by orders to be given,
And escort the unknown soldier up to heaven.

Compliantly they gathered from each region,
The G.A.R., the D.A.R., the Legion,
Veterans of wars—Mexican, Spanish, Haitian—
Trustees of the patriotism of the nation;

Key Men, Watchmen, shunning circumlocution,
The Sons of the This and That and of the Revolution;
Not to forget, there gathered every man
Of the Confederate Veterans and the Ku-Klux Klan.

The Grand Imperial Marshal gave the sign;
Column on column, the marchers fell in line;
Majestic as an army in review,
They swept up Washington's wide avenue.

Then, through the long line ran a sudden flurry,
The marchers in the rear began to hurry;
They feared unless the procession hastened on,
The unknown soldier might be risen and gone.

The fear was groundless; when they arrived, in fact,
They found the grave entirely intact.
(Resurrection plans were long, long past completing
Ere there was thought of re-enforced concreting.)

They heard a faint commotion in the tomb,
Like the stirring of a child within the womb;
At once they saw the plight, and set about
The job to dig the unknown soldier out.

They worked away, they labored with a will,
They toiled with pick, with crowbar, and with drill
To cleave a breach; nor did the soldier shirk;
Within his limits, he helped to push the work.

He, underneath the débris, heaved and hove
Up toward the opening which they cleaved and clove;
Through it, at last, his towering form loomed big and bigger—
"Great God Almighty! Look!" they cried, "he is a nigger!"

Surprise and consternation and dismay
Swept over the crowd; none knew just what to say
Or what to do. And all fell back aghast.
Silence—but only an instant did it last.

Bedlam: They clamored, they railed, some roared, some bleated;
All of them felt that somehow they'd been cheated.
The question rose: What to do with him, then?
The Klan was all for burying him again.

The scheme involved within the Klan's suggestion
Gave rise to a rather nice metaphysical question:
Could he be forced again through death's dark portal,
Since now his body and soul were both immortal?

Would he, forsooth, the curious-minded queried,
Even in concrete, re-entombed, stay buried?
In a moment more, midst the pile of broken stone,
The unknown soldier stood, and stood alone.

V

The day came to a close.
And heaven—hell too—was filled with them that rose.
I shut the pearly gate and turned the key;
For Time was now merged into Eternity.

I gave one last look over the jasper wall,
And afar descried a figure dark and tall:
The unknown soldier, dust-stained and begrimed,
Climbing his way to heaven, and singing as he climbed:
Deep river, my home is over Jordan,
Deep river, I want to cross over into camp-ground.

Climbing and singing—
Deep river, my home is over Jordan,
Deep river, I want to cross over into camp-ground.

Nearer and louder—
Deep river, my home is over Jordan,
Deep river, I want to cross over into camp-ground.

At the jasper wall—
Deep river, my home is over Jordan,
Deep river,
Lord,
I want to cross over into camp-ground.

I rushed to the gate and flung it wide,
Singing, he entered with a loose, long stride;
Singing and swinging up the golden street,
The music married to the tramping of his feet.

Tall, black soldier-angel marching alone,
Swinging up the golden street, saluting at the great white throne.
Singing, singing, singing, singing clear and strong.
Singing, singing, singing, till heaven took up the song:
Deep river, my home is over Jordan,
Deep river, I want to cross over into camp-ground.

VI

The tale was done,
The angelic hosts dispersed,
but not till after
There ran through heaven
Something that quivered
'twixt tears and laughter.

PART FOUR

CULTURAL CRITICISM

CULTURAL CRITICISM

James Weldon Johnson's impressive body of cultural criticism is essential to a full and complex understanding of the history and uses of black cultural production for the period 1900 to 1930. The three essays that appear in this section are representative of Johnson's contributions in the domain of cultural criticism.

"Native African Races and Culture," published in 1927 as part of the series of occasional papers sponsored by the Slater Fund, is an important essay for the intellectual labor it seeks to perform. Johnson's objective is to document the "African background of the Negro" in the vital area of cultural production, thus repositioning persons of African descent as contributors to world culture and, by extension, African Americans as contributors and shapers of American culture. This is an argument that precedes by more than a decade a similar argument that the anthropologist Melville Herskovits would make in his landmark work *The Myth of the Negro Past* (1941).

In the essay "The Dilemma of the Negro Author," first published in *The American Mercury* in 1928, Johnson examines the vital question of audience for African American writers. He posits that African American writers are confronted with the problem of the "double" or "divided audience, an audience made up of two elements with differing and often opposite and antagonistic points of view." Johnson maintains that there is something approaching a solution to this artistic dilemma through what he terms the "fusion" or the creation of a "common audience out of white and black America." Johnson introduces an additional layer of complexity to the debate on audience and culture occurring during this period. The most well-known exchange of views on these vital matters, one in which Johnson played an influential role, is captured in George Schuyler's "The Negro-Art Hokum" (1926) and Langston Hughes's "The Negro Artist and the Racial Mountain" (1926).

In "Race Prejudice and the Negro Artist," which appeared in *Harper's* in 1928, Johnson offers commentary on the strategy of "the art approach to the Negro problem." While heartened by the strides made by black artists within the context of the Harlem Renaissance or New Negro Movement, Johnson asserts that black expression in the arts is far from new; what is "new" is the "evaluation and public recognition" black artists were receiving during the period of the 1920s.

These three essays serve the dual function of providing us with an opening into the scope and complexity of the cultural formations in African America, while concurrently providing us with an analysis of the debates and major figures who shaped and were shaped by this dynamic sphere. As a writer who turned to the essay in order to theorize thc complexity of formations in African American culture, Johnson is a pioneering figure in a tradition of thought that includes such figures as W.E.B. Du Bois, Zora Neale Hurston, Sterling A. Brown, Richard Wright, James Baldwin, Ralph Ellison, Amiri Baraka, Alice Walker, Stanley Crouch, Toni Morrison, and Charles Johnson.

Native African Races and Culture

The African continent, with its eleven million square miles, almost four times as large as the United States of America, has a history reaching to the very dawn of human consciousness and of written or carven record. It has been not only a cradle of races and nations, but of refining arts, technology and crafts as well. Vast folk migrations have passed through the African continent from one end to the other; with the consequence that it now holds in its population of well above two hundred millions, the most diverse races, nations and languages imaginable.

For Americans, Africa and more particularly African Negroes have derived their chief significance from slavery. To speak of the Negro was to refer to a man of color, usually thought of as "black," brought on a slave ship to America, without possessions, without culture or aptitude, who had to learn laboriously the language of the country to which he had been brought, as well as the simplest tasks imposed upon him. The descendants of the slave labored under the disabilities which had been imposed upon him. They were at first denied the possession of human souls. They were thought of as being nearer to the beast than to man. All their achievements, whether they attained to the rank of artisan or eventually began to take their place in industry, science and the arts, were attributed to their new environment. They were held to be the beneficiaries of their new home. They had brought nothing with them. What they became, what they are, is attributed entirely to the beneficence of their home in the Western Hemisphere.

To adopt this point of view, as it has been generally adopted in the United States, is to ignore the African background of the Negro. That background is both an ancient and a richly varied one. To that background it is the purpose in the following pages to give brief consideration.

AFRICAN RACES

To begin with, there is no single and uniform Negro type or race. The most careful and scientific writers on the subject of African races have found it virtually impossible to give any definition of what constitutes a Negro since not only in stature, in physical conformation, but in skin color as well there is infinite variation among the African peoples. Thus, as Du Bois says, "the mulatto ... is as typically African as the black man," and Sir Harry Johnston attributes to African races an admixture of Caucasian blood varying from one-half to one-thirty-second. While his generalizations are not meant to be taken as exact or literal, it may be worth while to give here his estimates of the proportion of "white" or "Caucasian" blood in native African peoples:

RACE	PROPORTION OF CAUCASIAN BLOOD
Hima	½
Masai-Latuka	¼ to ⅛
Suk-Turkana-Elgumi	⅛
Nilotic	1/24
Bantu	1/16 to 1/32
West African	None
Pygmy	"
Bushman (Hottentot)	"

This same author divides the native Negro inhabitants of the African continent into three main groups: first, "the Negro in general," ranging from Abyssinia on the East Coast to Senegal and from Lake Chad to Cape Colony in the South; second, the Congo Pygmy; and third, the Hottentot Bushman, living in the southern triangle of the Continent. In the northern two-thirds of the African Continent are more than one hundred "separate and independent language families" each group of languages being "so separate from the other and without outside affinities that any one of them might be Asiatic or American so far as special African affinities were concerned." In the southern one-third of the African Continent, on the other hand, there is but one language-family, the Bantu; its only rival being the Bushman-Hottentot tongues which, together with the Sandawi in East Africa, are spoken by, at most, 50,000 people as against the 40,000,000 who at the time Sir Harry Johnston wrote spoke the Bantu tongues.

The descriptions of these races, even to one who has not seen individuals or pictures of individuals, will give some idea of the diversity which prevails. Thus the pygmies, whose existence was at first doubted, and who were believed to be the invention of explorers with a taste for tall stories about short people, are a tiny race, often less than five feet tall, inhabiting the Congo forests of Central Africa, living chiefly by hunting and trapping. Their color is variously described as being coffee brown, red and light yellow. In those northern portions of Africa, bordering on the southern fringe of the Sahara desert, and extending across the continent at its widest, known as the Sudan, are a bewildering variety of races, of all colors and forms. The Fellatahs, Nigritians, Berbers and Arabs, all with different degrees of Negro admixture, vary in color from light brown, and almost white, to a dark brown. The Ewe speaking peoples in the western part of this area, on the coast and in the countries adjoining the coast, have a strong Moorish cast of feature, some of them with reddish hair. Dowd quotes Canot as saying of the Fellatah girls: "I do not think the forms of these Fellatah girls, with their complexions of freshest bronze, are excelled in symmetry by the women of any other country."

In what Dowd calls the northern and the southern cattle zones of Africa, where cattle keeping is the main occupation of the natives, are the Masai, whose "aristocratic class" averages about six feet in height, are "spare in figure and recall the 'Apollo type,' " whose young women "are especially pleasing in their physiognomy." On the plateau west of Lake Victoria, one of the Great Lakes of Africa, are the Bahima, "a tall, and finely formed race, of nutty-brown color, with almost European features. They have oval faces, thin lips and straight noses." In the southern part of the Continent are a group of races, including the Hottentot, Kaffir, Zulu, Basuto, Makololo, Herrero, Matabele, etc., whose colors and statures are as varied as those of other races of Africa. Thus, to traverse in a swift birds-eye glance the races of this ancient Continent, the Continent of mystery, is to range from the Pygmies of the Congo forests to the Turkana-Suk, one of the tallest races living on the surface of the globe. The late Captain Wellby met with a district in which he estimated the average height of the men as being seven feet; and Sir Harry Johnston found very tall men, a number of them as tall as six feet six inches.

ORIGIN OF THE AFRICAN RACES

While the culture of ancient Egypt, the land of pyramids and of the sphinx, of colossal statuary and enormous temples, is well known to Americans, it is not often called to mind that the Negro played an important part in Egyptian civilization, that Egyptian civilization not only radiated downward into Africa, but that the Negro furnished rulers, officers, artisans, as well as a substantial part of the population during Egypt's long history. The ancient chronicler, one of the first and greatest historians, Herodotus, as Du Bois points out, alluded to the Egyptians as "black and curly-haired." And measurements in the tombs of Egyptian nobles of the eighteenth dynasty indicate that Negroes then formed at least one-sixth of the higher class.

In the chief art museums of Europe, in the Egyptian collections of the Metropolitan Museum of Art in New York and in the Boston Museum of Fine Arts, are beautifully carved heads and full statues of Egyptian rulers, many of them plainly bearing evidence, in Negro cast of features, of the part played by the Negro in Egypt's history. Is it not significant that the features of the great Sphinx are negroid?

Just where and how the race called Negro originated is in dispute and constitutes a question to which no completely satisfactory answer may be given. Johnston believes that the Pygmies are nearest the basic Negro race; that they were driven deeper and deeper into the recesses of the Congo forest by successive invasions from the North, the chief invaders being the group of races now known as Bantu; that there was a strong admixture from time to time of Hamitic peoples who crossed the Red Sea from Arabia or wandered down from Egypt. Dr. Alexander Francis Chamberlain, in the *Journal of Race Development,* 1911, indicates the part which Negroes played in ancient Egypt. He points out that Nefertari, Queen of Egypt, was a Negro woman of great beauty, who lived about 1700 B.C., was highly honored and venerated, and had many monuments erected in her honor. This author states that "the Egyptian race itself in general had a considerable element of Negro blood, and one of the prime reasons why no civilization of the type of that of the Nile arose in other parts of the Continent, if such a thing were at all possible, was that Egypt acted as a sort of channel by which the genius of Negroland was drafted off into the service of Mediterranean and Asiatic culture. In this sense Egyptian civilization may be said, in some respects, to be of Negro origin." He points out further that Ethiopian women, "black but comely," as wives of satraps or governors of provinces, and kings, were often the real rulers of Oriental provinces and empires. Negro poets were known in Damascus and other Oriental cities. The presence of Egyptian types among the peoples further south in the continent is repeatedly commented upon by explorers and writers. Among the Bahima in the Uganda Protectorate have been noticed again and again "a type of face startingly Egyptian in its main features, and sometimes not much darker in complexion."

What part, if any, the early Phoenician traders and their Carthaginian descendants played in contributing to the formation of the African races remains a matter of conjecture. There is, however, no doubt whatever that Moors and Arabs, all the races inhabiting northern Africa, as well as many inhabiting the Near East, have not only absorbed Negro strains but have been absorbed during the invasions, folk-wanderings and commerce on the African Continent.

POLITICAL ORGANIZATION

In the Sudan especially once existed great empires and kingdoms testifying to the organizing power of the Negro and of African races. These empires were not confined to the Sudan. There were powerful leaders and dynasties in the heart of Africa, and in South Africa as well. In the Uganda protectorate, for example, which centers in the great African Lakes at the headwaters of the Nile, Johnston estimates that the history of these kingdoms extends as far back as the 14th century of our era. This author re-tells the legend of what he calls the "Norman of Central Africa," a conqueror whom he thus compares with William the Conqueror who led the Normans to a conquest of the Anglo-Saxon population of England. His name, so legend tells, was Muganda or "the brother," and he came with a pack of dogs, a woman, a spear, and a shield to the Katonga Valley. He was a poor man but so successful in hunting that large numbers of the aboriginal Negroes flocked to him for flesh. They finally became so devoted to him as to invite him to become their chief. He accepted and soon "erected his principality into a strong and well-organized power." "The Kings of Uganda," says Johnston, "kept up their prestige, maintained their wealth, and asserted their influence over the aristocracy by the continual raids they made over the adjacent countries of Busoga, Bukedi, Unyoro, Toro and even Ruanda... The limit of their power to the west at times was only the wall of the Congo Forest. Mr. Lionel Decle, in his extended explorations of the country immediately north of Tanganyika, found in a village an ancient Uganda shield, supposed to have been there about a hundred years, and according to the traditions of the natives it was obtained from one of the warriors of a Uganda expedition who fell in battle against the people of Burindi. These powerful Negro kings maintained a certain civilization and a considerable amount of law and order in the territories which they governed."

The history of these kingdoms extends back for hundreds of years. They were not merely the sudden and evanescent creations of some chieftian, but were established empires with regular succession of rulers, a hierarchy of court officials and provincial governors, and all the ceremony incidental to such a political structure. "So far as tradition goes," says Sir Harry Johnston, "the Bahima of Ankole can trace the genealogy of their kings for about 300 years back. The Baganda can recall their kings of a period as far distant as the fifteenth century. The genealogy of the Uganda sovereigns includes thirty-six names (prior to the present king); and if the greater part of the earlier names are not myths, this genealogy, reckoning an average of fifteen years' reign to each monarch, would take us back to the middle of the fourteenth century... Assuming that they are to be reduced because they contain repetitions or imaginary or concurrent names, one is still entitled to assume that Uganda, Unyoro, and perhaps Ankole and Karagwe to the south, have been settled kingdoms under dynasties of Hamitic (Gala?) origin for five hundred years." Dowd reports that at the time of Stanley's visit the empire of the Waganda covered an area of 70,000 square miles. "Up to the recent domination by the British," says Dowd, "the Waganda were governed by an emperor who had a well-organized government. His council included a prime minister, several princesses, a chief butler, chief baker, and a commander of the army and navy. There were feudal lords ruling over provinces and owing allegiance to the king." Stanley estimated the fighting force at 25,000 men and reported that on campaigns the army was accompanied by women and children who carried spears and other weapons, besides provisions and water.

In the southern triangle of the African Continent, especially on the eastern side, are remains of walled cities, which seem to indicate powerful empires that have passed from the memory of man.

But even in recent times the South African races have demonstrated their organizing power. Dowd tells of the Kaffir tribes: "Their military life and habit of manipulating men has developed a degree of constructive imagination far beyond that of any other races of Africa. Their strategy in war and diplomacy in politics would do credit to any race; and some of their military leaders have been not inaptly compared to Caesar. In 1852, when Sir George Cathcart invaded Basutoland, his army was led into a trap by the simple stratagem on the part of the native leader, Moshesh, of exposing an immense herd of cattle in a position on the Berea mountain where their capture appeared easy. The British army was surprised, defeated and forced to retreat."

It is, of course, in the regions just south of the Sahara, in the Sudan and adjacent territories, that the most elaborate political organization has lasted even to our day. Kingdoms in the Sudan existed for centuries, with mosques, archives and towns, having flourishing fairs attended by thousands of people. These fairs were thoroughly policed, good order being scrupulously maintained, with an elaborate procedure for trying such cases as arose out of disputes or breaches in good order. A. B. Ellis states that Oyo or Yoruba was a powerful kingdom at least as early as 1724. George W. Ellis says of these kingdoms in northwestern Africa: "Some of the kings—possessing two capitals, and living in fortified castles that had glass windows and were decorated with sculptures and painting—had pageantries of the most stately magnificence. Indeed, when England, Germany, and France were just emerging from barbarism in intellectual, scientific, industrial and political development, some of these dynasties had attained a comparatively high degree of civilization; and geographers and historians mention Ghana, Timbuctu, and other interior towns as the resorts for the rich, the learned and the pious of all countries."

A description of the magnificent ceremonies incidental to a reception held by the king of Ashanti was noted in 1817 by Mr. Bowditch of the Royal African Company, and reprinted by A. B. Ellis: "Our observations en passant," wrote Mr. Bowditch, "had taught us to conceive a spectacle far exceeding our original expectations; but they had not prepared us for the extent and display of the scene which here burst upon us: an area of nearly a mile in circumference was crowded with magnificence and novelty. The king, his tributaries, and captains, were resplendent in the distance, surrounded by attendants of every description, fronted by a mass of warriors which seemed to make our approach impervious. The sun was reflected, with a glare scarcely more supportable than the heat, from the massive gold ornaments which glistened in every direction. More than a hundred bands burst at once on our arrival, with the peculiar airs of their several chiefs; the horns flourished their defiances, with the beating of innumerable drums and metal instruments, and then yielded for a while to the soft breathings of their long flutes, which were truly harmonious; and a pleasing instrument, like a bagpipe without the drone, was happily blended. At least a hundred large umbrellas, or canopies, which could shelter thirty persons, were sprung up and down by the bearers with brilliant effect, being made of scarlet, yellow and the most showy cloths and silks, and crowned on the top with crescents, pelicans, elephants, barrels, and arms and swords of gold; they were of various shapes, but mostly dome.... The king's messengers, with gold breastplates, made way for us, and we commenced our round, preceded by the canes and the English flag." Mr. Bowditch estimated the number of warriors present at this memorable scene at not less than 30,000. Ellis reports that Ashanti has been known to Europeans as a kingdom since the middle of the seventeenth century; "and their military superiority, which has secured the capital from destruction by other tribes, has enabled them to preserve the remains, and with them the memories, of former rulers."

Two forces in Africa, especially contributed to the formation and the maintenance of the powerful native kingdoms. One was the walled and fortified city with its regular social, religious and family institutions. The other was the market, which is one of the unique developments of the African Continent. Chamberlain says of the latter: "The institution of the market and the fair, e. g., among the Negro peoples of the Sudan and the development out of it of the village, the town and the city, are one of the most interesting phenomena in all the history of human culture. Among the questions involved in the evolution of the market and the fair are: the greater share of women in public and semi-public activities; the breaking down of the narrowness of mere tribal boundaries and clan-instincts, consequent upon the gathering together of so many people at repeated intervals; the movement toward abolition of war through the institutions of the marketplace and the prohibition of all hostile acts during the time of fairs and markets, etc.; the amalgamation of peoples resulting from the ultimately permanent character of these markets and fairs, and the absorption of those conducting them more or less into the general population by the consolidation of the temporary city without the walls with the old city within them; the influence upon the general honesty and morality of the community of the increasing importance of the right of asylum, the protection of the stranger within and without the gates, the necessity of honest weights and measures; the autonomy of the market, the market-tax with its corollary of protection of free-trade; the market-holiday and its relation to religious and other festivals and ceremonial occasions, etc."

It will be seen that in the case of African Negroes as indeed with all other races, political institutions beginning in such apparently simple needs as the desire to exchange commodities in markets have permeated every phase of life, leading to the development of cities, of kingdoms and empires and ceremonial life on a large scale.

The simplest village life of some of the African tribes has developed forms of common action which might well be emulated by more "civilized" and complex communities. Land is often held in common, being regarded as much a necessity of existence as water or air. And problems of land ownership are thus disposed of in a way to support all the population without either extreme wealth on the one hand or the contrast of terrible poverty on the other. Even in those tribes where slavery has been practiced it has taken a form less destructive than it took among white peoples. African slaves were for the most part regarded as members of the family and often amassed wealth surpassing that of their owners.

The law-abiding nature of the native African has often been commented upon by travellers and explorers. "The fondness of the African tribes for settling their disputes by recourse to courts is well known," says Herskovits. "Penalties for theft, murder, adultery, and other offenses are apparently fixed and understood by these courts; and, in general, the parties to a dispute abide by the decision of the court, even where the machinery of enforcement seems to be lacking." Of the treatment of slaves Dowd says: "Waitz was right in his contention that, as a rule, slaves are better treated among savages than among civilized people, for the reason first, that the savage master does not place so much value upon time and labor and hence does not rush his slaves, and second, that savage masters do not draw such tight class distinctions."

The extent of native African villages may be gathered when it is borne in mind that in a single town of the Latuka tribe, for example, there might be as many as 10,000 to 12,000 head of cattle. One tribe in the Sahara, the Tibbus, observed Denham, had 5,000 camels.

Among the Hausas, "legislation was in the hands of the governor of the state or city acting in conjunction with a council of rich men or nobles. Among the Yorubas it was in the hands of the king and local governor or councils, but sometimes the whole people assembled and made and administered the laws. In each state there was a council of chiefs and elders, and a two-thirds vote was required for the enactment of a law." The Hausas, among other tribes, had a clearly developed code of law and police maintained order at their markets. In this connection it should be borne in mind that the institution of police, paid out of public moneys, is a very late development in the history of European cities, wealthy people in England and on the Continent taking their retainers and servants with them for protection against robbers when going out after dark.

The decay of these states and governments and the stagnation of culture and civilization may be traced directly to the African slave trade. Slave trading threw the greater part of the Continent into chaos and in the four hundred years during which it existed cost Africa, it is estimated, one hundred million souls.

RELIGION

Religion takes a prominent place, perhaps the most prominent place, in the lives of most primitive peoples. It is of course often intimately involved in the practice of witchcraft. Among the African tribes as among the ancient Greeks, legends of gods were made to account for natural forces, Shango being the God of Thunder among the tribes of the West Coast and innumerable deities taking the place of the gods and nymphs and demons of Greek mythology. A. B. Ellis says that "the general bias of the Negro mind has been in favor of selecting the firmament for the chief Nature-god, instead of the Sun, Moon or Earth; and in this respect the natives resemble the Aryan Hindus, Greeks, and Romans, with whom Dyaus pitar, Zeus, and Jupiter equally represented the firmament."

All natural activities are of course attributed to personal forces. Deaths are supposed to have been caused by malevolence and sorcery; and Ellis points out that among the Yoruba on the Slave Coast of West Africa old women, like those in England when witchcraft was an article of faith, often acknowledged themselves witches when accused and charged themselves with deaths which had occurred in the community.

The rhythmic sense for which many of the African peoples are noted finds its expression in their religious dances. We quote again from Ellis's important work, The Yoruba-Speaking Peoples of the Slave Coast of West Africa: "Dancing was, with the Greeks, intimately connected with worship; as Lucian says, 'You cannot find a single ancient mystery in which there is not dancing;' and on the Gold and Slave Coasts every god of note has his own dance, which is sacred to him, and known only to the initiated. The religion of ancient Greece has been obscured by a great deal of later poetic imagery; but, when we look into it closely, it is found to be similar to that of the Yorubas, and was no doubt produced when the Greeks were in a like intellectual condition."

Among the tribes inhabiting the Sudan and North Africa, many are adherents of Islam. The Vai, for example, are Moslems for they have been taught that the Negro has played an honorable part in the military history and achievements of that religion. "By the best informed Muhammadans," says George W. Ellis, "the Africans are made to feel a pride in the fact that their race is recognized in the Koran, which contains a chapter inscribed to a Negro, and the Muhammad was in part descended from an African and had a Negro as his confidant in Arabia. It is pointed out that Negroes figured prominently in the progress of Islam, and on one occasion slew a rival of Muhammad. It is said that the prophet greatly admired a Negro poet of ante-Islamic times and regretted that he had never seen him. The Vai Negroes thus feel a close relationship to the Koranic faith. As we have seen, they name their children after Muhammad and the prophets as if they were their kinsmen. They delight to think of and commune with the great masters of their faith as equals. Their boys may be seen writing in the sand these names and the words of the Koran."

The spread of the Islamic faith throughout Africa has, of course, been hastened by the Arab traders, who for centuries have not only been plying the coasts of the African Continent but have been penetrating its deserts and jungles in search of gold, ivory, rare stones and woods and other products, as well as slaves.

The function of the medicine man and the priest in African tribal life is so varied and far-reaching that only a few aspects of it can be even touched upon here. But it should be borne in mind, first of all, that his practices are in no wise limited merely to superstitious gestures, dances, amulets, etc. In fact, some of the outstanding medical discoveries of Europe had been made in a prior form by the medicine men of Africa: for example, that flies and mosquitoes are the purveyors of disease. This discovery had been made among the Yoruba, whose medical men attributed smallpox to a most powerful and evil spirit, Shankpanna, whose agents and messengers are flies and mosquitoes. In other parts of Africa the medicine men have learned how to set bones, puncture the lung in cases of pleurisy, and administer a multitude of remedies as well as poisons concocted from shrubs, flowers and trees known to them only.

Dowd points out that the medicine men "do not always resort to magic or rely upon spirits and deities, but have a considerable knowledge of materia medica, and treat diseases on purely scientific principles; that is to say, they examine the patient, locate the seat of the disease and prescribe certain diet and medicines."

On the West Coast, the religion of the natives has been brought to the point of a well-established and thoroughly organized priesthood, which is in reality a guild or fraternity, requiring special training and apprenticeship as well as special initiation. Among the Yoruba there are three orders of priests, with well recognized grades. Knowledge of the mysteries of the gods is transmitted from generation to generation and the numbers of priests were augmented from time to time either by people devoting themselves or being devoted by relatives or masters to this life-profession. Among the Tshi-speaking people of the West Coast a novitiate of as long as three years was required, the novices living in retirement and receiving instruction from priests in the secrets of the craft. Dancing formed a special part of their education and they had to undergo many months of instruction and practice before being allowed to appear in public. The dance was performed to the sound of drums, and it was during the dance that the priest became inspired, or "possessed," by a god and let fall oracular utterances. These utterances, says A. B. Ellis, differ in no essential particular from the replies given by the oracle of Delphi in Greece to suppliants for divine guidance.

The beliefs of African tribes are of course exceedingly various. "The striking resemblance which the Yoruba religious system bears to that of the ancient Greeks can scarcely have escaped notice," says Ellis. "The spirits of the trees answer to the Hama-dryads, and we have river-gods and sea-spirits and metamorphosis to a brook, spring, or lagoon is common, and we have one example of a girl being transformed, like Daphne, into a shrub."

Among the Tshi-speaking peoples the word *kra* is used to designate the spirit of a living man, or the spirit which dwells in him and to which sacrifice is made in return for the protection it affords. A similar spirit is supposed to inhere in inanimate objects. The word *kra* does not correspond to the European idea of soul, but is rather a guardian spirit, who leaves a man after his death. Dreams are supposed to represent the adventures of the *kra* or guardian spirit during sleep.

The part played by the fetish in West African life has been so thoroughly investigated by A. B. Ellis that it is best perhaps to quote his own words on this subject. He states that "the words 'fetish' and 'Fetishism' are absolutely unknown to all Negroes except such as have come into contact with Europeans, and have learned them from them.... The word 'fetish' is of Portuguese origin, and it is a corruption of fetico, an amulet or charm. At the time of the Portuguese discoveries in West Africa, that is to say, from about 1441 to 1500, Catholic Europe abounded in relics of saints, charmed rosaries, images, and crosses, which were, in the majority of cases, regarded by their wearers as amulets or charms." The Portuguese, Mr. Ellis continued, applied the word only to the worship of inanimate objects. "The practice of propitiating by offering beings who are believed to dwell in the woods or mountains, the rivers or the sea, is not fetishism. Neither can the worship of idols be so termed, for the idol is merely the representation of an absent god, or the symbol of an idea, and has of itself no supernatural or superhuman power or quality."

Mr. Ellis sums up as follows his conclusions on this subject: "So far from fetishism being peculiarly characteristic of the religion of the Negro of the Gold Coast, I am of opinion that the Negro is remarkably free from it.... Along with the belief that fetishism is the chief characteristic of the religion of the Negroes of the Gold Coast has grown up a belief that they fancy they can coerce their gods, and force them to do what they wish. I have read also, in at least one book, that the natives beat their gods if their prayers are unanswered. To this I can only say that, after an experience of the Gold Coast extending over thirteen years, I have never heard of, much less witnessed, anything of the kind, although I have made inquiries in every direction. The idea of coercion as applied to a deity appears to be quite foreign to the mind of the Negro, who rather seeks to gain his ends by adulation and offerings.... Moreover, as the native of the Gold Coast firmly believes in the intangible individuality of his gods, it is difficult to see how he could suppose himself able to ill-treat them."

INDUSTRY, ART, MANNERS

It is nothing short of amazing how thoroughly the African races have adapted themselves to the climatic variations of the Continent, using the opportunities it afforded for cattle raising, hunting, agriculture and commerce. Moreover, at a very early era, so early as to incline leading anthropologists to attribute to Africans its invention, they were smelting iron. They are among the first races to raise cattle and use their milk. Professor Franz Boas in an address at Atlanta University gave the following summary of the cultural contribution of African native races:

"While much of the history of early invention is shrouded in darkness, it seems likely that at a time when the European was still satisfied with rude stone tools, the African had invented or adopted the art of smelting iron.... It seems not unlikely that the people that made the marvelous discovery of reducing iron ores by smelting were the African Negroes. Neither ancient Europe, nor ancient western Asia, nor ancient China knew iron and everything points to its introduction from Africa. At the time of the great African discoveries towards the end of the past century, the trade of the blacksmith was found all over Africa, from north to south and from east to west. With his simple bellows and a charcoal fire he reduced the ore that is found in many parts of the continent and forged implements of great usefulness and beauty. Due to native invention is also the extended early African agriculture, each village being surrounded by its garden patches and field in which millet is grown. Domesticated animals were also kept; in the agricultural regions chickens and pigs, while in the arid parts of the country where agriculture is not possible, large herds of cattle were raised. It is also important to note that the cattle were milked, an art which in early times was confined to Africa, Europe and Northern Asia, while even now it has not been acquired by the Chinese. The occurrence of all these arts of life points to an early and energetic development of African culture."

Professor Boas points to the products of native workmen, the blacksmith, the weaver, wood-carver and the potter as furnishing "cultural achievements of no mean order."

But it is in the most rudimentary adjustments to climate and geographic peculiarities that the genius of the native races is shown. Dowd tells how the Bushmen, living in the waterless Kalahari desert and having often to go without water for several days, made even this environment yield them liquid. When they came to the dried bed of a river or pond, in pursuit of game, they would take a long reed and make a primitive filter by tying long grass around one end of this tube. They would then push the filter end as deep as possible into the muddy soil, allowing the water to slowly penetrate the filter. The water would then be drawn up by suction and discharged into an egg shell.

Again, in the case of the Hottentots, they had developed a complete system of counting and numbers, on a decimal basis, arising from the necessity of keeping track of their large herds of cattle. Native industries and crafts, still widely dispersed in Africa, were immeasurably more so before the advent of cheaply made and cheaply sold articles of European manufacture. For example, the Ashanti people knew how to make "cotton fabrics, turn and glaze earthenware, forge iron, fabricate instruments and arms, embroider rugs and carpets, and set gold and precious stones." Abyssinia in 1914 was estimated to have twenty million head of sheep and goats in addition to great herds of cattle. A Somali family would have an average of from 200 to 300 goats and sheep, 10 to 40 camels and 10 to 20 cows. Among the Galla tribes, cultivation of the soil was undertaken with a hoe and a wooden plow drawn by oxen. Throughout the grain-raising parts of Africa, travelers and explorers have reported seeing granaries and storehouses in connection with the native villages. In the zone inhabited by the redoubtable warriors of the Niam-Niam, the handcrafts include copper and iron work, the making of hoes, weapons, knives, pottery, wood carvings, basket work, bark cloth, copper rings, etc. They, like many other Negro tribes furnish clever smithywork. Of these same Niam-Niam, the explorer Schweinfurth wrote that: "Nowhere in any part of Africa, have I ever come across a people that in every attitude and every motion exhibited so thorough a mastery of all the circumstances of war and of the chase as these Niam-Niam."

The fashioning of musical instruments is one of the industries to be found throughout the length and breadth of Africa. "Uganda is a land of music and musicians," says Dowd. "It possesses a great variety of native musical instruments such as the drum, horn, rattles, bells, flute, harp, etc., with many additions since the introduction of European civilization. 'Every little goatherd has a flute,' says Tucker, 'and almost every other man who walks along the road is playing on a reed flageolet.'.... The natives are very fond of singing and a professional class of singers is employed by the king to enliven his court."

Sir Harry Johnston speaks of the Baganda as being especially versed in the making and playing of flutes, which they manufacture from the thick canes of sorghum, elephant grass, sugar cane, bamboos and other wood. They have too the *kinanda,* an instrument consisting of slips of iron and resonant wood fastened to a sounding board and twanged by the fingers. This same tribe had developed a decimal system of calculation before the advent of Europeans or Arabs, and had words for every multiple of ten up to twenty millions. Sir Harry Johnston says of the Baganda that they are a people "so naturally polite and artistic that they may in time justify the title which the author of this book has several times applied to them—'The Japanese of Central Africa.' " Their country provides them with different colored clay and this they have utilized in the manufacture of fine pottery further beautified with a plumbago glaze. Cups, vases and milk pots made by the people are to be seen in the British Museum. They have also developed a variety of basket work, like the Bahima, who weave some of the baskets so fine that they can contain milk without leakage.

The politeness and ceremonial considerateness of the Baganda has received exceptional tribute from Johnston: "Their chiefs are certainly native gentlemen who possess a degree of tact which many Europeans might imitate. I do not think I have ever been bored by a Muganda. If they come on a visit, they rise to go at the right moment. When you are travelling through their country, and arrive at a camp near the residence of a big chief, he would never dream of paying you a visit until he had first ascertained that you had rested from your fatigue, and that his presence would be agreeable." The Bahima, too, use flutes, also lyres and drums. In the modern kingdom of Ankole were found three special drums hundreds of years old and possessing ceremonial significance.

The musical development of the Niam-Niam, according to Schweinfurth, led even to a primitive kind of opera or drama with one man as the whole caste. "There is a singular class of professional musicians who make their appearance decked out in the most fantastic way with feathers, and covered with a promiscuous array of bits of wood and roots, and all the pretentious emblems of magic art, the feet of earth-pigs, the shells of tortoises, the beaks of eagles, the claws of birds, and teeth in every variety.... Whenever one of this fraternity presents himself, he at once begins to recite all the details of his travels and experiences in an emphatic recitative, and never forgets to conclude by an appeal to the liberality of his audience." Another explorer reports the recitation by troubadours, to the accompaniment of a musical instrument, of the deeds of their ancestors. And Dowd speaks of the sham fighting of the Niam-Niam during the war dance as an embryonic drama.

Chamberlain refers to the variety of musical instruments scattered throughout Negro Africa: "Negro Africa possesses many varieties of drums, and of stringed instruments akin to the harp and the violin, etc. Indeed all stages necessary for the development of the harp from the simplest form to the instrument as we find it among the ancient Egyptians previous to its dispersal over Asia and Europe are to be met with on African soil, and the attribution of its invention to some Negro people is quite reasonable, on the evidence in hand. And the same thing, with somewhat less certainty, perhaps, may be said of the violin. In the characteristically African marimba, or xylophone, we have the beginnings of the piano and closely related musical instruments, in which case, one of its names, 'the Negro piano,' assumes a new significance. The 'pot drum' so-called, and perhaps another variety or two of that instrument, originated also in Negro Africa. The *goura* of certain South African peoples is a curious musical instrument which still awaits adoption or modification by civilized man."

One phase of African handiwork which has of late years been acclaimed throughout the civilized world is reflected in the wood carvings, of ceremonial masks and figures, also the famous bronze castings found in Benin. The first exhibition of African carvings as works of art was held in 1914 in New York, at the famous laboratory known as "291." Here during a series of related exhibitions, showing the foundations of modern art expression and the relationship between the various forms of expression, African wood carvings were exhibited as part of a series featuring the work of the celebrated modern artists, Picasso, Braque and Picabia. That these primitive artists and many others had been profoundly influenced by the work of the primitive carvers was clearly shown. In connection with this first exhibition at 291 Fifth Avenue, of African sculpture, Marius De Zayas, himself a caricaturist of distinction, wrote a notice explicitly showing the indebtedness of modern artists to this source of inspiration. Mr. De Zayas found in this Negro art of wood carving the point of departure for what is now known as "abstract of representation." "Negro art," wrote Mr. De Zayas, "has reawakened in us a sensibility obliterated by an education, which makes us always connect what we see with what we know—our visualization with our knowledge, and makes us, in regard to form, use our intellect more than our senses." Besides the artists named, perhaps the outstanding sculptor of the present generation, the Rumanian, Constantin Brancusi, has been profoundly and avowedly influenced by the plastic work of the African Negro carvers.

It is not merely in the plastic arts that the Negro Africans have distinguished themselves. Despite the belief formerly widespread that they lacked a literature, their languages are rich and expressive and almost all tribes have many proverbs and tales embodying folk wisdom and tribal and individual experience of life. A. B. Ellis, among others, has collected numbers of these proverbs and cites, for example, the following as showing the shrewd wit of the Yoruba people:

> Boasting is not courage.
> He who forgives ends the quarrel.
> Do not attempt that you cannot bring to a good end.
> He who marries a beauty marries trouble.
> A poor man has no relations.
> He who annoys another only teaches him to strengthen himself.
> When the jackal dies the fowls do not mourn, for the jackal never brings up a chicken.
> Birth does not differ from birth; as the free man was born so was the slave.
> A fugitive does not stop to pick the thorns from his foot, neither does he make choice of his sauce.

These proverbs are part of a native literature not the less real and widespread because unwritten. It includes innumerable fables, among them the stories of the hare and the tortoise, and other animal tales which very likely were brought by slaves to America to form the basis for the Uncle Remus and other collections.

"The Yoruba folk-lore tales are very numerous," says Ellis. "A reciter of tales ... is a personage highly esteemed, and in great demand for social gatherings. Some men, indeed, make a profession of story-telling, and wander from place to place reciting tales.... As among the Ewe tribes, the professional story-teller very often uses a drum, with the rhythm of which the pauses in the narrative are filled up.... The professional story-teller must not be confounded with the ... narrator of the national traditions, several of whom are attached to each king or paramount chief, and who may be regarded as the depositories of the ancient chronicles."

There remains by way of conclusion to say a word as to the morality of African tribal life. That customs vary widely is a fact familiar even to travellers among civilized nations. The variation among the races of Africa is of course wide and includes such extremes as cannibalism and infanticide, as well as excessive cruelty in warfare. However, testimony is abundant to the prevalence of well-established codes as well, which are scrupulously lived up to and enforced. The segregation of young girls among the Vai in the institution known as the Gree-gree bush, and the careful avoidance by all males of any violation of its sanctity is only one instance in point. "The Negro tribe that has no moral conceptions is yet to be discovered and described," wrote George W. Ellis. "Of the dozen or more in Liberia none are so low but what they have 'Gree-gree bushes' or institutions for the special instruction and protection of their girls; laws regulating marriage and defining crime, and numerous customs the purpose of which is to secure respect for the aged, obedience to parents, reverence for the fetish gods, and to save the captured in war from the pangs of death."

The conclusion to be drawn even from a superficial study of conditions in the great continent of Africa is that men there as in other parts of the globe are human, exhibiting every variety of human disposition and aptitude. And the more the native races are studied the more complex, fascinating and profound are seen to be their cultural inheritance and gifts to the rest of the world.

It is long since Africa was known as the land of mystery. It is now being opened up by railroads, highways, and will doubtless more and more afford nourishment, raw materials, and produce of every variety to the rest of the world. In the circumstances it behooves intelligent people to inform themselves about the achievements of the peoples native to this vast and rich continent, peoples whose achievement, incidentally, cast an illuminating light upon the rapid progress and development under strange conditions, in an alien environment, of the Negro in America.

The Dilemma of the Negro Author

The Negro author—the creative author—has arrived. He is here. He appears in the lists of the best publishers. He even breaks into the lists of the best-sellers. To the general American public he is a novelty, a strange phenomenon, a miracle straight out of the skies. Well, he *is* a novelty, but he is by no means a new thing.

The line of American Negro authors runs back for a hundred and fifty years, back to Phillis Wheatley, the poet. Since Phillis Wheatley there have been several hundred Negro authors who have written books of many kinds. But in all these generations down to within the past six years only seven or eight of the hundreds have ever been heard of by the general American public or even by the specialists in American literature. As many Negro writers have gained recognition by both in the past six years as in all the generations gone before. What has happened is that efforts which have been going on for more than a century are being noticed and appreciated at last, and that this appreciation has served as a stimulus to greater effort and output. America is aware today that there are such things as Negro authors. Several converging forces have been at work to produce this state of mind. Had these forces been at work three decades ago, it is possible that we then should have had a condition similar to the one which now exists.

Now that the Negro author has come into the range of vision of the American public eye, it seems to me only fair to point out some of the difficulties he finds in his way. But I wish to state emphatically that I have no intention of making an apology or asking any special allowances for him; such a plea would at once disqualify him and void the very recognition he has gained. But the Negro writer does face peculiar difficulties that ought to be taken into account when passing judgment upon him.

It is unnecessary to say that he faces every one of the difficulties common to all that crowd of demon-driven individuals who feel that they must write. But the Aframerican author faces a special problem which the plain American author knows nothing about—the problem of the double audience. It is more than a double audience; it is a divided audience, an audience made up of two elements with differing and often opposite and antagonistic points of view. His audience is always both white America and black America. The moment a Negro writer takes up his pen or sits down to his typewriter he is immediately called upon to solve, consciously or unconsciously, this problem of the double audience. To whom shall he address himself, to his own black group or to white America? Many a Negro writer has fallen down, as it were, between these two stools.

It may be asked why he doesn't just go ahead and write and not bother himself about audiences. That is easier said than done. It is doubtful if anything with meaning can be written unless the writer has some definite audience in mind. His audience may be as far away as the angelic host or the rulers of darkness, but an audience he must have in mind. As soon as he selects his audience he immediately falls, whether he wills it or not, under the laws which govern the influence of the audience upon the artist, laws that operate in every branch of art.

Now, it is axiomatic that the artist achieves his best when working at his best with the materials he knows best. And it goes without saying that the material which the Negro as a creative or general writer knows best comes out of the life and experience of the colored people in America. The overwhelming bulk of the best work done by Aframerican writers has some bearing on the Negro and his relations to civilization and society in the United States. Leaving authors, white or black, writing for coteries on special and technical subjects out of the discussion, it is safe to say that the white American author, when he sits down to write, has in mind a white audience—and naturally. The influence of the Negro as a group on his work is infinitesimal if not zero. Even when he talks about the Negro he talks to white people. But with the Aframerican author the case is different. When he attempts to handle his best known material he is thrown upon two, indeed, if it is permissible to say so, upon three horns of a dilemma. He must intentionally or unintentionally choose a black audience or a white audience or a combination of the two; and each of them presents peculiar difficulties.

If the Negro author selects white America as his audience he is bound to run up against many long-standing artistic conceptions about the Negro; against numerous conventions and traditions which through age have become binding; in a word, against a whole row of hard-set stereotypes which are not easily broken up. White America has some firm opinions as to what the Negro is, and consequently some pretty well fixed ideas as to what should be written about him, and how.

What is the Negro in the artistic conception of white America? In the brighter light, he is a simple, indolent, docile, improvident peasant; a singing, dancing, laughing, weeping child; picturesque beside his log cabin and in the snowy fields of cotton; naïvely charming with his banjo and his songs in the moonlight along the lazy Southern rivers; a faithful, ever-smiling and genuflecting old servitor to the white folks of quality; a pathetic and pitiable figure. In a darker light, he is an impulsive, irrational, passionate savage, reluctantly wearing a thin coat of culture, sullenly hating the white man, but holding an innate and unescapable belief in the white man's superiority; an everlastingly alien and irredeemable element in the nation; a menace to Southern civilization; a threat to Nordic race purity; a figure casting a sinister shadow across the future of the country.

Ninety-nine one-hundredths of all that has been written about the Negro in the United States in three centuries and read with any degree of interest or pleasure by white America has been written in conformity to one or more of these ideas. I am not saying that they do not provide good material for literature; in fact, they make material for poetry and romance and comedy and tragedy of a high order. But I do say they have become stencils, and that the Negro author finds these stencils inadequate for the portrayal and interpretation of Negro life today. Moreover, when he does attempt to make use of them he finds himself impaled upon the second horn of his dilemma.

II

It is known that art—literature in particular, unless it be sheer fantasy—must be based on more or less well established conventions, upon ideas that have some room in the general consciousness, that are at least somewhat familiar to the public mind. It is this that gives it verisimilitude and finality. Even revolutionary literature, if it is to have any convincing power, must start from a basis of conventions, regarding of how unconventional its objective may be. These conventions are changed by slow and gradual processes—except they be changed in a flash. The conventions held by white America regarding the Negro will be changed. Actually they are being changed, but they have not yet sufficiently changed to lessen to any great extent the dilemma of the Negro author.

It would be straining the credulity of white America beyond the breaking point for a Negro writer to put out a novel dealing with the wealthy class of colored people. The idea of Negroes of wealth living in a luxurious manner is still too unfamiliar. Such a story would have to be written in a burlesque vein to make it at all plausible and acceptable. Before Florence Mills and Josephine Baker implanted a new general idea in the public mind it would have been worse than a waste of time for a Negro author to write for white America the story of a Negro girl who rose in spite of all obstacles, racial and others, to a place of world success and acclaim on the musical revue stage. It would be proof of little less than supreme genius in a Negro poet for him to take one of the tragic characters in American Negro history—say Crispus Attucks or Nat Turner or Denmark Vesey—, put heroic language in his mouth and have white America accept the work as authentic. American Negroes as heroes form no part of white America's concept of the race. Indeed, I question if three out of ten of the white Americans who will read these lines know anything of either Attucks, Turner or Vesey; although each of the three played a rôle in the history of the nation. The Aframerican poet might take an African chief or warrior, set him forth in heroic couplets or blank verse and present him to white America with infinitely greater chance of having his work accepted.

But these limiting conventions held by white America do not constitute the whole difficulty of the Negro author in dealing with a white audience. In addition to these conventions regarding the Negro as a race, white America has certain definite opinions regarding the Negro as an artist, regarding the scope of his efforts. White America has a strong feeling that Negro artists should refrain from making use of white subject matter. I mean by that, subject matter which it feels belongs to the white world. In plain words, white America does not welcome seeing the Negro competing with the white man on what it considers the white man's own ground.

In many white people this feeling is dormant, but brought to the test it flares up, if only faintly. During his first season in this country after his European success a most common criticism of Roland Hayes was provoked by the fact that his programme consisted of groups of English, French, German, and Italian songs, closing always with a group of Negro Spirituals. A remark frequently made was, "Why doesn't he confine himself to the Spirituals?" This in face of the fact that no tenor on the American concert stage could surpass Hayes in singing French and German songs. The truth is that white America was not quite prepared to relish the sight of a black man in a dress suit singing French and German love songs, and singing them exquisitely. The first reaction was that there was something incongruous about it. It gave a jar to the old conventions and something of a shock to the Nordic superiority complex. The years have not been many since Negro players have dared to interpolate a love duet in a musical show to be witnessed by white people. The representation of romantic love-making by Negroes struck the white audience as somewhat ridiculous; Negroes were supposed to mate in a more primeval manner.

White America has for a long time been annexing and appropriating Negro territory, and is prone to think of every part of the domain it now controls as originally—and aboriginally—its own. One sometimes hears the critics in reviewing a Negro musical show lament the fact that it is so much like white musical shows. But a great deal of this similarity it would be hard to avoid because of the plain fact that two out of the four chief ingredients in the present day white musical show, the music and the dancing, are directly derived from the Negro. These ideas and opinions regarding the scope of artistic effort affect the Negro author, the poet in particular. So whenever an Aframerican writer addresses himself to white America and attempts to break away from or break through these conventions and limitations he makes more than an ordinary demand upon his literary skill and power.

At this point it would appear that a most natural thing for the Negro author to do would be to say, "Damn the white audience!" and devote himself to addressing his own race exclusively. But when he turns from the conventions of white America he runs afoul of the taboos of black America. He has no more absolute freedom to speak as he pleases addressing black America than he has in addressing white America. There are certain phases of life that he dare not touch, certain subjects that he dare not critically discuss, certain manners of treatment that he dare not use—except at the risk of rousing bitter resentment. It is quite possible for a Negro author to do a piece of work, good from every literary point of view, and at the same time bring down on his head the wrath of the entire colored pulpit and press, and gain among the literate element of his own people the reputation of being the prostitutor of his talent and a betrayer of his race—not by any means a pleasant position to get into.

This state of mind on the part of the colored people may strike white America as stupid and intolerant, but it is not without some justification and not entirely without precedent; the white South on occasion discloses a similar sensitiveness. The colored people of the United States are anomalously situated. They are a segregated and antagonized minority in a very large nation, a minority unremittingly on the defensive. Their faults and failings are exploited to produce exaggerated effects. Consequently, they have a strong feeling against exhibiting to the world anything but their best points. They feel that other groups may afford to do otherwise but, as yet, the Negro cannot. This is not to say that they refuse to listen to criticism of themselves, for they often listen to Negro speakers excoriating the race for its faults and foibles and vices. But these criticisms are not for the printed page. They are not for the ears and eyes of white America.

A curious illustration of this defensive state of mind is found in the Negro theatres. In those wherein Negro players give Negro performances for Negro audiences all of the Negro weaknesses, real and reputed, are burlesqued and ridiculed in the most hilarious manner, and are laughed at and heartily enjoyed. But the presence of a couple of dozen white people would completely change the psychology of the audience, and the players. If some of the performances so much enjoyed by strictly Negro audiences in Negro theatres were put on, say, in a Broadway theatre, a wave of indignation would sweep

Aframerica from the avenues of Harlem to the canebrakes of Louisiana. These taboos of black America are as real and binding as the conventions of white America. Conditions may excuse if not warrant them; nevertheless, it is unfortunate that they exist, for their effect is blighting. In past years they have discouraged in Negro authors the production of everything but *nice* literature; they have operated to hold their work down to literature of the defensive, exculpatory sort. They have a restraining effect at the present time which Negro writers are compelled to reckon with.

This division of audience takes the solid ground from under the feet of the Negro writer and leaves him suspended. Either choice carries hampering and discouraging conditions. The Negro author may please one audience and at the same time rouse the resentment of the other; or he may please the other and totally fail to rouse the interest of the one. The situation, moreover, constantly subjects him to the temptation of posing and posturing for the one audience or the other; and the sincerity and soundness of his work are vitiated whether he poses for white or black.

The dilemma is not made less puzzling by the fact that practically it is an extremely difficult thing for the Negro author in the United States to address himself solely to either of these two audiences. If he analyzes what he writes he will find that on one page black America is his whole or main audience, and on the very next page white America. In fact, psychoanalysis of the Negro authors of the defensive and exculpatory literature, written in strict conformity to the taboos of black America, would reveal that they were unconsciously addressing themselves mainly to white America.

III

I have sometimes thought it would be a way out, that the Negro author would be on surer ground and truer to himself, if he could disregard white America; if he could say to white America, "What I have written, I have written. I hope you'll be interested and like it. If not, I can't help it." But it is impossible for a sane American Negro to write with total disregard for nine-tenths of the people of the United States. Situated as his own race is amidst and amongst them, their influence is irresistible.

I judge there is not a single Negro writer who is not, at least secondarily, impelled by the desire to make his work have some effect on the white world for the good of his race. It may be thought that the work of the Negro writer, on account of this last named condition, gains in pointedness what it loses in breadth. Be that as it may, the situation is for the time one in which he is inextricably placed. Of course, the Negro author can try the experiment of putting black America in the orchestra chairs, so to speak, and keeping white America in the gallery, but he is likely at any moment to find his audience shifting places on him, and sometimes without notice.

And now, instead of black America and white America as separate or alternating audiences, what about the combination of the two into one? That, I believe, is the only way out. However, there needs to be more than a combination, there needs to be a fusion. In time, I cannot say how much time, there will come a gradual and natural rapprochement of these two sections of the Negro author's audience. There will come a breaking up and remodeling of most of white America's traditional stereotypes, forced by the advancement of the Negro in the various phases of our national life. Black America will abolish many of its taboos. A sufficiently large class of colored people will progress enough and become strong enough to render a constantly sensitive and defensive attitude on the part of the race unnecessary and distasteful. In the end, the Negro author will have something close to a common audience, and will be about as free from outside limitations as other writers.

Meanwhile, the making of a common audience out of white and black America presents the Negro author with enough difficulties to constitute a third horn of his dilemma. It is a task that is a very high test for all his skill and abilities, but it can be and has been accomplished. The equipped Negro author working at his best in his best known material can achieve this end; but, standing on his racial foundation, he must fashion something that rises above race, and reaches out to the universal in truth and beauty. And so, when a Negro author does write so as to fuse white and black America into one interested and approving audience he has performed no slight feat, and has most likely done a sound piece of literary work.

The American Mercury, 1928

Race Prejudice and the Negro Artist

What Americans call the Negro problem is almost as old as America itself. For three centuries the Negro in this country has been tagged with an interrogation point; the question propounded, however, has not always been the same. Indeed, the question has run all the way from whether or not the Negro was a human being, down—or up—to whether or not the Negro shall be accorded full and unlimited American citizenship. Therefore, the Negro problem is not a problem in the sense of being a fixed proposition involving certain invariable factors and waiting to be worked out according to certain defined rules. It is not a static condition; rather, it is and always has been a series of shifting interracial situations, never precisely the same in any two generations. As these situations have shifted, the methods and manners of dealing with them have constantly changed. And never has there been such a swift and vital shift as the one which is taking place at the present moment; and never was there a more revolutionary change in attitudes than the one which is now going on.

The question of the races—white and black—has occupied much of America's time and thought. Many methods for a solution of the problem have been tried—most of them tried *on* the Negro, for one of the mistakes commonly made in dealing with this matter has been the failure of white America to take into account the Negro himself and the forces he was generating and sending out. The question repeated generation after generation has been what shall we do with the Negro?—

ignoring completely the power of the Negro to do something for himself, and even something to America. It is a new thought that the Negro has helped to shape and mold and make America. It is, perhaps, a startling thought that America would not be precisely the America it is to-day except for the powerful, if silent, influence the Negro has exerted upon it—both positively and negatively. It is a certainty that the nation would be shocked by a contemplation of the effects which have been wrought upon its inherent character by the negative power which the Negro has involuntarily and unwittingly wielded.

A number of approaches to the heart of the race problem have been tried: religious, educational, political, industrial, ethical, economic, sociological. Along several of these approaches considerable progress has been made. To-day a newer approach is being tried, an approach which discards most of the older methods. It requires a minimum of pleas, or propaganda, or philanthropy. It depends more upon what the Negro himself does than upon what someone does for him. It is the approach along the line of intellectual and artistic achievement by Negroes, and may be called the art approach to the Negro problem. This method of approaching a solution of the race question has the advantage of affording great and rapid progress with least friction and of providing a common platform upon which most people are willing to stand. The results of this method seem to carry a high degree of finality, to be the thing itself that was to be demonstrated.

I have said that this is a newer approach to the race problem; that is only in a sense true. The Negro has been using this method for a very long time; for a longer time than he has used any other method, and, perhaps, with farther-reaching effectiveness. For more than a century his great folk-art contributions have been exerting an ameliorating effect, slight and perhaps, in any one period, imperceptible, nevertheless, cumulative. In countless and diverse situations song and dance have been both a sword and a shield for the Negro. Take the Spirituals: for sixty years beginning with their introduction to the world by the Fisk Jubilee Singers, these songs have touched and stirred the hearts of people and brought about a smoothing down of the rougher edges of prejudice against the Negro. Indeed, nobody can hear Negroes sing this wonderful music in its primitive beauty without a softening of feeling toward them.

What is there, then, that is new? What is new consists largely in the changing attitude of the American people. There is a coming to light and notice of efforts that have been going on for a long while, and a public appreciation of their results. Note, for example, the change in the reaction to the Spirituals. Fifty years ago white people who heard the Spirituals were touched and moved with sympathy and pity for the "poor Negro." To-day the effect is not one of pity for the Negro's condition, but admiration for the creative genius of the race.

All of the Negro's folk-art creations have undergone a new evaluation. His sacred music—the Spirituals; his secular music—Ragtime, Blues, Jazz, and the work songs; his folk lore—the Uncle Remus plantation tales; and his dances have received a new and higher appreciation. Indeed, I dare to say it is now more or less generally acknowledged that the only things artistic that have sprung from American soil and out of American life, and been universally recognized as distinctively American products, are the folk creations of the Negro. The one thing that may be termed artistic, by which the United States is known the world over, is its Negro-derived popular music. The folk creations of the Negro have not only received a new appreciation; they have—the Spirituals excepted—been taken over and assimilated. They are no longer racial, they are national; they have become a part of our common cultural fund. Negro secular music has been developed into American popular music: Negro dances have been made into our national art of dancing; even the plantation tales have been transformed and have come out as popular bedtime stories. The Spirituals are still distinct Negro folk songs, but sooner or later our serious composers will take them as material to go into the making of the "great American music" that has so long been looked for.

But the story does not halt at this point. The Negro has done a great deal through his folk-art creations to change the national attitudes toward him; and now the efforts of the race have been reinforced and magnified by the individual Negro artist, the conscious artist. It is fortunate that the individual Negro artist has emerged; for it is more than probable that with the ending of the creative period of Blues, which seems to be at hand, the whole folk creative effort of the Negro in the United States will come to a close. All the psychological and environmental forces are working to that end. At any rate, it is the individual Negro artist that is now doing most to effect a crumbling of the inner walls of race prejudice; there are outer and inner walls. The emergence of the individual artist is the result of the same phenomenon that brought about the new evaluation and appreciation of the folk-art creations. But it should be borne in mind that the conscious Aframerican artist is not an entirely new thing. What is new about him is chiefly the evaluation and public recognition of his work.

II

When and how did this happen? The entire change, which is marked by the shedding of a new light on the artistic and intellectual achievements of the Negro, the whole period which has become ineptly known as "the Negro renaissance," is the matter of a decade; it has all taken place within the last ten years. More forces than anyone can name have been at work to create the existing state; however, several of them may be pointed out. What took place had no appearance of a development; it seemed more like a sudden awakening, an almost instantaneous change. There was nothing that immediately preceded it which foreshadowed what was to follow. Those who were in the midst of the movement were as much astonished as anyone else to see the transformation. Overnight, as it were, America became aware that there were Negro artists and that they had something worth while to offer. This awareness first manifested itself in black America, for, strange as it may seem, Negroes themselves, as a mass, had had little or no consciousness of their own individual artists. Black America awoke first to the fact that it possessed poets. This awakening followed the entry of the United States into the Great War. Before this country had been in the war very long there was bitter disillusionment on the part of American Negroes—on the part both of those working at home and those fighting in France to make the world safe for democracy. The disappointment and bitterness were taken up and voiced by a group of seven or eight Negro poets. They expressed what the race felt, what the race wanted to hear. They made the group at large articulate. Some of this poetry was the poetry of despair, but most of it was the poetry of protest and rebellion. Fenton Johnson wrote of civilization:

I am tired of work; I am tired of building up somebody else's civilization.
Let us take a rest, M'lissy Jane.

You will let the old shanty go to rot, the white people's clothes turn to dust, and the Calvary Baptist Church sink to the bottomless pit.
Throw the children into the river; civilization has given us too many. It is better to die than it is to grow up and find out that you are colored.
Pluck the stars out of the heavens. The stars mark our destiny. The stars marked my destiny.
I am tired of civilization.

Joseph Cotter, a youth of twenty, inquired plaintively from the invalid's bed to which he was confined:

Brother; come!
And let us go unto our God.
And when we stand before Him
I shall say,
"Lord, I do not hate,
I am hated.
I scourge no one,
I am scourged.
I covet no lands,
My lands are coveted.
I mock no peoples,
My people are mocked."
And, brother, what shall you say?

But among this whole group the voice that was most powerful was that of Claude McKay. Here was a true poet of great skill and wide range, who turned from creating the mood of poetic beauty in the absolute, as he had so fully done in such poems as "Spring in New Hampshire," "The Harlem Dancer," and "Flame Heart," for example, and began pouring out cynicism, bitterness, and invective. For this purpose, incongruous as it may seem, he took the sonnet form as his medium. There is nothing in American literature that strikes a more portentous note than these sonnet-tragedies of McKay. Here is the sestet of his sonnet, "The Lynching":

Day dawned, and soon the mixed crowds came to view
The ghastly body swaying in the sun:
The women thronged to look, but never a one
Showed sorrow in her eyes of steely blue;

And little lads, lynchers that were to be,
Danced round the dreadful thing in fiendish glee.

The summer of 1919 was a terrifying period for the American Negro. There were race riots in Chicago and in Washington and in Omaha and in Phillips County, Arkansas; and in Longview, Texas; and in Knoxville, Tennessee; and in Norfolk, Virginia; and in other communities. Colored men and women, by dozens and by scores, were chased and beaten and killed in the streets. And from Claude McKay came this cry of defiant despair sounded from the last ditch:

If we must die—let it not be like hogs
Hunted and penned in an inglorious spot.

Oh, Kinsmen! We must meet the common foe;
Though far outnumbered, let us still be brave,
And for their thousand blows deal one death blow!
What though before us lies the open grave?
Like men we'll face the murderous, cowardly pack,
Pressed to the wall, dying, but—fighting back!

But not all the terror of the time could smother the poet of beauty and universality in McKay. In "America," which opens with these lines:

Although she feeds me bread of bitterness,
And sinks into my throat her tiger's tooth,
Stealing my breath of life, I will confess
I love this cultured hell that tests my youth.

he fused these elements of fear and bitterness and hate into verse which by every test is true poetry and a fine sonnet.

The poems of the Negro poets of the immediate post-war period were widely printed in Negro periodicals; they were committed to memory; they were recited at school exercises and public meetings; and were discussed at private gatherings. Now, Negro poets were not new; their line goes back a long way in Aframerican history. Between Phillis Wheatley, who as a girl of eight or nine was landed in Boston from an African slave ship in 1761, and who published a volume of poems in 1773, and Paul Laurence Dunbar, who died in 1906, there were more than thirty Negroes who published volumes of verse—some of it good, most of it mediocre, and much of it bad. The new thing was the effect produced by these poets who sprang up out of the war period. Negro poets had sounded similar notes before, but now for the first time they succeeded in setting up a reverberating response, even in their own group. But the effect was not limited to black America; several of these later poets in some subtle way affected white America. In any event, at just this time white America began to become aware and to awaken. In the correlation of forces that brought about this result it might be pointed out that the culminating effect of the folk-art creations had gone far toward inducing a favorable state of mind. Doubtless it is also true that the new knowledge and opinions about the Negro in Africa—that he was not just a howling savage, that he had a culture, that he had produced a vital art—had directly affected opinion about the Negro in America. However it may have been, the Negro poets growing out of the war period were the forerunners of the individuals whose work is now being assayed and is receiving recognition in accordance with its worth.

III

And yet, contemporaneously with the work of these poets a significant effort was made in another field of art—an effort which might have gone much farther at the time had it not been cut off by our entry into the War, but which, nevertheless, had its effect. Early in 1917, in fact on the very day we entered the War, Mrs. Emily Hapgood produced at the Madison Square Garden Theater three plays of Negro life by Ridgley Torrence, staged by Robert Edmond Jones, and played by an all-Negro cast. This was the first time that Negro actors in drama commanded the serious attention of the critics and the general public. Two of the players, Opal Cooper and Inez Clough, were listed by George Jean Nathan among the ten actors giving the most distinguished performances of the year. No one who heard Opal Cooper chant the dream in the "Rider of Dreams" can ever forget the thrill of it. A sensational feature of the production was the singing orchestra of Negro performers under the direction of J. Rosamond Johnson—singing orchestras in theaters have since become common. The plays moved from the Garden Theater to the Garrick, but the stress of war crushed them out. In 1920, Charles Gilpin was enthusiastically and universally acclaimed for his acting in "The Emperor Jones." The American stage has seldom seen such an outburst of acclamation. Mr. Gilpin was one of the ten persons voted by the Drama League as having done most for the American theater during the year. Most of the readers of these pages will remember the almost national crisis caused by his invitation to the Drama League Dinner. And along came "Shuffle Along"; and all of New York flocked to an out of the way theater in West Sixty-third Street to hear the most joyous singing and see the most exhilarating dancing to be found on any stage in the city. The dancing steps originally used by the "policeman" in "Shuffle Along" furnished new material for hundreds of dancing men. "Shuffle Along" was actually an epoch-making musical comedy. Out of "Shuffle Along" came Florence Mills, who, unfortunately, died so young but lived long enough to be acknowledged here and in Europe as one of the finest singing comediennes the stage had ever seen and an artist of positive genius. In 1923 Roland Hayes stepped out on the American stage in a blaze of glory, making his first appearances as soloist with the Boston Symphony Orchestra and later with the Philharmonic. Few single artists have packed such crowds into Carnegie Hall and the finest concert halls throughout the country as has Roland Hayes; and, notwithstanding the éclat with which America first received him, his reputation has continued to increase and, besides, he is rated as one of the best box-office attractions in the whole concert field. Miss Marian Anderson appeared as soloist with the Philadelphia Symphony Orchestra and in concert at the Lewisohn Stadium at New York City College. Paul Robeson and J. Rosamond Johnson and Taylor Gordon sang Spirituals to large and appreciative audiences in New York and over the country, giving to those songs a fresh interpretation and a new vogue.

Paul Robeson—that most versatile of men, who has made a national reputation as athlete, singer, and actor—played in Eugene O'Neill's "All God's Chillun" and added to his reputation on the stage, and, moreover, put to the test an ancient taboo; he played the principal role opposite a white woman. This feature of the play gave rise to a more acute crisis than did Gilpin's invitation to the Drama League Dinner. Some sensational newspaper predicted race riots and other dire disasters, but nothing of the sort happened; the play went over without a boo. Robeson played the title role in a revival of "The Emperor Jones" and almost duplicated the sensation produced by Gilpin in the original presentation. There followed on the stage Julius Bledsoe, Rose McClendon, Frank Wilson, and Abbie Mitchell, all of whom gained recognition. At the time of this writing each of these four is playing in a Broadway production. Paradoxical it may seem, but no Negro comedian gained recognition in this decade. Negro comedians have long been a recognized American institution and there are several now before the public who are well known, but their reputations were made before this period. The only new reputations made on the comedy stage were made by women, Florence Mills and Ethel Waters. In addition there are the two famous Smiths, Bessie and Clara, singers of Blues and favorites of vaudeville, phonograph, and radio audiences. Of course there is Josephine Baker, but her reputation was made entirely in Europe. Nevertheless, these magical ten years have worked a change upon Negro comedy. Before Miller and Lyles brought "Shuffle Along" to New York, managers here could hardly conceive of a Negro musical comedy playing a Broadway house. When Williams and Walker, Cole and Johnson, and Ernest Hogan were in their heyday, people who wanted to see them had to go to theaters outside the great white-light zone. George Walker died before the "new day," and up to his retirement from the stage he kept up a constant fight for a chance for his company to play a strictly Broadway theater. Since "Shuffle Along," hardly a season has passed without seeing one or more Negro musical comedies playing in the finest theaters in New York. In fact, Negro plays and Negro performers in white plays on Broadway have become usual occurrences.

Odd has been the fate of the younger poets who were instrumental in bringing about the present state of affairs. It is a fact that none of them, with the exception of Claude McKay, quite succeeded in bridging over into it. Three of them, Roscoe Jamison, Lucian Watkins, and Joseph Cotter, are dead, all dying in their youth. Fenton Johnson is almost silent. And Claude McKay has for the past four or five years lived practically in exile. However, several of the older writers are busily at work, and there has sprung up in the last three or four years a group of newer creative writers. Countee Cullen and Langston Hughes have achieved recognition as poets. Jean Toomer, Walter

White, Eric Walrond, and Rudolph Fisher have made a place among writers of fiction. And Claude McKay, after a period of silence as a poet, has published his *Home to Harlem,* a generally acclaimed novel. These are names that carry literary significance, and they take their places according to individual merit in the list of the makers of contemporary American literature. In addition, there are more than a score of younger writers who are not yet quite in the public eye, but will soon be more widely known. Writers such as these are bound to be known and in larger numbers, because their work now has the chance to gain whatever appreciation it merits. To-day the reagents that will discover what of it is good are at work, the arbiters of our national letters are disposed to regard their good work as a part of American literature, and the public is prepared to accept it as such. This has not always been the case. Until this recent period, the several achievements in writing that have come to light have been regarded as more or less sporadic and isolated efforts, and not in any sense as having a direct relation to the national literature. Had the existing forces been at work at the time, the remarkable decade from 1895 to 1905, which brought forth Booker T. Washington's *Up from Slavery,* W. E. Burghardt Du Bois's *The Souls of Black Folk,* Charles Chestnutt's stories of Negro life, and Paul Laurence Dunbar's poetry, might have signaled the beginning of the "Negro literary renaissance."

During the present decade the individual Negro artist has definitely emerged in three fields, in literature, in the theater, and on the concert stage; in other fields he has not won marked distinction. To point to any achievement of distinction in painting the Negro must go back of this decade, back to H. O. Tanner, who has lived in Europe for the past thirty-five years; or farther back to E. M. Bannister, who gained considerable recognition a half century ago. Nevertheless, there is the work of W. E. Scott, a mural painter, who lives in Chicago and has done a number of public buildings in the Middle West, and of Archibald J. Motley, who recently held a one-man exhibit in New York which attracted very favorable attention. The drawings of Aaron Douglas have won for him a place among American illustrators. To point to any work of acknowledged excellence in sculpture the Negro must go back of this decade to the work of two women, Edmonia Lewis and Meta Warrick Fuller, both of whom received chiefly in Europe such recognition as they gained. There are several young painters and sculptors who are winning recognition. But the strangest lack is that with all the great native musical endowment he is conceded to possess, the Negro has not in this most propitious time produced a single outstanding composer. There are competent musicians and talented composers of songs and detached bits of music, but no original composer who, in amount and standard of work and in recognition achieved, is at all comparable with S. Coleridge-Taylor, the English Negro composer. Nor can the Negro in the United States point back of this decade to even one such artist. It is a curious fact that the American Negro through his whole history has done more highly sustained and more fully recognized work in the composition of letters than in the composition of music. It is the more curious when we consider that music is so innately a characteristic method of expression for the Negro.

IV

What, now, is the significance of this artistic activity on the part of the Negro and of its reactions on the American people? I think it is twofold. In the first place, the Negro is making some distinctive contributions to our common cultural store. I do not claim it is possible for these individual artists to produce anything comparable to the folk-art in distinctive values, but I do believe they are bringing something fresh and vital into American art, something from the store of their own racial genius: warmth, color, movement, rhythm, and abandon; depth and swiftness of emotion and the beauty of sensuousness. I believe American art will be richer because of these elements in fuller quantity.

But what is of deeper significance to the Negro himself is the effect that this artistic activity is producing upon his condition and status as a man and citizen. I do not believe it an overstatement to say that the "race problem" is fast reaching the stage of being more a question of national mental attitudes toward the Negro than a question of his actual condition. That is to say, it is not at all the problem of a moribund people sinking into a slough of ignorance, poverty, and decay in the very midst of our civilization and despite all our efforts to save them; that would indeed be a problem. Rather is the problem coming to consist in the hesitation and refusal to open new doors of opportunity at which these peoples are constantly knocking. In other words, the problem for the Negro is reaching the plane where it is becoming less a matter of dealing with what he is and more a matter of dealing with what America thinks he is.

Now, the truth is that the great majority of Americans have not thought about the Negro at all, except in a vague sort of way and in the form of traditional and erroneous stereotypes. Some of these stereotyped forms of thought are quite absurd, yet they have had their opinions and attitudes regarding their fellow colored citizens determined by such a phrase as, "A nigger will steal," or "Niggers are lazy," or "Niggers are dirty." But there is a common, widespread, and persistent stereotyped idea regarding the Negro, and it is that he is here only to receive; to be shaped into something new and unquestionably better. The common idea is that the Negro reached America intellectually, culturally, and morally empty, and that he is here to be filled—filled with education, filled with religion, filled with morality, filled with culture. In a word, the stereotype is that the Negro is nothing more than a beggar at the gate of the nation, waiting to be thrown the crumbs of civilization. Through his artistic efforts the Negro is smashing this immemorial stereotype faster than he has ever done through any other method he has been able to use. He is making it realized that he is the possessor of a wealth of natural endowments and that he has long been a generous giver to America. He is impressing upon the national mind the conviction that he is an active and important force in American life; that he is a creator as well as a creature; that he has given as well as received; that he is the potential giver of larger and richer contributions.

In this way the Negro is bringing about an entirely new national conception of himself; he has placed himself in an entirely new light before the American people. I do not think it too much to say that through artistic achievement the Negro has found a means of getting at the very core of the prejudice against him, by challenging the Nordic superiority complex. A great deal has been accomplished in this decade of "renaissance." Enough has been accomplished to make it seem almost amazing when we realize that there are less than twenty-five Negro artists who have more or less of national recognition; and that it is they who have chiefly done the work. A great part of what they have accomplished has been done through the sort of publicity they have secured for the race. A generation ago the Negro was receiving lots of publicity, but nearly all of it was bad. There were front page stories with such headings as, "Negro Criminal," "Negro Brute." Today one may see undesirable stories, but one may also read stories about Negro singers, Negro actors, Negro authors, Negro poets. The connotations of the very word "Negro" have been changed. A generation ago many Negroes were half or wholly ashamed of the term. To-day they have every reason to be proud of it.

For many years and by many methods the Negro has been overcoming the coarser prejudices against him; and when we consider how many of the subtler prejudices have crumbled, and crumbled rapidly under the process of art creation by the Negro, we are justified in taking a hopeful outlook toward the effect that the increase of recognized individual artists fivefold, tenfold, twentyfold, will have on this most perplexing and vital question before the American people.

Harper's, 1928

PART FIVE

AUTOBIOGRAPHY

AUTOBIOGRAPHY: SELECTIONS FROM *ALONG THIS WAY*

Published to great critical acclaim in 1933, Johnson's autobiography, *Along This Way,* is the portrait of a self-described race man and cosmopolite, of a poet, and also of an unafraid leader of his race. The selected chapters reprinted here span the period of Johnson's birth and boyhood in Jacksonville, Florida, and his education at Atlanta University (now Clark-Atlanta University). Chapter two provides us with a beautiful portrait of the loving, stable, and somewhat prosperous family into which Johnson was born in Jacksonville, Florida, just a few years after the Civil War. Here he reflects upon the special character of his relationship with his mother, Helen Louis Dillet, born in Nassau, Bahamas, on August 4, 1842, and reared in New York. Dillet's influence upon her son was manifest in a number of ways. It was she who provided her firstborn with an example of resistance to racism, and who, very importantly, taught him to read before he entered primary school, introduced him to the pleasures of reading, and was his music teacher. This chapter also contains Johnson's earliest remembrances of his father, James Johnson, who was born a freeman in Richmond, Virginia, on August 26, 1830, and, as a boy, went to New York to find his place in an America on the verge of civil war. In contrast to his wife, who possessed the sensibility of an artist, Johnson senior, as his son remembers, was initally a remote figure, which is so often the condition of working fathers. It is clear, however, that James Johnson loved his son, as he would leave him oranges, nuts, and raisins under the sleeping boy's pillow. It was his father who gave the future writer a children's library, which he kept until his death, and it was from his father's example that the future diplomat would develop his facility with languages, particularly Spanish.

There is the education Johnson received at home, and there is the education he received beyond the home. The latter is mainly the subject of chapter seven, wherein Johnson recalls his journey by train from Jacksonville to Atlanta at the age of sixteen to attend the preparatory school of Atlanta University. He writes that he attended the school for one year after which he entered Atlanta University as a freshman. Though Johnson was disappointed in Atlanta, he flourished at the school. It was at Atlanta University, led by the Yale-educated Horace Bumstead, that Johnson was initiated, in ways deeper than the preparation provided by his parents, into the complexities of the color line. While race, as he recalls, was not a feature of the curriculum, it completely imbued the atmosphere, spirit, and culture of the institution. During his six years of study at Atlanta University Johnson not only learned to negotiate the color line but also the rather Byzantine set of rules that governed all contact between male and female students, rules that bore the deep imprint of the most rigid customs of Victorian society. Johnson reveals to us that it was during the course of his undergraduate studies (he would later earn a master of arts from Columbia University) that his friendship with D——, that is, J. Douglass Whetmore, deepened. After matriculating from Atlanta University, Whetmore would cross the color line and pass for white. Johnson memorialized his friendship with Whetmore by taking him as the model for his protagonist in *The Autobiography of an Ex-Coloured Man.*

In these carefully chosen chapters from *Along This Way,* Johnson describes the singular set of factors that shaped his childhood, adolescence, and early manhood. These foundational experiences constitute the expanding floor upon which the mature Johnson would stand and lead both his race and nation at the beginning of the twentieth century. As Johnson would have us understand, this was a period during which lynching was commonplace, when segregation was a defining feature of civil society, and when black cultural production would soon be regarded not only as a means of advancing the argument for black citizenship but also, more transgressively and extravagantly, as an example of a national art.

When *Along This Way* was published Johnson was sixty-two years old and at the height of his national and international power and influence, which he wore lightly and with considerable dignity. The publication of Johnson's autobiography was heralded as a landmark event by both blacks and whites, as is evident in the uniformly positive response to the volume. The poet Countee Cullen wrote to Johnson to observe that the autobiography "is a fine and enviable road to have travelled, and you have described it in masterly fashion." "I have just completed the reading of your recent, *Along This Way*," writes the poet Frank S. Horne in a letter to Johnson, and "I hasten to say that it has been a most pleasant and exhilarating experience."

The scholar Benjamin Brawley regarded the autobiography as an inspirational work: "You can know that your faith in yourself and your willingness to blaze a trail will be an inspiration to many." The poet Gwendolyn Bennett wrote to Johnson in a similar vein: "You are wondering, no doubt, why the book, except for its literary merit, excited me so much. I don't think you can possibly realize what reading that book means to a young Negro who with one or two talents finds himself lost in the labyrinth of things that must be done and ways to do them and yet live." Similarly, the journalist and writer George Schuyler praised Johnson for the rare portrait of black life the autobiography provides and its inspirational elements: "While it will certainly prove instructive to the white reader, to the young Negro it should serve as an inspiration. It presents a side of Negro society that has so far received very little attention. It is happily free of defeatism, and if young Aframerica needs anything today it is hope and encouragement."

Carl Van Vechten, who established the James Weldon Johnson Memorial Collection of Negro Arts and Letters at Yale University in honor of Johnson after his death in an automobile accident in 1938, was characteristically effusive in his praise: "I not only read the book, but I read it at one sitting and took away from it a breathless kind of awe. It is a great performance, great in its reticence, great in its outpouring. You say so much and you suggest so much more.... I can imagine that for those who know nothing about you it will come almost as a thunderbolt of excitement. It stands with the GREAT autobiographies and it is your best book to date, unquestionably.... You write a simple, sonorous English which is both highsounding and unaffected. You have to go back to Defoe for a comparison."

"Having just finished reading your latest book ALONG THIS WAY," writes the industrialist John D. Rockefeller to Johnson, "I want to tell you how much I enjoyed it from every point of view. It was, of course, particularly interesting to me because of our friendship, but I would have wanted to have read it anyway. I knew that you had had a very varied career, but I had not begun to realize how really all inclusive it was. There is hardly a field which you did not at least touch. To congratulate you on the book," observes Rockefeller, "would be trite to say the least. However I did want you to know how much pleasure I had derived from reading it."

Having written to Johnson for advice on *Moses, Man of the Mountain*, at the time a novel in progress, the novelist and anthropologist Zora Neale Hurston, who often in her correspondence with Johnson addressed him affectionately as "Lord Jim," praised the autobiography and also reported its popularity among academicians: "I am reading ALONG THIS WAY now. It is *grand*! My sister and I used to go around the house claiming things like that—what you and your brother did at the what-not. By the way, Prof. France of Rollins College is having it read in his class. Prof. Sproul in English (his sister married Dorothy Peter's brother) is using it in his classroom also."

Joel E. Spingarn, Johnson's fellow freedom fighter within the framework of the NAACP, provided an assessment of the autobiography that reveals the depth of their long friendship: "It is a noble book, dear Jim, this record of your life. I hardly realized how many important things there were of which you could say *magna pars fui,* and the record of them is worthy of the experiences. Always you seem to see visions and yet have your feet on the ground, to combine imagination and common sense as only one who is both poet and statesman could." Spingarn closes his letter to his friend thusly: "Your book is full of wise things, the result of a very rich experience, from which you have been able, as few men have, to gather the final flower and fruit. I congratulate you from my heart."

As one of the pillars in the temple of culture remembered as the Harlem Renaissance, Johnson nurtured and supported many writers, including the poet Langston Hughes who telegraphed his enthusiasm for *Along This Way:* "GREETINGS AND CONGRATULATIONS ON PUTTING INTO LIVING WORDS A LIFE SO WELL

LIVED BRAVO ENCORE AND A SECOND VOLUME AFTER YOU HAVE LIVED A LOT MORE ALONG THIS WAY."

Johnson's *Along This Way* continues to speak to us across time and geography; it remains an influential work of enduring significance for a variety of reasons. First, there is the example of Johnson as both race man and cosmopolite who sought always to transcend the parochialism of American life. More, it is a record of a life richly lived and for which Johnson offers frank, honest, and revealing commentary. As one of the principal architects of the Harlem Renaissance and a leading figure in the modern civil rights movement, Johnson's autobiography is vital to understanding the ways in which the arts and progressive coalition politics advanced the national vision set forth in the founding documents of state. Above all, as a signal work of autobiography the beautiful and brave record of Johnson's life is one which reveals, again and again, the meaning, the costs, and the possibilities of American citizenship.

SELECTIONS FROM *ALONG THIS WAY*

CHAPTER II

I was born June 17, 1871, in the old house on the corner; but I have no recollection of having lived in it. Before I could be aware of such a thing my father had built a new house near the middle of his lot. In this new house was formed my first consciousness of home. My childish idea of it was that it was a great mansion. I saw nothing in the neighborhood that surpassed it in splendor. Of course, it was only a neat cottage. The house had three bedrooms, a parlor, and a kitchen. The four main rooms were situated, two on each side of a hall that ran through the center of the house. The kitchen, used also as a room in which the family ate, was at the rear of the house and opened on a porch that was an extension of the hall. On the front a broad piazza ran the width of the house. Under the roof was an attic to which a narrow set of steps in one of the back rooms gave access.

But the house was painted, and there were glass windows and green blinds. Before long there were some flowers and trees. One of the first things my father did was to plant two maple trees at the front gate and a dozen or more orange trees in the yard. The maples managed to live; the orange trees, naturally, flourished. The hallway of the house was covered with a strip of oilcloth and the floors of the rooms with matting. There were curtains at the windows and some pictures on the walls. In the parlor there were two or three dozen books and a cottage organ. When I was seven or eight years old, the organ gave way to a square piano. It was a tinkling old instrument, but a source of rapturous pleasure. It is one of the indelible impressions on my mind. I can still remember just how the name "Bacon" looked, stamped in gold letters above the keyboard. There was a center marble-top table on which rested a big, illustrated Bible and a couple of photograph albums. In a corner stood a what-not filled with bric-a-brac and knick-knacks. On a small stand was a glass-domed receptacle in which was a stuffed canary perched on a diminutive tree; on this stand there was also kept a stereoscope and an assortment of views photographed in various parts of the world. For my brother and me, in our childhood (my brother, John Rosamond, was born in the new house August 11, 1873), this room was an Aladdin's cave. We used to stand before the what-not and stake out our claims to the objects on its shelves with a "that's mine" and a "that's mine." We never tired of looking at the stereoscopic scenes, examining the photographs in the album, or putting the big Bible and other books on the floor and exploring for pictures. Two large conch shells decorated the ends of the hearth. We greatly admired their pink, polished inner surface; and loved to put them to our ears to hear the "roar of the sea" from their cavernous depths. But the undiminishing thrill was derived from our experiments on the piano.

When I was born, my mother was very ill, too ill to nurse me. Then she found a friend and neighbor in an unexpected quarter. Mrs. McCleary, her white neighbor who lived a block away, had a short while before given birth to a girl baby. When this baby was christened she was named Angel. The mother of Angel, hearing of my mother's plight, took me and nursed me at her breast until my mother had recovered sufficiently to give me her own milk. So it appears that in the land of black mammies I had a white one. Between her and me there existed an affectionate relation through all my childhood; and even in after years when I had grown up and moved away I never, up to the time of her death, went back to my old home without paying her a visit and taking her some small gift.

I do not intend to boast about a white mammy, for I have perceived bad taste in those Southern white people who are continually boasting about their black mammies. I know the temptation for them to do so is very strong, because the honor point on the escutcheon of Southern aristocracy, the *sine qua non* of a background of family, of good breeding and social prestige, in the South is the Black Mammy. Of course, many of the white people who boast of having had black mammies are romancing. Naturally, Negroes had black mammies, but black mammies for white people were expensive luxuries, and comparatively few white people had them.

When I was about a year old, my father made a trip to New York, taking my mother and me with him. It was during this visit that I developed from a creeping infant into a walking child. Without doubt, my mother welcomed this trip. She was, naturally, glad to see again the city and friends of her girlhood; and it is probable that she brought some pressure on my father to make another move—back to New York. If she did, it was without effect. I say she probably made some such effort because I know what a long time it took her to become reconciled to life in the South; in fact, she never did entirely. The New York of her childhood and youth was all the United States she knew. Latterly she had lived in a British colony under conditions that rendered the weight of race comparatively light. During the earlier days of her life in Jacksonville she had no adequate conception of her "place."

And so it was that one Sunday morning she went to worship at St. John's Episcopal Church. As one who had been a member of the choir of Christ Church Cathedral she went quite innocently. She went, in fact, not knowing any better. In the chanting of the service her soprano voice rang out clear and beautiful, and necks were craned to discover the singer. On leaving the church she was politely but definitely informed that the St. John's congregation would prefer to have her worship the Lord elsewhere. Certainly she never went back to St. John's nor to any other Episcopal church; she followed her mother and joined Ebenezer, the colored Methodist Episcopal Church in Jacksonville, and became the choir leader.

Racially she continued to be a nonconformist and a rebel. A decade or so after the St. John's Church incident Lemuel W. Livingston, a student at Cookman Institute, the Negro school in Jacksonville founded and maintained by the Methodist Church (North), was appointed as a cadet to West Point. Livingston passed his written examinations, and the colored people were exultant. The members of Ebenezer Church gave a benefit that netted for him a purse of several hundred dollars. There was good reason for a show of pride, Livingston was a handsome, bronze-colored boy with a high reputation as a student, and appeared to be ideal material for a soldier and officer. But at the Academy he was turned down. The examining officials there stated that his eyesight was in some manner defective. The news that Livingston had been denied admission to West Point was given out at a Sunday service at Ebenezer Church. When at the same service the minister announced "America" as a hymn, my mother refused to sing it.

My mother was artistic and more or less impractical and in my father's opinion had absolutely no sense about money. She was a splendid singer and she had a talent for drawing. One day when I was about fifteen years old, she revealed to me that she had written verse, and showed me a thin sheaf of poems copied out in her almost perfect handwriting. She was intelligent and possessed a quick though limited sense of humor. But the limitation of her sense of humor was quite the normal one: she had no relish for a joke whose butt was herself or her children; my father had the rarer capacity for laughing even at himself. She belonged to the type of mothers whose love completely surrounds their children and is all-pervading; mothers for whom sacrifice for the child means only an extension of love. Love of this kind often haunts the child in later years. He runs back again and again through all his memories, searching for a lapse or a lack or a falling short in that love so that he might in some degree balance his own innumerable thoughtlessnesses, his petty and great selfishnesses, his failures to begin to understand or value the thing that was once his like the air he breathed; and the search is vain.

The childhood memories that cluster round my mother are still intensely vivid to me; many of them are poignantly tender. I am between five and six years old.... In the early evening the lamp in the little parlor is lit.... If the weather is chilly, pine logs are sputtering and blazing in the fireplace.... I and my brother, who is a tot, are seated on the floor.... My mother takes a book and reads.... The book is *David Copperfield*.... Night after night I follow the story, always hungry for the next installment.... Then the book is *Tales of a Grandfather*.... Then it is a story by Samuel Lover. I laugh till the tears roll down my cheeks at the mishaps of Handy Andy. And my brother laughs too, doubtless because he sees me laughing.... My mother's voice is beautiful; I especially enjoy it when she mimics the Irish brogue and Cockney accents.... My brother grows sleepy.... My mother closes the book and puts us both to bed—me feverish concerning the outcome of David's affairs or thrilling over the exploits of Wallace or Robert the Bruce, or still laughing at Andy. She tucks us in and kisses us good-night. What a debt for a child to take on!

She was my first teacher and began my lessons in reading before ever I went to school. She was, in fact, the first colored woman public school teacher in Florida, and, when my school days began at Stanton, the central school in Jacksonville for colored children, she was one of the teachers there. And that, perhaps, is why I have no sharp recollection of just when I started school. I have a blurred and hazy picture in my memory of being in a large room with fifty, maybe sixty boys and girls, most of whom were several years older than I. The picture of the teacher is fainter, and would probably be fainter still had I not afterwards come to know that she was Diana Grant, the wife of the man who was for a number of years the pastor of Ebenezer Church. But I recall more clearly my sense of discomfort. The room was too crowded; some of the children I was packed in with were not clean, I rebelled at the situation.

At this point there must have been some sort of a hiatus, I remember nothing further about that class and classroom, but I do remember distinctly being in a larger, less crowded room with nicer children and with a young lady named Carrie Sampson as my teacher. At once I fell in love with Miss Sampson, and small wonder, she was so lovely. When the time came for me to leave her class, the honor of promotion seemed to be no recompense for my desolation. I wanted to continue without end my education at her feet. It took persuasion and some sterner measures to induce a change of mind, if not of heart. The episode forms a pleasant memory of childhood, and the knowing that this my earliest judgment upon living beauty disclosed such exacting standards has always been a matter of certain pride to me. I saw my teacher many times when I was no longer a child, and I know she was one of the most beautiful women I have ever seen.

The development of the ability to read opened up for me a world of wonders that I never grew tired of exploring. My father gave me my first own books, a "library," consisting of seven volumes packed in a cardboard case four and a half inches high, three inches wide, and two inches deep. I still have the books, they are intact, but show the passage of the years. Each book contains a story about good little girls and good and bad little boys. I need not add that each story pointed a wholesome lesson. I list them: *Peter and His Pony, The Tent in the Garden, Harry the Shrimper, The White Kitten, Willie Wilson the Newsboy,* and *The Water Melon.*

Peter and His Pony opens thus:

> "Dear papa," said Peter one morning to his father, "you said when I was nine years old, you would give me a pony to ride on. Don't you know that I shall be nine years old in three months' time? and will you keep your promise?"
>
> Mr. Howard smiled at Peter's eagerness, and said, "I promised to give you a present of a pony when you should be nine years of age, provided you were sufficiently careful to be trusted with the charge of it; for, though I can afford to buy you a pony, I cannot afford to keep a man to clean and look after it."
>
> "Oh, father," cried Peter, "I will do all that. I will brush his coat every day, and feed him regularly. I shall be fond of him, and he will be fond of me. If you will be so kind as to let me have a pony, I shall be very happy."
>
> "I do not doubt that you will be very happy if I give you a pony," replied Mr. Howard; "but before I promise to give you one, I wish to be quite sure that the pony will be happy also; and if he is not well cleaned and regularly fed, and his shoes looked carefully after, he will not be happy."
>
> "Dear papa," said Peter, "I do assure you that I will always attend to my pony before I eat my breakfast—you may be sure he shall want for nothing."
>
> "Very well," said Mr. Howard, "I will think upon what you have said, and will let you know at the proper time what I intend to do."

Peter got the pony on his ninth birthday, and was very faithful in attending him. But for just once Peter neglected his duties, and when he rode that day the pony lost a shoe, cut his foot, and went lame. Peter's negligence brought upon him the retribution of being deprived for a month of the pleasure of riding.

The chief effect of the story on me was a long season of importuning my father to buy me a pony—the which I never got.

I finished these little books in short order, and looked for stronger meat. In fact, my father had underestimated my stage of development;

my mother's readings had already carried me far beyond books of this grade. I read for myself *Pickwick Papers,* some of the *Waverly Novels, Pilgrim's Progress,* the fairy tales of the Brothers Grimm, and took my first dip into poetry through Sir Walter Scott. I think that of these books the stories by the Brothers Grimm made the deepest effect. These stories left me haunted by the elusiveness of beauty—elusiveness, its very quintessence. Years after, when I read Keats's *Ode to a Nightingale* the thought flashed through my mind that for one whose spirit had not been thus pervaded in childhood it would be impossible even to catch at the tenuous beauty in:

> The same that oft-times hath
> Charm'd magic casements, opening on the foam
> Of perilous seas, in faery lands forlorn.

I exhausted the little supply in our parlor and began laying hands on any book that came within my reach. I remember one day when I was absorbed in a novel I had got hold of with the title, as I remember it, *Vashti—Or Until Death Do Us Part,* my mother said to me, "You had better leave that book till you are older." How good were her grounds for censorship I cannot tell but I remember that I finished the book without, I think, doing myself any appreciable harm. Several years later I began buying regularly two magazines published for boys, *Golden Days* and *Golden Argosy.*

My mother was also my first music teacher. She had less than ordinary proficiency on the organ and piano, but she knew enough to give me and my brother a start. Before we began to learn our notes and the keys of the instrument, we used to stand, whenever we were allowed, close by on either side while she picked out hymns or other simple pieces. It was our great delight, my brother at one end of the keyboard and I at the other, to chime in with what were then wholly futuristic harmonies.

Pardonable sentiment does not make me completely forget that my mother's love was not manifested in unchanging gentleness. There were times when her love or her sense of responsibility for the kind of men her two boys would grow up to be prompted sterner treatment. Then the mental or moral lesson would be impressed upon us otherwise than through our intellectual processes or our higher emotions.

Whenever I was spanked my brother always received vicariously whatever benefits there might be. When I cried he cried even more piteously or more lustily than I. These spankings were literally dark moments in my life. It was not the stinging sensation of the sole of the slipper or the back of the hairbrush that I dreaded, for the force applied was never excessive; it was the moment of darkness that terrified me. My mother's method was to put my head face down between her knees. This made the operation convenient for her, but it had on me somewhat the effect of a total eclipse of the sun on primitive peoples; the world was blotted out and, in addition, I underwent the horrors of the sensation of being smothered.

One instance stands out almost singly in my mind. Often a spanking comes to a child like a thunderclap out of a clear sky, and he doesn't fully realize why he is being punished. He suffers it like the brave man, who dies but once. But one evening after dark I and my brother, being in possession of a few pennies, conspired to run around the corner to Mrs. Handy's grocery store and buy two "prize" boxes of candy. We went without giving notice or asking permission. On starting back I became immediately aware of the gravity of the situation. With each step homeward my forebodings increased. I recognized the inevitable and had a thousand foretastes of it. When I entered the house it was with as heavy a sense of sin as any infant conscience could carry. However, summoning all the gayety we could, we exhibited the baubles we had won—these trinkets, not the candy, were the chief objects of our desires—but that did not stay the hand of fate.

Before my spanking days were entirely over, I took the matter up frankly with my mother and made a plea for open-air spanking. I conceded her right to punish me when I did wrong, but protested against having my eyes and nose and mouth buried in the dark depths of her skirts. She didn't fall back on parental prerogatives, but yielded me the point.

My Richmond grandmother's advice to my father about not sparing the rod and spoiling the child had no effect on him; not once in his life did he lay a finger in punishment on me or my brother. Nevertheless, by firmness and sometimes by sternness, he did exercise a strong control over us. But I am fogy enough to believe that the spankings my mother gave me did me good.

I cannot remember when I did not know my mother, but I can easily recall the at first hazy and then gradually more distinct notions about my father. My impressions of him began to take shape from finding under my pillow in the mornings an orange, some nuts, and raisins, and learning that he had put them there after I had gone to sleep. Shortly after my father got to Jacksonville the St. James Hotel was built and opened. When it was opened he was the headwaiter, a job he held for twelve or thirteen years. Doubtless the hotel had been planned, and may even have been under construction, before he arrived; probably this was the definite prospect before him when he set out for Jacksonville. The St. James was for many years the most famous and the most fashionable of all the Florida resort hotels. A number of summers my father was the headwaiter at some mountain or seaside hotel in the North. So in my babyhood and first days of childhood I didn't see very much of him. His work at the St. James took him from home early in the mornings to see breakfast served, and he remained at the hotel until dinner was finished, by which time I had been put away in the little bed in which I slept. It was from the hotel that he brought the fruit and sweets that he put under my pillow. I remember, too, that our Sunday dinner always came from the hotel. It was brought in a hamper by one of the waiters, and the meat was usually fricasseed chicken.

I got acquainted with my father by being taken to the hotel to see him. As soon as Rosamond was big enough, he was taken too. My mother never went; one of the waiters fetched us until we were old enough to go alone. These visiting days were great days for us: the wide steps, the crowded verandas, the music, the soft, deep carpets of the lobby; this was a world of enchantment. My first definite thought about the hotel was that it belonged to my father. True, there was always around in the office a Mr. Campbell, a rather stooped man with a short reddish beard, who habitually gave me a friendly pat on the shoulder, and who evidently had something to do with the place. But just to the right, at the entrance to the big dining-room stands my father, peerless and imposing in full-dress clothes; he opens the door and takes me in; countless waiters, it seems, are standing around in groups; my father strikes a gong and the waiters spring to their stations and stand like soldiers at attention. I am struck with wonder at the endless rows of tables now revealed, the glitter of silver, china, and glass, and the array of napkins folded so that they look like many miniature white pyramids. Another gong, and the waiters relax, but one of them tucks a napkin under my chin and serves me as though I were a princeling. Then, with desires of heart and stomach satisfied and a quantity of reserves tied in a napkin, I am tucked away in a corner. Again the gong, the doors are thrown open, the guests stream in. My father snaps his fingers, waiters jump to carry out his orders, and guests smile him their thanks. He lords it over everything that falls within my ken. He is, quite obviously, the most important man in the St. James Hotel.

This childish portrait needs, of course, some rectification. No boy can make a fair estimate of his father. I was thirty years old before I was able to do it. The average boy all along thinks highly of his mother. In manhood he is likely even to sentimentalize her faults into tender virtues. With his male parent it is not so; his opinion goes through a range of changes and tends to be critical rather than sentimental. Up to ten a boy thinks his father knows everything; at twenty he indulgently looks upon the "old man" as a back number or, maybe, something less complimentary; at thirty, if the boy himself has any sense, he recognizes all of his father's qualities pretty fairly.

My father was a quiet, unpretentious man. He was naturally conservative and cautious, and generally displayed common sense in what he said and did. He never went to school; such education as he had was self-acquired. Later in life, I appreciated the fact that his self-development was little less than remarkable. He had a knowledge of general affairs and was familiar with many of the chief events and characters in the history of the world. I have the old sheepskin bound volume of *Plutarch's Lives* which he owned before I was born. He had gained by study a working knowledge of the Spanish language; this he had done to increase his value as a hotel employee. When he was a young man in New York, he attended the theater a good deal, and, before I was aware of where the lines came from or of what they meant. I used to go around the house parroting after him certain snatches from the Shakespearean plays. I particularly recall: "To be or not to be; that is the question" and "A horse! a horse! my kingdom for a horse!"

The quality in my father that impressed me most was his high and rigid sense of honesty. I simply could not conceive of him as a party to any monetary transaction that was questionable in the least. I think he got his greatest satisfaction in life out of the reputation he had built up as a man of probity, and took his greatest pride in the consequent credit standing that he enjoyed. This element in his character was a source of gratification to my pride and also, more than once, to my needs. One instance of double gratification was when I was at home in Jacksonville in 1910, just a few weeks before I was to be married. My father and mother discussed an appropriate gift to me and, finally, to my undisguised joy, decided upon a check for a thousand dollars. My father, excusably, did not have a thousand dollars in cash; but he said to me, "My boy, we'll go down town tomorrow and see if we can get the money." We went the next morning to one of the principal banks and my father spoke with John C. L'Engle, the president. The transaction was put through without any delay; he got the money on his note, without collateral security, without even an endorser. I was as proud to see him able to do such a thing as I was glad to have the money.

In the narrow sense, he was an unsociable man. My mother liked company; and when I was a boy we frequently had company at the house; occasionally there was a party. I, too, liked the company and the extra nice things to eat that were always a concomitant—especially ice cream of which in my whole life I have never had too much. My father took practically no part in these affairs. In his opinion the entertaining of company as "company" was a waste of time and money.

Yet he was not devoid of graces. He played the guitar well as a solo instrument, a use seldom made of it now. He possessed a vein of eloquence and had a good ear for the well-turned phrase. He liked to get off pithy aphorisms. He keenly enjoyed witticisms, particularly his own. Some of the latter, through repetition, became fixed in my mind. On a hot afternoon he would say to me, "Bubs, draw a fresh bucket of water from the well, and be sure to get it from the north side." Or on a still hotter afternoon, "Son, suppose while you're resting you take the ax and chop a little wood." Not infrequently he would achieve a penetrating truth. It was not until he was in his middle forties that he became a church member, when he was past fifty he became a preacher; one day, after he had been a preacher for some years, he said to me, "My boy, do you know I was never *compelled* to associate with bad people until I joined the church?"

He was a jolly companion for a boy, and I loved to be with him and go about with him. He made my first kites. He was adept at folding paper, and he made me windmills and fashioned little boats to be sailed in a tub. He made shadow-figures on the wall at night. He took me and my brother to places along the river where we could paddle about and learn to swim. After we were big enough to trot around with him, he played with us a good deal in this way during the times between hotel seasons. Before I was able to hold the instrument on my knees he began to teach me the guitar. I had to stand up to it in the same manner in which a player stands up to a bass viol. By the time I was ten years old I was, for a child, a remarkable performer—I judge; for I remember people, sometimes guests from the hotel, coming to our house to hear me play.

My father was a man of medium size, but constitutionally strong. One of the traditions of the home was that he was never sick. His color was light bronze, and so, a number of shades darker than that of my mother. She at fifty bore more than a slight resemblance to the later portraits of Queen Victoria; so much so that the family doctor christened her "Queen," a name to which she afterwards answered among her intimate friends.

The years as they pass keep revealing how the impressions made upon me as a child by my parents are constantly strengthening controls over my forms of habit, behavior, and conduct as a man. It appeared to me, starting into manhood, that I was to grow into something different from them; into something on a so much larger plan, a so much grander scale. As life tapers off I can see that in the deep and fundamental qualities I am each day more and more like them.

CHAPTER VII

Now I entered a period which, for excitement, surpassed anything in my experience. For months my father and mother had been forming plans for sending me off to school, and the time for carrying out those plans was drawing nearer day by day. My parents had reviewed information about several schools: Howard University, Fisk University, Atlanta University, Biddle (now Johnson C. Smith) University, and Hampton Institute. My father at first favored Hampton. He had practical ideas about life, one of them being that every boy should learn a trade. I think, too, he had a sentimental leaning toward Hampton because of the fact that he was by birth a Virginian. We, for I was taken into conference, finally decided on Atlanta University. Just what was the determining factor in this choice I do not remember. Perhaps my mother and I merely outvoted my father. Most likely it was the fact that Atlanta was nearest.

I was on the eve of an adventure, and its lure was powerful, but I had my moments of misgivings. I was leaving the familiar sights and objects and associations that had so far made up life for me. I was stepping off a well-known path upon a strange road. I watched my mother preparing me for the journey, but I could not know the anxious love she put into the task. Yet I am now sure that she knew she was packing my kit for me to take a road that would ultimately lead very far from the place where she stood.

Ricardo had been urging his people to let him go to Atlanta University with me. He argued that it would help him to achieve more quickly the object for which he had been sent to the United States; namely, to learn English and study dentistry. He was sincere, but I think he had also caught some of my enthusiasm and wanted to try the new experience. I think, too, he was loath to have me go and leave him in Jacksonville. There had grown between us a strong bond of companionship; and what was, perhaps, more binding, the bond of language. Up to that time my proficiency in Spanish was much greater than his in English; so he never exerted himself to speak to me except in his own language. Anyone who has undergone the agony of having to express himself inadequately in a foreign language knows what a sweet relief it is to find somebody who understands his mother tongue. Ricardo found that relief in me. There were things he could say to me which, if expressed in English, would have made him feel embarrassed. Among these were the confidences regarding his love affairs. These affairs were numerous but always intense. I had gone through phases of love common to a boy's lot; I had felt the pull and tug of that mysterious force; indeed, involved in my misgivings about leaving Jacksonville was Jennie, a golden-hued, fifteen-year-old bit of femininity, and my heart's desire; but the idea that love could be the frenzied, frantic thing it was with Ricardo was not yet within my comprehension. One night after we had gone to bed he actually frightened me. He complained emphatically of violent pains in and round his heart; the indications were that that organ was about to break or explode. I called my mother and she came in and gave him a dose of tincture of lavender. My sympathy cooled when he divulged to me that the attack was caused by a sudden passion he had conceived for Jennie, my own heart's desire.

The letter and the money came from Havana. Ricardo was to go with me to Atlanta University. I was glad that I would have a friend and companion from the start. D—— and I had long expected that we should go off to school together, but early in the summer he confided to me that he was going to run away from home. His mother, whom he loved very dearly, had died when he was small. His father married a second wife, who died shortly afterwards. He then took a third wife. D——'s second stepmother was very kind to him, but his father, always harsh, grew harsher. I tried to dissuade my friend from his plan to leave home. I begged him to stick it out until he got off to school. However, he did run away and go to New York. And so I was doubly glad that Ricardo was going with me. On the night my mother was putting the final touches on my packing there was a rumbling sound; the house trembled and swayed; we rushed downstairs and out, and became aware that there was an earthquake. This was a part of the tremor that came to be known as the Charleston Earthquake, and bore no relation whatever to the fact that I was leaving Jacksonville.

Ricardo and I boarded the train that left Jacksonville at night and arrived in Atlanta the next morning. We had first-class tickets, and my father put us in the first-class car. (This was the year in which Florida passed its law separating the races in railroad cars, and it was just being put into operation; a matter that I, at least, was then ignorant of.) We had a good send-off; many of our friends, boys and girls, came to bid us good-by. My heart's desire, looking very pretty, was there, and kept quite close to my mother. I wonder if keeping close to my mother was one of those feminine traits that a girl of fifteen knows intuitively. At any rate, the effect on me was full, and I clearly remember how strangely I was stirred by this simple, perhaps incidental, matter of juxtaposition. We got aboard midst a lot of noisy chatter that enabled me to cover up my choked condition when I kissed my mother good-by.

The train pulled out and we settled down comfortably in one seat after having arranged our packages, among which was a box of lunch. In those days no one would think of boarding a train without a lunch, not even for a trip of two or three hours; and no lunch was a real lunch that did not consist of fried chicken, slices of buttered bread, hard-boiled eggs, a little paper of salt and pepper, an orange or two, and a piece of cake. We had a real lunch and were waiting only for the train to get fully under way before opening it. A number of colored people had got on the train but we were the only ones in the first-class car. Before we could open our lunch the conductor came round. I gave him the tickets, and he looked at them and looked at us. Then he said to me gruffly, "You had better get out of this car and into the one ahead." "But," I answered, "we have first-class tickets; and this is the first-class car, isn't it?" It is probable that the new law was very new to him, and he said not unkindly, "You'll be likely to have trouble if you try to stay in this car." Ricardo knew there was something wrong but didn't fully understand the conversation or the situation, and asked me, "*¿Que dice?*" (What is he saying?) I explained to him what the conductor was trying to make us do; we decided to stay where we were. But we did not have to enforce the decision. As soon as the conductor heard us speaking a foreign language, his attitude changed; he punched our tickets and gave them back, and treated us just as he did the other passengers in the car. We ate our lunch, lay back in our seats, and went to sleep. We didn't wake up until it was broad daylight and the engine was puffing its way up through the gullies of the red clay hills on which Atlanta sits.

This was my first impact against race prejudice as a concrete fact. Fifteen years later, an incident similar to the experience with this conductor drove home to me the conclusion that in such situations any kind of a Negro will do; provided he is not one who is an American citizen.

Atlanta disappointed me. It was a larger city than Jacksonville, but did not seem to me to be nearly so attractive. Many of the thoroughfares were still red clay roads. It was a long time before I grew accustomed to the bloody aspect of Atlanta's highways. Trees were rare and there was no city park or square within walking distance. The city was neither picturesque nor smart; it was merely drab. Atlanta University was a pleasant relief. The Confederate ramparts on the hill where the school was built had been leveled, the ground terraced, and grass and avenues of trees planted. The three main buildings were ivy-covered. Here was a spot fresh and beautiful, a rest for the eyes from what surrounded it, a green island in a dull, red sea. The University, as I was soon to learn, was a little world in itself, with ideas of social conduct and of the approach to life distinct from those of the city within which it was situated. When students or teachers stepped off the campus into West Mitchell Street, they underwent as great a transition as would have resulted from being instantaneously shot from a Boston drawing room into the wilds of Borneo. They had to make an immediate readjustment of many of their fundamental notions about life. When I was at the University, there were twenty-odd teachers, of whom all, except four, were white. These white teachers by eating at table with the students rendered themselves "unclean," not fit to sit at table with any Atlanta white family. The president was Horace Bumstead, a cultured gentleman, educated at Yale and in Germany, yet there was only one white door in all Atlanta thrown open to him socially, the door of a German family. No observance of caste in India was more cruelly rigid. The year before I entered, the state of Georgia had cut off its annual appropriation of $8000 because the school stood by its principles and refused to exclude the children of the white teachers from the regular classes.

I was at the University only a short time before I began to get an insight into the ramifications of race prejudice and an understanding of the American race problem. Indeed, it was in this early period that I received my initiation into the arena of "race." I perceived that education for me meant, fundamentally: preparation to meet the tasks and exigencies of life as a Negro, a realization of the peculiar responsibilities due to my own racial group, and a comprehension of the application of American democracy to Negro citizens. Of course, I had not been entirely ignorant of these conditions and requirements, but now they rose before me in such sudden magnitude as to seem absolutely new knowledge. This knowledge was no part of classroom instruction—the college course at Atlanta University was practically the old academic course at Yale; the founder of the school was Edmund Asa Ware, a Yale man, and the two following presidents were graduates of Yale—it was simply in the spirit of the institution; the atmosphere of the place was charged with it. Students talked "race." It was the subject of essays, orations, and debates. Nearly all that was acquired, mental and moral, was destined to be fitted into a particular system of which "race" was the center.

On the day of my arrival, the opening day, I took an examination and was assigned to the Junior Preparatory class. Ricardo was not examined. He was something of a puzzle. He had a good elementary education in Spanish, but no equivalent of it in English; so he was made a special student in one of the grammar school classes—the University then had such a department. For weeks he stuck to me as closely as he could; for he felt his status as a stranger more keenly than ever. His embarrassment seemed greatest in the dining hall, where he had to sit facing a whole row of girls. The dining hall was a large, bright room that took up the main part of the basement of North Hall, the girls' dormitory building. It was filled with long tables, at each of which ten or twelve girls sat on one side and about an equal number of boys on the other. Two teachers at a table acted as hosts; but there were not enough male teachers to go round, so at a number of tables an advanced student did the carving. And the position of carver was no sinecure. The various dishes of food were placed between the hosts. The carver asked each student, "What will you have?" The girls were served first. They were generally dainty and made certain choices. But from the boys' side there rolled out a monotonous repetition of "Some of each." Three-fourths of the boys would send back for a second helping with the request for "Some of each."

Ricardo and I talked Spanish at the table and this gave us pleasant notoriety; we could not have excited more curiosity and admiration had we been talking Attic Greek. Following strictly in the Yale tradition, the students at Atlanta University thought of a foreign language as something to be studied, not spoken. We were, naturally, assigned to the same room. It was a good-sized, clean, and comfortable room with a closet. In it were a table with a lamp, two chairs, a washstand with pitcher and basin, and a wooden slop-bucket. The floor was uncovered, except for a strip of carpet in front of the bed and an oil-cloth mat in front of the washstand. The walls were white and absolutely bare. There was not the slightest hint of decoration. The mattress on the bed was filled with fresh, sweet-smelling straw, and was fully two feet high before we started sleeping on it. When I first dived into it I felt as though I was plunging into the surf at Pablo Beach. We saw very little of each other during the day, except at meals; for on school days there were only about two hours, in the afternoons, that were not filled with duties of one kind or another. This proved to be the very thing that Ricardo needed, and he began mastering English with astonishing rapidity.

At some time during the day each student was required to put in one hour, at least, at work. It was the job of a group of a half-dozen boys to fill the wood bin in the kitchen every afternoon. We carried the wood in our arms, and I ruined a couple of good jackets keeping the kitchen fires burning. There was, however, an intangible recompense connected with this task that made us forget some of its irksomeness: the wood pile was located in the angle of the two wings of the girls' dormitory, and each boy could make a show of how much wood he could carry, while the unapproachable creatures looked down on him from their windows. I say "unapproachable," I ought to italicize the word, for there was no offense in the Atlanta University calendar that more perturbed the authorities than approaching a girl. A boy could see a girl upon a written application with the girl's name filled in, signed by himself and, if granted, countersigned by the president or dean. The caller was limited to twenty minutes in the parlor in North Hall; and he would find out that the matron was as particular about overtime as a long-distance telephone operator. He was also likely to overhear sundry remarks—in this day known as wisecracks—made by various girls as they passed to and fro in the halls and up and down the main staircase. For the "caller" could be spotted as soon as he struck the bridge on his way to North Hall, and word would be flashed from window to window and from room to room. If he was one of the constant sort, his visit did not arouse much interest, but, if he was of the other sort, it caused great speculation. Had the girls known how to gamble, they might have had exciting times betting on who the particular girl would be.

I found this whole procedure humiliating, and I made it a point of honor not to make out an application to call on a girl—a resolution I broke only twice during my six years, and for reasons that appeared to be sufficiently exigent. It might seem that these repressive regulations would have incited "sexy" talk among the boys, but they did not. The boys did talk a great deal about the girls across the bridge, but the talk was always on an expurgated, I might say, emasculated level. This was not prudery; it was idealism, and there was in it, too, something of an innate racial trait. There was an amazing absence of realistic discussion of sex; and no boy would have dared to bring the girls of North Hall into such a discussion. North Hall girls, love, and sex formed one of the spiritual mysteries. I remember that one day I was corrected by an older student in a group when I spoke of one of the teachers as "Miss." "We call her 'Miss' but she is really Mrs.," he said. This teacher was badly deformed, and, when I expressed mild surprise that she had found a husband, the whole group came down on my head. They pointed out to me that *true love* and physical passion were entirely distinct and unrelated—a doctrine that I found fully and forcibly set forth in the textbook on moral philosophy that I took up later in my course. This Sir Galahad attitude of the Atlanta University boys of that time appears to me in the present age in the light of a phenomenon.

The longest stretch of free time we had on school days was the two-hour period between the work hour and supper. The time on Sundays was pretty well filled; preaching in the morning, Sunday school in the afternoon, and prayer meeting at night. The couple of hours before the morning service we often whiled away walking about the campus, a sixty-five acre tract, part of it wooded. Saturday was our big day. We had to work two hours in the morning, but dinner was served at 1 o'clock and we had the whole afternoon up to supper time at 6. On Saturday afternoons during the fall there was usually a baseball game on. The baseball season closed with a big game on Thanksgiving Day. (We knew nothing about football until four or five years later, when it was encouraged by Professor Adams, who had been a player at Dartmouth.) These games were attended by the girls as well as the boys, and by crowds of townspeople. During the winter months Saturday afternoons were devoted to calling on friends in the city by those fortunate enough to know any Atlanta families. The girls also had the privilege, by permission, of visiting friends in town on this half-holiday. We would put on our best clothes—for Saturday not Sunday was the day we dressed up—and sally forth immediately after dinner. These afternoons formed one of the pleasantest parts of our student life; we met nice people, we would likely be offered something good to eat, and we ran a chance of meeting by accident, perhaps not wholly by accident, certain of the North Hall girls who might be visiting mutual friends.

I had been at the University a couple of weeks when, without notice, D—— appeared with his father. He had returned home from his runaway trip, and his father had agreed to let him come to Atlanta. I was glad and he was glad, for it meant that the thing we had dreamed about had come to pass. I took him to the matron, where we arranged to have a cot for him put in the room occupied by Ricardo and me. Three in a room made it a bit crowded, but the slight inconvenience didn't bother us because he was so anxious to tell me about his adventure in running away, and I wanted to talk to him about things at the University, most of them things that Ricardo would not be interested in or even understand. A good many nights, after lights were out and Ricardo had fallen asleep, D—— and I talked in subdued tones. In these talks we began to lay plans for the future: we would finish at Atlanta University, then we would study law and form a partnership.

D—— was assigned to the Freshman class; and I thought with vexation of the time I had lost with Mr. Culp as my teacher. He had some conditions to make up because Cookman Institute standards were not on a par with those of the preparatory school at the University, but this was no serious handicap for his quick mind, in fact, so quick that it often sped lightly over what should have been laboriously explored.

A few days after D——'s arrival I saw in the papers that the St. Louis Browns and another big league team were to play an exhibition game in Atlanta. I became feverish with desire to see them play. I especially wanted to see Arlie Latham, the famous third baseman of the Browns. Neither D—— nor Ricardo was much of a player, but they were both fans and caught my enthusiasm to see this game; in addition, it meant a half-day out of school for the three of us. I wrote out the application to be excused and took it to the proper authority. That authority, for the time, was Professor Francis. He read the application, looked up at me with his sharp, dark eyes, then read the application again, presumably, to be sure he had read it aright the first time. Meanwhile, there ran through my mind some of the things I had already picked up about him from the older boys. He was disliked by the majority because he was regarded as a snooper. It was said that he walked about the halls of the boys' dormitory at night with rubbers on; that he was not above listening at keyholes; that nothing delighted him more than to "find out something," and that he had tracked down numberless plots and acts against the established order of the institution. It was felt that he had no understanding of or sympathy with boyhood, and known that he made no allowances for the deeds done by those still in that semi-savage state. He was the university pastor and was not far from fanaticism in his religious zeal. The unpopularity of Professor Francis was offset by the popularity of Professor Chase, our teacher of Greek. Mr. Chase was a stocky man with a head like the pictured one of the poet Aristophanes. His ruddy face held two merry eyes and was fringed by a cropped, reddish beard. On cold days he wore a shawl in the manner of Abraham Lincoln. He spoke haltingly, but was always eloquent in his defense of the boys. It may have been more than a coincidence that the two most understanding men—from a boy's point of view—at Atlanta during my time were both from Dartmouth, Professor Chase and Professor Adams. It was the latter who gave us our first lessons in the finer points of football. Mr. Francis was from Yale, and was the embodiment of all the stern virtues then traditional of that great school.

This was my first personal contact with Mr. Francis, and the contact made it hard to believe him to be as bad as he was painted. While he pondered my application, I shyly studied him. I was a little awestruck. He, like Mr. Chase, was stocky and had a Greek philosopher's head, but his complexion was pallid, his eyes piercing, and his short beard—all the men teachers, except two, wore beards of varying hues—was dark and tinged with gray. He was gentle and softspoken; in fact, he almost purred when he spoke. I noted a furtiveness in his glance and manner that I afterwards recognized as a marked characteristic. While I waited he squirmed round in his swivel chair, frowned, plucked at his beard, and, picking up a ruler from his desk, gave his skull several resounding whacks. Then he turned and informed me in a kindly way that he had been connected with the University from its founding and that never before in its history had such a request been made—a request to be absent from classes to attend a ball game. Also he gave me to understand that had I been longer steeped in the spirit of the institution I would not have dreamed of making it. Perhaps my innocence or my ignorance appealed to him or it may have been that he was, after all, a humorist in disguise; at any rate, he turned suddenly to his desk and countersigned the application. I left his office hurriedly with the precious scrap of paper tucked away in my pocket. Among the three of us there was sufficient worldly wisdom to make us keep our holiday a secret.

There was a large crowd at the ball grounds, but we were there early and got good seats. On the way Ricardo bought a package of cigarettes and, as soon as we were seated, he and D—— lit up and began smoking. They, of course, offered me a smoke, but I declined. Furthermore, I tried to dissuade them, and once or twice snatched the lighted cigarettes from their mouths and threw them away. This last resort roused considerable anger in Ricardo, and he rolled at me a string of sonorous and untranslatable Spanish oaths. Now, I was not being actuated by any goody-goody motive. It was true that each of us on entering the University had signed the compulsory pledge to abstain from alcoholic drinks, tobacco, and profanity; and I did have some regard for my pledge; but of, at least, equal weight was my knowledge that smoking was considered an offense meriting suspension or even expulsion, and, as my knowledge on this point was, I knew, fuller than theirs, I was trying my best to give my two friends the benefit of it.

We were delighted with the game. Arlie Latham fulfilled all our expectations of him, both as a baseball player and comedian. We returned to the University happy and after supper got great satisfaction out of relating to our envious fellow students the story of the game.

The next day I was called to the president's office. I stood waiting while Mr. Francis fumbled over the papers on his desk as though he was searching anxiously for an important misplaced document. While still fumbling and not looking up he said to me very quietly, "Johnson, what about the smoking at the ball grounds yesterday?" I was astounded. If I had been given an instant in which to collect myself I should have responded with a straightforward, honest lie, in full keeping with the code of honor of normal boys, but he continued talking and rehearsed the whole scene as it had taken place, and even the conversation, almost word for word. I was stupefied. The three of us had looked around quite carefully when the smoking began, and had seen no one that we knew. I felt that I was witnessing a feat of black magic. Mr. Francis dismissed me without further questioning, and I went out wondering if he was going to press the matter or was merely giving me a confirming demonstration of his reputed powers as a detective. I am sure now that he did get a great kick out of the interview; and I suspect that all of his similar exploits were a source of great pleasure. When I left him I also knew that I had, undeservedly, gone up to the top notch in his estimation.

As soon as I could get to D—— and Ricardo I told them that the cat was out of the bag and jumping; and I gave them the best tip I could as to the direction she was taking. Their mystification was as great as mine. That night we talked of nothing else. Ricardo was indifferent about the outcome; Atlanta University didn't mean more to him than the privilege of smoking meant. What stirred him most was curiosity as to how Mr. Francis knew. But D—— was much concerned; he had just patched things up with his father, who not unreluctantly had agreed to send him to college; and he knew that his future and our joint plans for the future were at stake. He and I hoped that the incident was closed. Our hope rested on the fact that neither he nor Ricardo had been sent for. However, we decided that there was no use in going up against the indubitable powers possessed by Mr. Francis, and if they were sent for the only thing to do would be to make a clean breast of it. The summons came the following afternoon. Ricardo went in the strength of his indifference and D—— in the weakness of his concern. Mr. Francis rehearsed the scene and conversation over for them; and, as with me, gave not the slightest hint as to how the matter had become manifest to him. D—— was repentant, but Ricardo stated as plainly as possible that education or no education, he couldn't get along without smoking. He clinched his statement by saying, "Meester Francis, I wass born weet de cigarette in de mout." They were both admonished and reprieved. I think it was Ricardo's indifference rather than D——'s penitence that saved them. I am sure that Mr. Francis anticipated with pride that in the next catalogue of Atlanta University would be listed, "Ricardo Rodriguez Ponce, Havana, Cuba." And there was no way of punishing the compliant D—— while sparing the recalcitrant Ricardo.

I began my course in manual training in the carpenter shop. I enjoyed going to the industrial building as much as to any of my classes, except my Latin class. I had no exceptional difficulty with mathematics and I was interested in the subject, but I found that I had a love for language, and Latin meant more for me than mere class work. It was the same when I came to Greek, and French and German. Besides, I had found Latin to be my "snap" course. The similarity to Spanish, especially in the principal verbs, made it relatively easy for me; and through Caesar and Cicero and Vergil and Horace and Tacitus and Livy I read at sight many lines that cost my classmates much thumbing of dictionary and grammar. Work at the shops was fascinating. I liked the bright, sharp tools, the peculiar fragrance that clings to a carpenter's chest, the good smell of the wood as the saw cut into it or as the shavings came curling up through the plane, and the experience of making things. I caught glimpses of boys working at the forges, at the turning lathes and at the draughting tables. I was intensely interested in it all, and more than once wished that my father, who believed in a trade for every boy, could see me at work.

I had been going to the shops for quite a while before I saw the engineer; that is, the man who had charge of the engine room. He was a colored man, light yellow, with a mass of black hair, and a melancholy expression of the face that was deepened by a long, dark, drooping mustache. He looked like a reformed pirate, or as a pirate ought to look if he reformed. At first glance I wondered where I had seen the face before; I racked my brain, but, to my great irritation, could not tell. The rest of the day and somewhat through the night that face puzzled and haunted me. The next day at the shops I saw the man and looked at him long and hard. What happened? Did he for an instant give off a flicker that had already been caught on the film of my memory? I cannot say, but in a flash I knew him. He was the man who sat directly behind the three of us at the baseball game. In a following flash the workings of the occult powers of Mr. Francis were revealed in broad daylight, and they looked pretty mean.

On the ground floor of Stone Hall, the main building, was the general study room. It accommodated, perhaps, three hundred students, and was furnished with modern individual desks and chairs. In this room the boys and girls of the Preparatory and Normal departments sat and studied during school hours; from it they filed out on bells to the various classrooms for recitation. The daily devotional exercises were held there. The general study room was in charge of John Young, a graduate of the University and an instructor in Latin. Mr. Young was one of the handsomest men I have ever known—and he was one of the two men teachers who did not wear short beards. He had made a reputation as an excellent scholar and a fine athlete. All the boys were proud of him, and half the girls were in love with him. During my Middle Prep year he was preparing himself to go to Harvard for his Master's degree—the degree of Doctor of Philosophy was not then the *sine qua non* of the teaching profession. He expected to return to Atlanta as a full professor of Latin. He did enter Harvard, but died before he had finished the year—of a broken heart, they said; but that is another story. Students in the College department studied in their rooms and went over to Stone Hall for recitations. The study room and recitation rooms of the Grammar department were located in South Hall, the boys' dormitory building.

The big room in Stone Hall was a pleasant place for study. The greatest distraction for a boy was the presence of so many pretty girls. Certainly, I had seen girls before, but their place in the scheme of things had been extrinsic, casual, subsidiary. Now, all at once, they assumed a vital position. They kept up a constant assault on the center of my thoughts. I could relegate them to their old place when I was on the baseball field or with a group of boys on the campus or at work in the shops, even when reciting with them in class; but sitting silent in the study room I fell, whether I would or not, under their pervasive and disquieting allure. Of course, there was the natural explanation; but more than biology was involved; there was also an element of aesthetics. The majority of these girls came from the best-to-do colored families of Georgia and the surrounding states. They really made up a selected group. Atlanta University was widely known as a school that attracted this type. As a result, the proportion of tastefully dressed, good-mannered, good-looking girls was very high. I had never seen their like in such numbers. To look at them evoked a satisfying pleasure. They ranged in color from ebony black to milk white. At one end of the scale eyes were dark and hair crisp, and at the other, eyes were blue or gray and the hair light and like fine spun silk. The bulk of them ran the full gamut of all the shades and nuances of brown, with wavy hair and the liquid velvet eyes so characteristic of women of Negro blood. There was a warmth of beauty in this variety and blend of color and shade that no group of white girls could kindle. I have been in far places and lived in strange lands since I sat in that study room in Stone Hall but the idea has grown stronger and stronger that, perhaps, the perfection of the human female is reached in the golden-hued and ivory-toned colored women of the United States, in whom there is a fusion of the fierceness in love of blond women with the responsiveness of black.

The thing of essential value that I got out of sitting through two years in this big room did not come from what I studied, but from the increasing power I gained to apply my mind to what I was studying, the power to shut out from it what I willed. This, of course, is the known power without which there can be but small achievement of intellectual or spiritual growth. And I have since found in it a boon; the ability to withdraw from the crowd while within its midst has never failed to yield me the subtlest and serenest of pleasures.

I was not long in finding my rank as a fellow student; and that is a rank not less important than the one in scholarship. It is, at any rate, a surer indicator of how the future man or woman is going to be met by the world. I found that I possessed a prestige entirely out of proportion to my age and class. Among the factors to which this could be attributed were: my prowess as a baseball pitcher, my ability to speak a foreign language, and the presumable superiority in worldly wisdom that having lived in New York gave me. I think, at the time, D—— and

I were the only students who could boast of first-hand knowledge of the great city. I could boast of having traveled even to a foreign country. Another factor was my having a college student as my chum and roommate. D—— was only three months older than I, but he was more mature and far more sophisticated. Indeed, in his youth his face began to wear a jaded appearance; and, as a young man, he had a very low droop to the corners of his mouth. He had an unlimited self-assurance, while I was almost diffident; and he had inherited or acquired a good share of his father's roughness and coarseness. He had a racy style of speech, which I envied; but many of his choicest expressions I was unable to form in my own mouth. D—— was a *rara avis* at Atlanta University; nothing like him had ever before been seen in that cage. Yet he was popular with the boys and the girls, and, strange to say, even with the teachers. His very rakishness had a definite charm. And underneath his somewhat ribald manner he was tender-hearted and generous. Moreover, he was extremely good-looking, having, in fact, a sort of Byronic beauty. He was short and inclined to stoutness. When he was a small boy, he was fat. His head, large out of proportion to his height, was covered with thick, dark brown hair that set off his pale face and fine hazel eyes. The only thing that marred his looks was the frequent raising of the drooping corners of his mouth in a cynical curl. But speaking of his face as pale does not convey the full truth; for neither in color, features, nor hair could one detect that he had a single drop of Negro blood.

D—— was entirely at ease with the older boys and the young men of the College department; and in his take-it-for-granted way he made an opening with them for me. So almost from the start my closest associates were not among the boys of the Prep school but among the students of the College classes. I became the acknowledged fifth member of a combination made up of two Juniors, a Sophomore, and D——, calling themselves the "Big Four." We grouped ourselves whenever and wherever possible. We exchanged stories, information, and confidences; and we borrowed each other's money, generally for the purpose of paying for a late supper. Why a boy in boarding school can never get enough to eat will, I suppose, always remain a question. The meals in the dining room were never stinted, but we were always ready for a late, clandestine supper. There was an old man named Watson, whose job it was to tend the fine herd of cows owned by the school. He and his wife lived in a little house on the campus. We called this house "Little Delmonico" because the good woman, who was also a good cook, furnished on short notice a supper of fried chicken, hot biscuits, and all the milk we could drink for fifteen cents. Whenever we had the money, we were ready to run the gantlet after lights were out for one of these suppers. Terms were cash, but we paid willingly; and without seeking to know whence came the milk—or the chickens either. We also passed many hours in the room of one or the other of us playing whist or seven-up, with shades drawn, hat over keyhole, crack under door chinked, and muffled voices; for playing cards was listed among the cardinal sins. But the greater part of our time together was spent seriously. We talked the eternal race question over and over, yet always found something else to say on the subject. We discussed our ambitions, and speculated upon our chances of success; each one reassuring the others that they could not fail. There was established a bond of comradeship—among men, a nobler and more enduring bond than friendship.

It is not difficult for me to blot out forty-five years and sit again with these comrades of my youth. There is A——, tall, fair, slender, and elegant... peering near-sightedly through his heavy, gold-rimmed spectacles, but with his agile mind always balancing the possibilities and discovering the vantage. And H——, tall, too, but bronze-colored, broad-shouldered, heavy-jowled... in comparison with the ready, fluent A——, cumbrous of speech, using an almost Johnsonian vocabulary, and, when roused, vehemently eloquent. T——, brown, short, and jolly, with gray eyes looking out quizzically from his moon-round face... speaking in anecdotes as wiser men had spoken in parables... always fresh stories, stories of black and white in the South, stories which, although we roared at them, we knew to have their points buried deep in the heart of the race question. And D——, worldly-wise, dare-devilish, self-confident, and combative... invincible on his own ground, but in danger when he exposed a superficial knowledge of other things to the adroitness of A——, to the honest logic and common sense of H——, to the humor of T——, before which what any one of the rest of us posited might be blown away like dust before a strong puff of breath. We talked, we argued, we nursed ambitions and dreams; but none of us could foretell. There is no way of getting a peep behind that dark curtain, which simply recedes with each step we take toward it; leaving in front all that we can ever know. In truth, if some mysterious being had appeared in our midst and announced to A—— that he would rise to the highest office in the church; to H—— that he was to become the most influential and powerful Negro of his time in our national politics; to T—— that he was to have his heart's desire granted in being widely recognized as a typically brilliant Georgia country lawyer; and to D—— that he was to be one of the most prosperous colored lawyers in the country, a member of the Jacksonville city council, and an important factor in Florida politics, we should all, probably, have been incredulous—but that is exactly what was behind the dark curtain. And it was also behind the dark curtain that before these lines would be written each of the four would have passed beyond the boundary of past, present, and future.

I now began to get my bearings with regard to the world and particularly with regard to my own country. I began to get the full understanding of my relationship to America, and to take on my share of the peculiar responsibilities and burdens additional to those of the common lot, which every Negro in the United States is compelled to carry. I began my mental and spiritual training to meet and cope not only with the hardships that are common, but with planned wrong, concerted injustice, and applied prejudice. Here was a deepening, but narrowing experience; an experience so narrowing that the inner problem of a Negro in America becomes that of not allowing it to choke and suffocate him. I am glad that this fuller impact of the situation came to me as late as it did, when my apprehension of it could be more or less objective. As an American Negro, I consider the most fortunate thing in my whole life to be the fact that through childhood I was reared free from undue fear of or esteem for white people as a race; otherwise, the deeper implications of American race prejudice might have become a part of my subconscious as well as of my conscious self.

I began also in this period to find myself, to think of life not only as it touched me from without but also as it moved me from within. I went in for reading, and spent many of the winter afternoons that settle down so drearily on the bleak hills of North Georgia absorbed in a book. The university library was then the Graves Memorial Library. It contained ten thousand or so volumes, an array of books that seemed infinite to me. Many of the titles snared me, but I was often disappointed to find that the books were written from the point of view of divine revelation and Christian dogma or with a bald moral purpose. Among all the books in the Graves Library it was from books of fiction that I gained the greatest satisfaction. I read more Dickens; I read George Eliot; I read *Vanity Fair,* and that jewel among novels, *Lorna Doone.* It was during this period that I also read with burning interest Alphonse Daudet's *Sapho,* a book which was not in the library but was owned by one of the boys and circulated until it was all but worn out. The episode in which Sapho is carried up the flight of stairs left a disquieting impression on my mind that lingered long.

Before I left Stanton I had begun to scribble. I had written a story about my first plug (derby) hat. Mr. Artrell thought it was fine, and it made a hit when I read it before the school. Now an impulse set me at writing poetry, and I filled several notebooks with verses. I looked over these juvenilia recently and noted that the first of my poems opened with these three lines:

> Miserable, miserable, weary of life,
> Worn with its turmoil, its din and its strife,
> And with its burden of grief.

I did not follow this vein. Perhaps even then I sensed that there was already an over-supply of poetry by people who mistake a torpid liver for a broken heart, and frustrated sex desires for yearnings of the soul. I wrote a lot of verses lampooning certain students and teachers and conditions on the campus. However, the greater part of my output consisted of rather ardent love poems. A number of these latter circulated with success in North Hall, and brought me considerable prestige as a gallant. It has struck me that the potency possessed by a few, fairly well written lines of passionate poetry is truly astounding, and altogether disproportionate to what really goes into the process of producing them. It is probable that the innate hostility of the average man toward the poet has its basis in this fact.

My chief shortcoming as an Atlanta University student I quickly recognized. It was my inaptitude as a public speaker. I was astonished to see boys no older than I rise and without fear or hesitation discourse upon weighty subjects; the weightier the subject, the more fluent the discourse. All the outstanding university orators were personages. They thrilled the large audiences that filled the chapel on special occasions; and the applause they received was without question a higher kind of approbation than the cheers given the players on the baseball field. The renown of several of the best speakers had spread beyond Atlanta. I determined to make as much of an orator out of myself as possible. I joined the Ware Lyceum, the debating society of the Preps, and looked forward to the time when I might shine in the Phi Kappa, the College society. I do not brag when I say that I achieved a measure of success. The first time I took part in a debate in the Ware Lyceum I was almost as terror-stricken as I was when I attempted my first Sunday school recitation. In my Sophomore year I won first prize in the principal oratorical contest; and in the following year I gained a tie with another speaker for that honor. Before I left Atlanta I had learned what every orator must know: that the deep secret of eloquence is rhythm—rhythm, set in motion by the speaker, that sets up a responsive rhythm in his audience. For the purpose of sheer persuasion, it is far more important than logic. There is now doubt as to whether or not oratory is an art—curiously, it is the only art in which the South as a section has gained and held preeminence—if it may still be classed among the arts, it is surely the least of them all. Oratory, it cannot be denied, has its uses; it has been of tremendous use to me. But the older I grow, the more I am inclined to get away from it. For rhetorical oratory I have absolute distrust. My faith in the soundness of judgment in a man addicted to opium could not be less than that in a man addicted to rhetorical oratory. Rhetorical oratory is the foundation upon which all the humbug in our political system rests.

These new activities crowded out music, and I hardly ever touched the piano during all my student days. I did, however, keep my guitar with me, and played it often. In my last two or three years I sang bass on the college quartet. I gave only the time required by the rules to religious observance. I attended all the Sunday services, because they were compulsory; but the Wednesday night prayer meetings, group prayer meetings in the reception room of the matron, and other voluntary activities I renounced. I did this at some cost. The school was founded in the missionary spirit and, although the original zeal had subsided, it was still quite high. Students who were religiously observant still enjoyed certain preferences. I am sure that I lowered Mr. Francis's first estimate of me very much; and he was, at the time, the administrative head of the institution. The preaching service on Sunday mornings was sometimes interesting. Not so much could I say for Sunday school in the afternoons. I already knew by heart the Bible stories and the lessons for the young to be drawn from them. The Sunday evening prayer meetings bored me terribly. They were conducted by Mr. Francis, and included the singing of hymns (in which he always joined loudly, and also always in a different key), a religious talk by him on student conduct, and brief admonitions by certain of the students to the others. Some students fulfilled their obligations by repeating Bible verses. These quotations were most often apropos of no subject under consideration.

I doubt not that there were students who enjoyed these prayer meetings and were spiritually benefited, but I believe the main effect was to put a premium on hypocrisy or, almost as bad, to substitute for religion a lazy and stupid conformity. I remember that in my Middle Prep year, being, for reasons that I shall presently relate, without a roommate, the matron assigned to me a new student, a loutish young fellow, in order that he might come under my refining influence; that is, by example or otherwise, I was to be the inculcator of proper ideas about bathing, changing clothes, keeping teeth brushed and shoes shined, and about other niceties that would bring him up to Atlanta University standards. A good many new boys stood in need of this kind of tutorship. A few of the boys from the back country, who all their lives had been passing in and out of their houses over one or two steps at most, had to learn even how to go up and down stairs. I have seen such boys, generally free and easy in their movements, clinging desperately to the handrail while they painfully made their way up or down; and I realized that people who trip lightly up and down long flights of stairs are really performing a difficult acrobatic stunt, mastered by long years of practice. There was not much in common between me and my new roommate, but I did my best to be faithful to my trust. Each night during study hour he would sit gloomily pondering his books for a while, then would undress and kneel down to say his prayers. And each night after I had finished studying I would wake him up and make him get into bed. One night I didn't feel very well, and went to bed first, leaving him to finish studying and say his prayers. When the rising bell woke me the next morning he was still on his knees. The time it took to get him awake and limbered up enough to dress himself made me late for breakfast.

One day late in the spring, not far from commencement time, I received another summons to see Mr. Francis in his office. I was curious but not worried. When I appeared before him, he was more direct and accusatory than he was on the former similar occasion. He at once put to me a series of questions that sounded like an echo of that famous list once propounded by Cicero to Catiline.

"Where were you yesterday afternoon?"

"Well, I was called to practice with the team, and I spent most of the afternoon on the ball field."

"Didn't you go out on West Hunter Street sometime during the afternoon?"

"No, sir."

"Didn't you go with some other boys to a place where you bought a bottle of wine and drank it, and smoked cigarettes?"

"No, sir."

The interview ended with Mr. Francis somewhat nonplussed. I was ignorant of what may have happened, but I saw D—— right away and told him about the inquisition I had been put through. His face blanched. He had not breathed a word to me; and now he did not need to. The "Big Four" got together at night, and I met with them. The facts were: the four had the afternoon before walked far out on West Hunter Street—this section of it only a clay road leading into the country—to a place where an old German (he may have been an Italian) cultivated a small vineyard and manufactured home-made wine; they had bought a bottle of his wine, drunk it, and smoked cigarettes. The meeting resolved itself into a board of strategy. We discussed the matter from every angle. I ventured the opinion that Mr. Francis, judging from the questions he had asked me, had firsthand knowledge of the whole affair. It was decided that one of the number be sent out to the old vintner to find out just what the situation was. T—— was selected to go. The night was stormy. We waited anxiously with lights out for him to return. It would have been better if any one of the others had gone and left T—— to keep our spirits up. He came back wet, spattered and stained with red clay. His report confirmed our worst fears. Mr. Francis had been out and seen the old man, and wheedled and wrung from him all that had taken place. The old man had given descriptions of persons, not names, because he didn't know the names. And that explained why I had been called; he had described one of the boys as having gray eyes, and my gray eyes being the most pronounced feature of my face had led Mr. Francis to send for me. How he overlooked the fact that T——'s eyes were gray we could not say. Probably, too, the old man repeated to Mr. Francis the first names, as well as he could remember them, that he heard the boys address each other by.

The evidence appeared to be overwhelming. How Mr. Francis got his first clue we never found out. Maybe he saw the four boys leave the campus together, and shadowed them. It is possible that some neighbor or some passerby saw the boys go into the old vintner's place, and reported the fact. Professor Chase pleaded for the boys in the faculty meeting that tried the case with tears streaming down his cheeks. But Mr. Francis with a majority could not be moved; and each of the four received a sentence of indefinite suspension. That night all of them showed wretchedness. T—— did attempt a story or two, but for the first time his efforts failed to provoke even a smile. D——, despite his superb self-confidence, was terribly broken up. He thought with dread of the effect of the news on his relations with his father. Through a part of the night he wept quietly, and I wept with him. The verdict cast a gloom over the whole school. Four such boys could not be sent away from a very small college without making a mighty hole in it. None of the four ever went back to Atlanta University.

I sometimes speculate on what might have happened had I not been called for baseball practice that spring afternoon. Would I have gone with the "Big Four"? If I had, would I have stood out? Would I have tried to dissuade them, and if so, could I have succeeded? Or would I have followed along and been sent away too? Of course, I cannot answer any one of these questions. But I do know that I have always been glad that I did not make myself liable for such punishment. For, in spite of petty regulations and a puritanical zeal, Atlanta University was an excellent school. In spite of the fact that its code of moral conduct was as narrow as it was high, it was an excellent school. Its reputation for thorough work and scholarship was unsurpassed by any similar institution in the country; and the breadth of the social ideas that it carried out practically was, perhaps, unequaled. I have at times thought that, in some degree, its training might have cramped and inhibited me. But generally I have felt that for me there was probably no better school in the United States.

There is now and has been for some time a cry going up against the inadequacy of our school methods and their results. Without doubt, there is ground for complaint. But, at the same time, it is too easy to lose sight of the fact that not the school nor the teachers, but the student is the preponderant factor in education. The student who claims that he is handicapped or miscast for life through the mere inadequacy of the methods used for his instruction would not have profited discernibly more from the most superior methods in vogue or, as yet, only on paper. A good share of the complaint against the elementary schools rises out of the disappointment of fond and overambitious parents who look for a miracle. No kind of school can do the impossible; and any school that turns out the bulk of its students with a fair degree of developed mental and physical control may feel well satisfied with its work. In the higher institutions, teaching increases in importance as a factor; there must be both great teachers and capable students for the achievement of real education, but great teachers are almost as rare as great philosophers.

PART SIX

POLITICAL WRITING

POLITICAL WRITING: *NEGRO AMERICANS, WHAT NOW?*

Published in 1934, *Negro Americans, What Now?* is James Weldon Johnson's last major published work. As such, it is the distillation of his best thinking and writing in the genre of political writing. Other examples of Johnson's political writing include his editorials and such works as "Self-Determining Haiti" (1920), a report he wrote in his first year as Executive Secretary of the NAACP, which was published as four articles in *The Nation.* Reprinted here in its entirety, "the pamphlet," as Johnson called *Negro Americans, What Now?,* is a superbly reasoned, elegant, and concise summation of his views on what he terms the "American question," that is, the realization of full citizenship rights for African Americans. Addressing himself to African Americans, Johnson asserts that the "present time demands a plain and reasoned statement of the facts and an endeavour to devise ways and means to meet those facts." In the writing of this meditation on the state of the race, as it were, Johnson's chief objective is to outline "the racial situation as it exists today," and to point "to the ways which, I believe, lead out."

In masterful fashion, Johnson weighs the pro and cons of immigration and physical rebellion, of isolation and integration. He also offers a balanced assessment of such black institutions as the church and the press. In addition, he sets forth a vision of the kind of education that would best prepare black youth for leadership; methods for establishing meaningful relationships with American business and labor that would advance his goal of full social and political equality for African Americans; and the role of culture in realizing his program of group rights that seeks to establish a harmony with individual rights.

One of the important contributions that Johnson makes to black political discourse in *Negro Americans, What Now?* is what I would term his theory of citizenship, one which he offers as a model for all Americans. Johnson's theory of citizenship is called cosmopolitanism, which he believes is essential to the creation and maintenance of racial cooperation. He offers the following observations regarding the challenges and opportunities of cosmopolitanism:

> The establishment and maintenance of friendly interracial intercourse cannot be brought about without overcoming difficulties. The accomplishment at once demands of both sides a considerable cosmopolitanism of spirit and intellect. It is easy to live within the strict limits of one's own group; one knows its language; its language of words and of ideas; one knows all the questions that will come up and the answers; one does not have to extend himself. Social and intellectual intercourse on even the outskirts of cosmopolitanism is a more strenuous matter; and that is one of the reasons why most human beings prefer parochialism.

Writing of the social and political effects of a commitment to cosmopolitanism, Johnson maintains that out of "these relations have come numerous fine and lasting friendships and an effect on the whole race situation that is far-reaching, though it may not be entirely manifest."

Johnson's theory of citizenship or cosmopolitanism is enjoying a new vogue among scholars in the humanities and the social sciences. The new applications and adaptations of Johnson's concept of citizenship is additional evidence of his enduring relevance. In *Negro Americans, What Now?*, Johnson establishes the clear and powerful relationship between race and rights as well as sets forth a means of advancing the ideals of American democracy through the practice of a theory of citizenship he termed cosmopolitanism.

FOREWORD

It is not my intention that the title of this pamphlet should carry a prohibitive significance. Probably some white Americans will read what I have written. The significance of my title is that I am not particularly concerned with whether they do or do not. I am writing directly to my fellow Negro Americans, and on the American question which most deeply affects them.

To you, my fellows—

What I shall write will be put in the simplest, clearest, most economic English that I can use. If this little book should happen to fall into the hands of a Negro youth in the darkest center of the land, I should like to have him able not only to read it but to understand it. There was a day when rhetoric and oratory constituted the most generally used solvent for our problem. Indeed, for many years the problem was nightly "solved" by hundreds of orators on hundreds of platforms. That day is past. We know that the present time demands a plain and reasoned statement of the facts and an endeavor to devise ways and means to meet those facts.

I do not offer this pamphlet as a program. I do not believe that any one man or set of men can formulate a complete and practicable program. The most that can be done is to lay down certain lines along which a program may be worked out. This is all that I have here undertaken. Nor shall I devote any part of this booklet to cataloguing the wrongs we suffer and the humiliations that are put upon us. I do not rehearse them for the simple reason that we all know them by heart. The thing we seek to know is: what to do about them.

In the following pages I have, with the least possible amount of historical preliminaries and references and as fully as the brief compass of the pamphlet allows, outlined the racial situation as it exists today, and pointed to the ways which, I believe, lead out.

JAMES WELDON JOHNSON
Fisk University,
Nashville, Tennessee,
June 1934.

Negro Americans, What Now?

CHAPTER I
CHOICES

The world today is in a state of semi-chaos. We Negro Americans as a part of the world are affected by that state. We are affected by it still more vitally as a special group. We are not so sanguine about our course and our goal as we were a decade ago. We are floundering. We are casting about for ways of meeting the situation, both as Americans and as Negroes. In this casting about we have discovered and rediscovered a number of ways to which we have given more or less consideration. Let us see if we cannot by elimination reduce confusion and narrow down the limits of choice to what might be shown to be the one sound and wisc linc to follow.

EXODUS

Exodus has for generations been recurrently suggested as a method for solving the race problem. At the present time there is being fomented by some person or persons in Chicago a plan based on the idea of colonization. The plan calls for the setting aside of a state or territory of the United States exclusively for Negro Americans.

The idea of physical separation of the races as a solution antedates the Revolutionary War. Thomas Jefferson strongly expressed himself in favor of the colonization of the Negroes in some area on the coast of Africa. The first attempt, however, to put colonization into effect was made by Paul Cuffe, a free Negro and a shipowner of New Bedford, Massachusetts, who in 1815 transported at his own expense nine families to Africa. The first attempt on a grand scale was made in 1820, with the American Colonization Society and the United States government behind it—an attempt that culminated in the establishment of Liberia. At the outbreak of the Civil War there was another effort, fostered by a group within the race, and some two thousand colonists sought refuge in Haiti. The latest of the attempts on a large scale was the Garvey Movement. All of these efforts practically failed; that is, they had no effect on the problem and in no degree changed the condition of the race in the United States.

A century and a quarter ago deportation of the free Negroes might have been feasible; a half century later *that* was not a practicable undertaking; today the deportation or exodus of the Negro American population is an utter impossibility. Not within a bounded period could twelve million people be transported; and before that period was over the total number would be well above twelve million. Nor is there any place to which to take them. There are no more "vacant" places on earth; and no government in the world, with the barest possibility of Brazil as the exception, would welcome even one-twelfth the whole number; Liberia would no doubt be as reluctant as any. None of the tribes of colonial Africa would relish sharing their best lands with us merely because we and they are of somewhat the same complexion. The United States government might purchase territory somewhere and deport us. But that would involve a pretty stiff political job and a financial expenditure that would make the figures of the National Recovery program look small.

We may cross out exodus as a possible solution. We and the white people may as well make up our minds definitely that we, the same as they, are in this country to stay. We may be causing white America some annoyance, but we ourselves are not passing the time in undisturbed comfort. White America will simply have to sustain a situation that is of its own making, not ours.

PHYSICAL FORCE

Our history in the United States records a half-dozen major and a score of minor efforts at insurrection during the period of slavery. This, if they heard it, would be news to that big majority of people who believe that we have gone through three centuries of oppression without once thinking in terms of rebellion or lifting a finger in revolt. Even now there come times when we think in terms of physical force.

We must condemn physical force and banish it from our minds. But I do not condemn it on any moral or pacific grounds. The resort to force remains and will doubtless always remain the rightful recourse of oppressed peoples. Our own country was established upon that right. I condemn physical force because I know that in our case it would be futile.

We would be justified in taking up arms or anything we could lay hands on and fighting for the common rights we are entitled to and denied, if we had a chance to win. But I know and we all know there is not a chance. It is, I believe, among the certainties that some day, perhaps not very far off, native blacks of Africa will, by physical force if necessary, compel the whites to yield their extra privileges and immunities. The increasing inability of the great powers to spare the strength and resources necessary for maintaining imperialism will hasten the certainty. The situation of the African natives is, however, on one point at least, the reverse of our own—on the point of comparative numerical strength.

Yet, there is a phase of physical force that we in the United States should consider. When we are confronted by the lawless, pitiless, brutish mob, and we know that life is forfeit, we should not give it up; we should, if we can, sell it, and at the dearest price we are able to put on it.

THE REVOLUTION

Communism is coming to be regarded as the infallible solution by an increasing number of us. Those who look to the coming revolution (and why they should believe it is coming in the United States I see no good reason; it is obvious that the United States is going through revolutionary economic and social changes, but the changes do not point to Communism) seem to think it will work some instantaneous and magical transformation of our condition. It appears to me that this infinite faith in Communism indicates extreme *naïveté.* Those who hold this faith point to Soviet Russia as a land in which there is absolutely no prejudice against Negroes. This is an unquestioned fact, but I can see no grounds on which to attribute it to Communism. There was no prejudice against Negroes in Tsarist Russia. Tsarist Russia was the country that could honor a black Hannibal; the country that could make a mulatto Pushkin its national poet; the country in which university students in St. Petersburg could unhitch the horses from the carriage of Ira Aldridge, the black American tragedian, after his performance of Othello, and themselves draw him back to his hotel. The simple truth is: the *Russian people* have no prejudice against Negroes.

In considering Communism with respect to the Negro, the question before us, of course, is not how it works in Russia, but how it would probably work in the United States. If the United States goes Communistic, where will the Communists come from? They certainly will not be imported from Russia. They will be made from the Americans here on hand. We might well pause and consider what variations Communism in the United States might undergo.

I hold no brief against Communism as a theory of government. I hope that the Soviet experiment will be completely successful. I know that it is having a strong influence on the principal nations of the world, including our own. I think it is a high sign of progress that Negro Americans have reached the point of holding independent opinions on political and social questions. What I am trying to do is to sound a warning against childlike trust in the miraculous efficacy on our racial situation of any economic or social theory of government—Communism or Socialism or Fascism or Nazism or New Deals. The solving of our situation depends principally upon an evolutionary process along two parallel lines: our own development and the bringing about of a change in the national attitude toward us. That outcome will require our persevering effort under whatever form the government might take on.

It may be argued that although there is not and has not been any anti-Negro feeling in Russia, it is the country in which anti-Semitism was stronger than in any other, and that oppression and repression of the Jews have been greatly abated or entirely wiped out by Communism. Such an argument goes to prove the possibility that

Communism in the United States would wipe out oppression and repression of Negro Americans and give them a status of equality. I grant the possibility—what though it may not be realized miraculously and suddenly. I grant that if America should turn truly Communistic (by which I mean—if it should adopt and practice Communism without reservations, and not adapt it as it has adapted democracy and Christianity so as to allow every degree of inequality and cruelty to be practiced under them); that if the capitalistic system should be abolished and the dictatorship of the proletariat established, with the Negro aligned, as he naturally ought to be, with the proletariat, race discriminations would be officially banned and the reasons and feelings back of them would finally disappear.

But except to a visionary there are no indications that the present or prospective strength of Communism is able or will be able to work such a change, either by persuasion or by military coup. In the situation as it now exists it would be positively foolhardy for us, as a group, to take up the cause of Communistic revolution and thereby bring upon ourselves all of the antagonisms that are directed against it in addition to those we already have to bear. It seems to me that the wholesale allegiance of the Negro to Communistic revolution would be second in futility only to his individual resort to physical force.

I have said that there is no apparent probability that the United States will go over to Communism; but the same cannot be said about Fascism. Most of us, it is true, have for long years lived in the Fascist South; so it is hardly possible that we could fare worse under a national Fascist government. That may not be true as to other minorities. We should oppose with our utmost strength any encroachment of Fascism, for we have both a practical and a moral obligation to do all we can to defend the rights of other minorities, as well as our own.

ISOLATION OR INTEGRATION?

By this process of elimination we have reduced choices of a way out to two. There remain, on the one hand, the continuation of our efforts to achieve integration and, on the other hand, an acknowledgment of our isolation and the determination to accept and make the best of it.

Throughout our entire intellectual history there has been a division of opinion as to which of these two divergent courses the race should follow. From early times there have been sincere thinkers among us who were brought to the conclusion that our only salvation lies in the making of the race into a self-contained economic, social, and cultural unit; in a word, in the building of an *imperium in imperio.*

All along, however, majority opinion has held that the only salvation worth achieving lies in the making of the race into a component part of the nation, with all the common rights and privileges, as well as duties, of citizenship. This attitude has been basic in the general policy of the race—so far as it has had a general policy—for generations, the policy of striving zealously to gain full admission to citizenship and guarding jealously each single advance made.

But this question of direction, of goal, is not a settled one. There is in us all a stronger tendency toward isolation than we may be aware of. There come times when the most persistent integrationist becomes an isolationist, when he curses the White world and consigns it to hell. This tendency toward isolation is strong because it springs from a deep-seated, natural desire—a desire for respite from the unremitting, grueling struggle; for a place in which refuge might be taken. We are again and again confronted by this question. It is ever present, though often dormant. Recently it was emphatically brought forward by the utterances of so authoritative a voice as that of Dr. Du Bois.

The question is not one to be lightly brushed aside. Those who stand for making the race into a self-sufficient unit point out that after years of effort we are still Jim-Crowed, discriminated against, segregated, and lynched; that we are still shut out from industry, barred from the main avenues of business, and cut off from free participation in national life. They point out that in some sections of the country we have not even secured equal protection of life and property under the laws. They declare that entrance of the Negro into full citizenship is as distant as it was seventy years ago. And they ask: What is the Negro to do? Give himself over to wishful thinking? Stand shooting at the stars with a popgun? Is it not rather a duty and a necessity for him to face the facts of his condition and environment, to acknowledge them as facts, and to make the best use of them that he can? These are questions which the thinkers of the race should strive to sift clearly.

To this writer it seems that one of the first results of clear thinking is a realization of the truth that the making of the race into a self-sustaining unit, the creating of an *imperium in imperio,* does not offer an easier or more feasible task than does the task of achieving full citizenship. Such an *imperium* would have to rest upon a basis of separate group economic independence, and the trend of all present-day forces is against the building of any foundation of that sort.

After thoughtful consideration, I cannot see the slightest possibility of our being able to duplicate the economic and social machinery of the country. I do not believe that any other special group could do it. The isolationists declare that because of imposed segregation we have, to a large degree, already done it. But the situation they point to is more apparent than real. Our separate schools and some of our other race institutions, many of our race enterprises, the greater part of our employment, and most of our fundamental activities are contingent upon our interrelationship with the country as a whole.

Clear thinking reveals that the outcome of voluntary isolation would be a permanent secondary status, so acknowledged by the race. Such a status would, it is true, solve some phases of the race question. It would smooth away a good part of the friction and bring about a certain protection and security. The status of slavery carried some advantages of that sort. But I do not believe we shall ever be willing to pay such a price for security and peace.

If Negro Americans could do what reasonably appears to be impossible, and as a separate unit achieve self-sufficiency built upon group economic independence, does anyone suppose that that would abolish prejudice against them and allay opposition, or that the struggle to maintain their self-sufficiency would be in any degree less bitter than the present struggle to become an integral part of the nation? Taking into account human nature as it is, would not the achievement be more likely to arouse envy and bring on even more violent hatreds and persecutions?

Certainly, the isolationists are stating a truth when they contend that we should not, ostrichlike, hide our heads in the sand, making believe that prejudice is non-existent; but in so doing they are apostles of the obvious. Calling upon the race to realize that prejudice is an actuality is a needless effort; it is placing emphasis on what has never been questioned. The danger for us does not lie in a possible failure to acknowledge prejudice as a reality, but in acknowledging it too fully. We cannot ignore the fact that we are segregated, no matter how much we might wish to do so; and the smallest amount of common sense forces us to extract as much good from the situation as there is in it. Any degree of sagacity forces us at the same time to use all our powers to abolish imposed segregation; for it is an evil *per se* and the negation of equality either of opportunity or of awards. We should by all means make our schools and institutions as excellent as we can possibly make them—and by that very act we reduce the certainty that they will forever remain schools and institutions "for Negroes only." We should make our business enterprises and other strictly group undertakings as successful as we can possibly make them. We should gather all the strength and experience we can from imposed segregation. But any good we are able to derive from the system we should consider as a means, not an end. The strength and experience we gain from it should be applied to the objective of *entering into,* not *staying out of* the body politic.

Clear thinking shows, too, that, as bad as conditions are, they are not as bad as they are declared to be by discouraged and pessimistic isolationists. To say that in the past two generations or more Negro Americans have not advanced a single step toward a fuller share in the commonwealth becomes, in the light of easily ascertainable facts, an absurdity. Only the shortest view of the situation gives color of truth to such a statement; any reasonably long view proves it to be utterly false.

With our choice narrowed down to these two courses, wisdom and far-sightedness and possibility of achievement demand that we follow the line that leads to equal rights for us, based on the common terms and conditions under which they are accorded and guaranteed to the other groups that go into the making up of our national family. It is not necessary for our advancement that such an outcome should suddenly eradicate all prejudices. It would not, of course, have the effect of suddenly doing away with voluntary grouping in religious and secular organizations or of abolishing group enterprises—for example, Negro newspapers. The accordance of full civil and political rights has not in the case of the greater number of groups in the nation had that effect. Nevertheless, it would be an immeasurable step forward, and would place us where we had a fair start with the other American groups. More than that we do not need to ask.

CHAPTER II

FORCES AND RESOURCES

In following the line that leads to equal rights, we are advancing to a fight, not beating a retreat; so we should take careful account of our forces and resources.

OUR NUMERICAL STRENGTH

Our numerical strength is at once a force and a resource. Not all the apathy, prejudice, and opposition in the United States would be able to block the forward march of twelve million people—if they were formed into an intelligent, courageous, and persistent phalanx. Twelve million of us can be made a reservoir from which may be drawn almost all of the elements needed in our struggle. Before our numerical strength was as great as it is, we had already drawn from the reservoir certain elements and made them into active forces. We must now make those forces more effective, organize and perfect still other forces, and bring about a co-ordination of all of them for the achievement of our objective. Up to now we have shown no greater weakness than our inability or unwillingness to co-ordinate the forces that we have long had at hand. Aside from the handicapping effects of ignorance and inexperience, we have allowed pettinesses and jealousies, rivalries and downright meannesses, to interfere with and defeat worthy attempts at co-operation. By this time we ought to have learned a lesson.

THE NEGRO CHURCH

The Negro church is the most powerful and, potentially, the most effective medium we possess. The whole Christian church stands at this period in need of another Reformation: a sloughing off of outworn creeds and dogmas, and an application of its power to the working out of the present-day problems of civilization and of social and spiritual life. The Negro church stands in need of some special reforms.

First of all, the church together with the race as a whole must do a certain amount of clearing away in the religious field. We must stamp out as far as we can the bootleggers of religion, those parasites who, whenever they can get together a sufficient number of poor, hard-working women, will open a store-front or basement church and peddle a spurious brand of Christianity at a relatively exorbitant price. Some of these men may be sincere, but the majority of them are ignorant, lazy louts, who would be of greater value to themselves and to the race if they were put at manual labor. A more important task is the driving out of those lecherous, criminal scoundrels who, as spectacular figures, are a rather recent product. These self-anointed "bishops," "Messiahs," and "whatnots," whose central idea of a church is a holy harem, a sanctified system of concubinage, arouse only feelings of disgust and rage. They all belong in jail; and each of us who helps to land one there does a good service.

No one, no matter what may be his attitude on religion, can fail to be interested in the astonishing history of the Negro church, if he will only become acquainted with it; and once he is familiar with that history, he will be compelled to acknowledge the vital work the church has accomplished. Aside from what it has done in religion, education, and in charities, it has been a tremendous social force. When there was no other agency to do it, the church brought about cohesion and stabilization in a bewildered and leaderless mass.

But the church cannot sit back on the essential work it accomplished in slavery days and in the post–Civil War period; it cannot excuse existing shortcomings by pointing to its worthy record. It must thoroughly make the internal reforms that will better fit it to meet the responsibility for racial advancement that it should shoulder now.

The church must as nearly as it can abolish hypnotic religion, that religion which excites visions of the delights of life in the world to come, while it gives us no insight into the conditions we encounter in the world in which we now live. There is still to be found in the Negro church too much obsolete doctrine. In too many pulpits there are still to be heard terrific fulminations against dancing, theater-going, and card-playing from preachers who ignore or know nothing about the fundamental current questions of life. This stricture, of course, may also be applied to many white churches.

The church is devoting too much energy to raising money—money to meet mortgage payments on fine edifices. Denominational rivalries and competition in outward show have forced the church into the position of living above its means and of being left with no financial margin after the high cost of worshiping God in a sumptuous temple is met. Such conduct is as reprehensible in a congregation as it is in an individual. As to mere church buildings—the most affluent Negro congregation in the country requires no more and is warranted in having no more than a modest, adequate meetinghouse, beautiful because of its simplicity. When we think of the number of congregations, made up of people just this side of the poverty line, struggling to possess and maintain a building entirely beyond their needs and their means, we find it both tragic and absurd. This common extravagance leaves mighty few Negro congregations with anything like the margin of money they should have on hand to be devoted to applied Christianity.

Needless multiplication of congregations is a definite weakness in the church. It is a process by which its strength, resources, and effectiveness are dissipated. I was recently in a northern city of 75,000 inhabitants. The Negro population is about 1000. As in all similar situations, these colored people were disoriented and in an anomalous position. They were too numerous to go unnoticed into general community life, and not numerous enough to constitute a group unto themselves. Yet these 1000 Negroes have five churches, with a total membership of 204. One church is all they need, all they can support. One church might be made into an agency that would improve their industrial, social, and civic status, as well as their spiritual state. Five churches do not multiply, they nullify whatever strength and effectiveness the one church might have.

Denominational and individual rivalries make this question a difficult one. Some denominations have a degree of authority in the matter, and others have very little or none. Possibly all the denominations might sign a concordat and agree upon a maximum number of congregations for each of so many hundreds or thousands of Negro inhabitants in a given area; then proceed to carry out a policy of consolidation and, when necessary, of abolishment. By such a process each denomination would find itself the gainer in strength and resources. In almost every community the Catholic Church serves as a grand example of the conservation of power, an example we might well imitate.

The Negro church, notwithstanding, is the most powerful agency we command for moving forward the race as a mass. It is then not too much to call upon the church to meet the exigency as it met the situation confronting it in slavery days and in the post–Civil War period. The present task requires an intelligent, high-minded, upright ministry; and that kind of ministry the church must have. The ignorant preacher of the past performed the work that was before him as best he could. All honor to him for what he accomplished. But the day of the ignorant preacher is gone.

With the making of these needed internal reforms the church would again demand of Negro youth in our colleges and universities a consideration of the ministry as a career giving scope for the exercise of their highest and best powers. Thereby, the church would be made a field as attractive for well-educated and progressive youth as the fields of medicine, law, dentistry, and social work have become in recent years. In the meantime, earnest, forward-looking, spiritual-minded young men and young women in our colleges should not stand aside waiting for these reforms to be completed; they should go into the church and help to bring them about.

What would it not mean to have a Negro ministry working for the advancement of the race with the same degree of intelligence, zeal, and singleness of purpose with which the Catholic clergy works for the advancement of those who profess the Catholic faith?

THE NEGRO PRESS

The Negro press was, thirty years ago, a feeble and struggling medium. Thirty years ago many colored people who deemed themselves intelligent openly boasted that they never read Negro newspapers. The papers themselves did not offer much. They were, in the main, poorly written, wretchedly printed, and run as personal organs. Today the Negro press is powerful and, relatively speaking, rich. The leading periodicals are printed on high-speed web perfecting presses, they carry all the modern newspaper features, and are intelligently edited. The Negro press as a racial agency is today second only to the Negro church in the number of people reached and influenced.

It is needless to say that this new power entails new responsibilities. There is no doubt that Negro journalists with a social sense recognize that fact. It is probable that they are wrestling with the problem of directing the power of the machine that has been created into channels of high purpose, a problem that is not simple or easy. Many of the

Negro newspapers have become popular; and a popular periodical is an insatiable creature; it must continually be fed on circulation, circulation secured at almost any price. So the management of a popular periodical is constantly driven by the necessity of furnishing what it thinks the greatest number of people want. Once on that road, it must keep up an accelerating speed. It cannot turn back, it cannot stop, it cannot even slow down.

"Give people what they want" is a specious slogan. It implies that "the people" are continually demanding other and still other things that the press must supply; and that "what the people want" is consequently good. Of these two implications, neither is true. The facts are: popular periodicals exhaust ingenuity in supplying things which they hope "the people will want," and "what the people want" is often bad or without value.

"It is the business of a newspaper to give the news" is another specious slogan. Editors should regard themselves as intelligent and responsible members of society. Certainly one of their responsibilities is to judge whether or not the "news" they disseminate serves any good purpose whatever, and whether or not it is worth, at least, the paper on which it is printed. And any person of average intelligence is forced to say that an undue proportion of the "news" in American newspapers, from the biggest dailies to the weakest weeklies, is not worth that much.

I believe I am right when I say that the Negro press has a peculiar as well as a general relationship to its clientele; that the Negro editor has a relatively deeper responsibility to his public than the white editor has to his; that the service possible for the Negro press to render to Negro America is more vital than what the white press has to give to white America. I believe that Negro Americans will understand and accept this statement without discussion.

It then follows that Negro newspapers ought to be more than imitations of white newspapers. Without doubt, they should avoid copying the license of the sensational daily newspapers that appeal to morons and the morbid-minded. Of course, we have our share of morons, and they constitute a tempting field for greater circulation; but why not try to gratify their wants in some better way? Our newspapers should also avoid following the example of those white publications that make a feature of pornography. An examination of the vast number of salacious white periodicals published in the United States would incline one to think that sex has gone to the white man's head, transferred its seat to the imagination. When sex goes to the head, it loses its lusty, wholesome quality and begins to fester, to become maggoty. Sex with us is, in a large measure, still in the lusty, wholesome stage. Let's keep it there as long as we possibly can.

I do not see how the Negro press can escape the responsibility of facing the question of the net result, of the ultimate effect of its work on the race, especially on the younger generation. Is it to be satisfied with only the fortuitous benefits that may come from commercially successful journalism? Or is it to feel that commercial success gives it the resources and facilities for carrying out a definite and far-reaching plan? Is it through its news policy to run the risk of making itself an unconscious agent of defeatism? Or does it desire to place the stronger emphasis on the notes of courage and confidence and final victory?

I am not an impractical visionary. I myself have been a newspaperman. I know that in order for Negro newspapers to accomplish much good they must first be good *newspapers.* I feel, however, that they can be good newspapers and, at the same time, something beyond merely good newspapers.

The pre–Civil War Negro newspapers did a great work. They dedicated themselves to the Anti-Slavery cause, and had a large share in arousing and shaping public opinion. They quickened and inspired their readers, and gave them a voice that made itself heard. They played a significant part in creating the forces that led to the destruction of slavery. With this main object accomplished, they passed off the scene. Contemporary Negro newspapers have done a revolutionary thing—they have converted masses of Negro Americans into readers. Hundreds of thousands who formerly read nothing today read the Negro periodicals; and no Negro would today boast that he never reads a Negro newspaper. Because they have taught masses of Negro Americans to read, they have been able in an extraordinary degree to keep the race aware and awake. They have likewise had marked effect upon the consciousness of white America. In a number of crises their work has been invaluable. When the Dyer Anti-Lynching Bill was being pushed, the Negro newspapers were a great factor in keeping the whole race stirred up and determined on the issue; and copies that reached the desks of congressmen and senators gave those representatives of the people a new light on their fellow Negro Americans. This was a clear instance of the power possible for them to wield.

The Negro press has prepared a rich field; what the harvest is to be is a question that owners and editors should seriously consider.

ORGANIZATIONS

Organizations among us are without number. There is a popular idea that we do not organize, it is erroneous; the fact is we tend to over-organize. If all the Negro organizations in the United States marched in procession, they would be a month or more passing any given point. Most of them, however, are small, separate bodies, and their main purposes are decidedly minor. What we lack is the will and ability to organize for major purposes.

Our principal fraternal organizations are national in scope. They developed rapidly and reached a degree of power and prosperity which now appears to be on the wane. Our big fraternities have filled and are still filling a useful purpose, but the difference between them and the smaller organizations is mainly a difference in size and resources. Their functions and objectives are fundamentally the same. All of these organizations function as units for social intercourse and enjoyment. They provide a forum for lodge politics and arenas in which self-realization and preferment may be achieved. They also have an economic feature; they care for the sick and bury the dead. In many of them, however, burying the dead has called for a financial outlay so far out of proportion to that used in caring for the living as to make "the high cost of dying" a live question.

One of the big organizations established an educational fund, but, speaking generally, the great resources, numerical, social, and financial, of our powerful fraternal organizations have been utilized with hardly a thought given to the fundamental phases of the situation in which Negroes in the United States find themselves. Many thousands of dollars have been wasted on annual conventions of which the chief business was having a good time, on showy parades, and on ostentatious funerals. Hundreds of thousands of dollars have been put into ornate temples; and in many cases these temples have led to bankruptcy and mortgage foreclosures. Other hundreds of thousands of dollars have become bones of contention, and led to dissension and law suits. In too many instances the heading up of fraternal organizations has been developed into a lucrative business; in plain words, into a racket. Our fraternal organizations have in a number of ways done much good, but considering their strength and their peculiar opportunities as secret societies for doing vital service, they have in the larger racial affairs fallen short, they have failed.

The two chief organizations that devote their efforts and resources primarily to the questions which affect Negroes as citizens of this country are both interracial. They are the National Association for the Advancement of Colored People and the National Urban League. There is between these two organizations an understanding which makes for a rough division of the work into two fields, economic and civil. The Urban League has given its efforts to housing, health, and employment. The National Association has given its efforts to civil, legal, and constitutional rights. There has been, of course, some overlapping; the rights of the Negro in industry naturally involve his rights as a citizen.

Taking into account all their shortcomings and all the mistakes and failures they may have made, the overwhelming fact remains that both these organizations have done excellent and essential work. And neither of them has been given the support it has deserved.

There are also the (Southern) Commission on Interracial Co-operation, which has accomplished certain delicate and important things that could not have been accomplished through any other medium, and the Interracial Commission of the Federal Council of the Churches of Christ in America, which has been a strong factor among religious bodies.

THE CORRELATION OF ALL FORCES

A Super-Power

Now, these principal forces and resources that we have enumerated are far from negligible. Even at their weakest they are assets. Their actual strength is great. Their potential powers have not been estimated. It is the potential powers of these elements that I shall discuss at this point. They are the powers above and beyond those needed and employed in the normal functioning of these elements. And they are the powers before which the obstacles between us and our major goal would be compelled to yield.

How may we call these potential powers, these powers that will prove effective, into being? The simplicity of the process will probably throw doubt on the magnitude of the feat. It may be done through the complete correlation of the existing forces. The result will be not merely increased efficiency in all the various units and greater total strength; it will be the creation of an entirely new power, a superpower, a power that will be a fusion of all our energies. If we create this power and center its force upon the walls that stand between us and the common rights, guarantees, and privileges of citizenship, we can be confident of battering them down.

The practical method I suggest for the creation and utilization of this power is to channel our forces so that they will function through a central machine. I believe we have that machine at hand in the National Association for the Advancement of Colored People. I believe we could get the desired results by making that organization the nucleus, the synthesis, the clearing house, of our forces. It already has the experience, the skill, and, in good part, the machinery. It has proved itself honest, sincere, intelligent, and capable. For the purpose of achieving, maintaining, and safeguarding our citizenship rights, no other organization can be compared with it. Its policies and techniques have proved to be the most advantageous and effective that we have thus far been able to devise.

I know that this is not a wholly unanimous opinion. The statement I have made has been frequently put in the form of a question. I believe, however, that a study of the history and work of the association for the past twenty-five years and of the concurrent history of Negro Americans will furnish sufficient evidence to prove that the race has made positive gains through the efforts of the N.A.A.C.P. Its successful efforts to hold segregation within the limits of custom and prevent it from being put over into the realm of law; its leadership in the fight against lynching, and its keeping of that crime and other racial injustices before the conscience of the American people; and its half-dozen signal legal victories involving our constitutional rights are examples in point.

But there is another way of evaluating the work of the organization. When the N.A.A.C.P. was founded, the great danger facing us was that we should lose the vestiges of our rights by default. The organization checked that danger. It acted as a watchman on the wall, sounding the alarms that called us to defense. Its work would be of value if only for the reason that without it our status would be worse than it is. In cities where our numbers are large we still live grouped together in one or more "Negro sections." (Although here in Nashville, where I am writing, white and colored people live together rather indiscriminately in many of the sections.) But there is hardly a doubt that in such cities Negro Americans by this time would all have been sentenced *by law* to live in black ghettos if the N.A.A.C.P. had not won the Louisville Segregation Case, in which the Supreme Court declared residential segregation on grounds of race to be unconstitutional. I am taking it for granted that no one will be so shallow as to ask if there is any difference between segregation by social conventions and segregation by legal enactment. I believe also that the National Association laid the foundation for the restoration of the ballot to Negro Americans in the South through its victories in the Texas Primary Cases. The Negro lost the right to vote conferred on him by the Fourteenth and Fifteenth Amendments because the Supreme Court through hair-splitting sophistry and astute evasion emasculated both amendments to the point of nullification. The signs are now that the right to vote will be re-established through the decisions of that same court. There is a school that holds that these legal victories are empty. They are not. At the very least, they provide the ground upon which we may make a stand for our rights. In the North we have a fair degree of civil rights and in the South we have the right to battle for those rights because the Fourteenth and Fifteenth Amendments are in the constitution. Let us suppose them not there, and we reach a quick realization of the material importance of legal enactments. Or note the effect of adverse laws.

If we correlate our numerical strength, the strength of our religious and fraternal organizations, such political and economic power as we have, and the power of our press in a way to make the National Association for the Advancement of Colored People the spearhead of our forces, in a way that will enable it to shift the emphasis more and more from protest to action and more fully to translate declarations into deeds, and to widen its field to include all the fundamental phases of life that affect us as citizens, there are Negro Americans now born who will live to see the race accorded the common rights of citizenship on the same terms upon which they are accorded to the other groups in the nation.

The suggestion I make of the N.A.A.C.P. as the "central machine" has—and I hope it is not necessary for me to state this—no relation to the fact that for a number of years I was a member of the executive staff of the association and am still officially connected with the organization. I make it on what appear to me to be the undeniable facts of the situation. If plans for a more adequate and a more effective "central machine" are suggested, I should readily subscribe to them.

CHAPTER III

TECHNIQUES AND POLICIES

The race situation is not static, it is constantly shifting. It is not what it was a hundred years ago or fifty years ago or twenty or even ten years ago; and so the methods of meeting it have had to change. Nor has the situation in any one period been identically the same in all parts of the country. At the present time we find that in Massachusetts it demands or admits of certain methods; in Virginia, of other methods; and in Mississippi, of still other methods. A historical survey of the varying techniques and policies employed and followed through the past three hundred years and in the different sections of the country would be an important study. Such a study would furnish points of orientation that would aid in formulating and projecting new techniques and policies. It would also give a clear view of the progressive stages through which we have come, and show the juvenile quality of much of the criticism that each younger generation makes of the work of a former generation. Sound criticism here calls for weighing the question as to whether or not the methods followed were the most adequate that could be used under the circumstances. It would, for example, be absurd to criticize the runaway slaves for running instead of standing up and fighting it out.

But we leave that historical survey to some candidate for his doctorate, and take up a consideration of the techniques and policies that are current.

EDUCATION

Education from the beginning has been regarded as the principal factor in the working out of our problem. The missionaries who came South immediately after the Civil War and established schools, wiser than all the statesmen of their time (except the Negro legislators of the Reconstruction), realized that nothing very high could be built unless the groundwork of education was first laid. Our original faith in education was almost childish. There was a quite general belief that with education our whole racial problem would quickly vanish. We went at education feverishly, old as well as young, and took it in over a range that extended from Webster's *Blueback Speller* to Goodwin's *Greek Grammar.* No magical result took place; nevertheless, this desire of the Negro to acquire knowledge and his ability to assimilate it constitute the cornerstone of all that the race has reared since its emancipation. Had he lacked either this urge or this capacity, he would not have advanced or even held his ground.

There have been no magical results, but time has proved that our faith in education was not misplaced. It was the schools and colleges founded by the missionaries that made possible the generating of the internal motive power that has kept us going. Without that power we might have been pulled along a pace or two, but there could not have been any spontaneous and determined move forward on our own part. In other words, those schools and colleges accomplished the work of providing from within, intellectual leadership for a group so isolated that, lacking such leadership, it would have remained leaderless altogether.

But the time has come for us to go over our ideas of "education." The pattern we are following is, in the main, the one that was originally cut out for us; and it remains the same in form, whether we are learning the alphabet in a shack schoolhouse or studying for a degree in one of our universities. This original pattern is a good one. It is far superior to the fads and superb nonsense that go under the name of "modern education." Therefore, it should not be scrapped, but it needs to be extended.

The old pattern was designed to give us a sound general education, an education to fit us to take our places as intelligent American citizens. That idea of education is fundamental and right; for whatever may be the opinions and attitudes on the matter, the solid fact remains that we are, for good or ill, a part of American civilization. We may be segregated and Jim-Crowed, but there is no way to subtract or extract us from American life; so we must be prepared to keep adjusted to it, to keep pace with it. And that means that our institutions must give Negro youth as good, as broad, and as high an education as is correspondingly given to white youth.

But we need not only an education that will enable us to meet the general situation as American citizens, we need also an education that will enable us to meet our peculiar situation as Negro Americans. Now let us understand at once that this does not mean a separate and distinct kind of "education for Negroes." Such a course would simply lead to the Jim-Crowing of ourselves educationally and intellectually. What it does mean is that the general education given by our institutions should be extended so as to have direct application to our particular case.

Take history as it is commonly taught in our schools. It is taught from a textbook that completely ignores the Negro or mentions him only in condescending or derogatory terms. That is a bad sort of history to teach to white youth; when it is taught to Negro youth it is absolutely pernicious. The fact is, there is hardly an important page of American history that can be fully and truthfully written without reference to the Negro as a contributing factor. Then, for Negro youth to study American history and learn nothing of the part played by Negro Americans in the making of that history is an absurdity. Notwithstanding, it is pathetically true that there are thousands of Negro youth in our schools and colleges who have never read the life of Frederick Douglass or of Booker T. Washington; to whom Nat Turner and Denmark Vesey and Sojourner Truth and Harriet Tubman are not even names. These young people have nothing to stand on. They have no ground under their feet. It is idle to talk to them about race pride, when they know of nothing of which to be proud. Race pride cannot be pumped into them artificially, it must spring naturally from their knowledge of all that is best in racial history, and must rest upon a resulting faith in the strength and capacities of the race. Without this knowledge and faith they are suspended, and when the forces of prejudice strike them they have nothing to fall back on. Knowledge of the extraordinary history of the race in this country and of the men and women who have achieved high marks in that history is essential to them as a sustaining force. Such pride of race as this will not make them lesser but better American citizens; it will not tend to separate them from the national life but will make them a stronger component part of it.

It ought not be necessary to say that this extension of the teaching of American history so as to give it direct application cannot be accomplished by merely excerpting episodes and incidents and events and biographical sketches that are wholly restricted to the Negro, and teaching them as Negro history. To isolate the facts in that manner would be to teach history *in vacuo;* the student would fail to get the contextual sense of what he was being taught. This extension should be accomplished by bringing the Negro into true and proper relation to American history, and by showing in what manner and degree he has been a force in shaping it.

The main burden of achieving this end will fall on the teachers. The textbooks they are expected to use will be of no assistance—and the average teacher without a textbook is a babe in the woods. The lack in the textbooks will have to be made up for by wide reading, careful research, and hard study on the part of the individual teachers. And the teachers will also have to acquire skill in making the knowledge thus gained an integral part of American history. Indeed, the teaching of history to Negro youth should not confine itself to the experiences of the race in America, but should explore the achievements that lie in the African background. A study of the African cultural background will give our youth a new and higher sense of racial self-respect, and will disprove entirely the theory of innate race inferiority.

What I have said about the teaching of American history is to be said also about the teaching of economics, political science, sociology, literature, and other of the arts. It is something pretty close to a waste of time for Negro students to study the laws of economics without being given an interpretation of the effects of those laws on the economic and industrial plight of Negro Americans. In teaching the science of government, what is purely academic should be supplemented by inferences drawn from government as it is constituted, maintained, and enforced in the United States and the various states, and from its operation on Negro Americans as a group. I do not in the least advocate that our colleges become any part of political machinery or touched by partisan politics, but I firmly believe that special political education of Negro youth is a proper and necessary function for them. The political history of the race should be reviewed; independent political thinking should be inculcated; political rights and responsibilities should be explained, and preparation for exercising those rights and assuming those responsibilities should be given.

There are those who feel that youth in our colleges ought not thus be burdened with problems of race; that the injection of such matter vitiates the cultural quality of their education. Well, if our young men and young women after entering college are not yet ready to consider and get the clearest possible understanding of our problem of race, I don't know when they will be ready. Some of them have already been hit by this problem and are groping for help. All of them will run into it before they have had time to frame their diplomas. There is no escape from it; therefore, if our colleges turn these young people out on life without, at least, attempting to give them some sound attitudes toward the problem of race and some preparation for dealing with it, they are failing in their full duty.

The argument that this extension of the general to give it specific application has no place in cultural education, I would answer by saying that nothing I have suggested is extraneous. The history of Negro Americans is a part of American history. The economic condition of Negro Americans cannot be separated from our national economic conditions. The political position of Negro Americans plays an important part in our national politics; indeed, it is the basis of the entire political system in the Southern states, the system under which three-fourths of all the Negroes in the United States live.

Certainly, the problem of race can and should be studied and discussed. What is necessary for doing it is to suppress the emotional element as completely as possible, and to view the subject objectively; in a word, to strive to approach and consider the whole matter as nearly as possible in the scientific manner. In this way our own problem can be studied and discussed just as any historical phase of society may be studied and discussed. One of the first steps would be to show to Negro youth that they are not weighted with the only race problem in the world; that theirs is but a part of the universal problem of race.

VOCATIONAL EDUCATION as provided for Negro youth has been rendered almost wholly antiquated by the marvelous advance in technology. A generation ago the majority opinion of the country was that industrial training should be the basic if not the only education for Negro boys and girls. But most of the standard trades that have been taught in our industrial schools and which were once regarded as sure guarantees of a livelihood have been practically abolished; they are today mechanized processes. It is hardly worth the while for these schools to turn out old-style blacksmiths, wheelwrights, shoemakers, typesetters, or even carpenters. The change calls for a revolution in the plants of our industrial schools. Machine methods must be substituted for the old handicrafts. This substitution is, however, one that only the largest and richest of our institutions can afford to make.

And this gives rise to another difficulty. The old-fashioned artisan was more or less free to bargain as an individual for the exchange of his labor. The labor of the technological worker is subject to regulation by a guild or a union or a manufacturing concern. So, the pecuniary value of the most modern training our industrial schools might give depends very largely upon the success Negro Americans will have in becoming actually a part of organized labor.

And that is another question.

EDUCATION OF WHITE PEOPLE. For decades past, education as a factor in the solution of the race problem has been regarded in terms of "educating Negroes." The education of Negroes is, at most, but two-thirds of the work involved; the other third or more is the education of white people. The ignorance of white people concerning us constitutes one of our greatest obstacles. We should be perfectly willing to have white America know the whole truth about us, faults as well as virtues, and to take our chances on a fair opinion based on that truth. But that is far from being the case. The greater part of white America thinks of us in stereotypes; most of these stereotypes coming to them second-hand by way of the representation of Negro life and character on the stage and in certain books. In the main they are exaggerated, false, and entirely unlike our real selves.

And this brings us up against an important fact: what the greater part of white America merely *thinks* about us is an influential factor in making our *actual condition* what it is.

White people must be educated. They must be taught the truth about us. We need not fear their getting the bad along with the good;

for all of the bad there is, and more, they have already, and we have enough good points to overcome the bad, if we can get them over. White America must not only be made thoroughly conscious of the handicaps, injustices, and wrongs under which Negro Americans struggle, it must also be made familiar with the elements of strength and of excellency possessed by the race. And white America must learn not only about the material but also about the artistic and spiritual contributions that Negro Americans have made to our common cultural store.

Now, I wish that our colleges could devise a way of establishing special extension courses for white people; a few white schools are making a start. It is, I know, possible and practical for each intelligent Negro American to establish an extension course and become responsible for the education of, at least, one ignorant white American. Select your pupil. It will be well to select one not interested in colored people or not friendly toward them. Whenever a fair, sound, forcible article on the race question comes to your hand, clip it and send it to your pupil. Do likewise about worthy and notable achievements by Negro Americans. If a good and convincing book comes out, send it to him or her if you can afford to do so. Keep it up assiduously. There might be some pupils too hardboiled to respond to this sort of instruction, but the percentage that would respond would be very large. Sheer curiosity would lead many of them on. The cumulative effect of this education over a number of years cannot be overestimated.

I shall say more on this point under the topic, Stereotypes, Art, and Money.

POLITICS

For more than three-quarters of a century we have been, negatively, a powerful factor in national politics. We were immanent in the great political controversies that preceded the Civil War; we were the prime cause of the war itself; we are today the chief issue in keeping alive the political system known as the "Solid South." For a brief period we played a positive part, a part that has been greatly misrepresented and maligned, but which, when the whole scene is surveyed, makes an astonishingly creditable showing. There were Negro Americans in the legislatures and in high office in most of the

Southern states. There were a score of men in the House of Representatives and the United States Senate—men, it can be said, who did not at all rank below the average of present-day congressmen—although that is not saying very much. All in all, it looked as though politics would be the principal factor in establishing our equal citizenship rights. But with the fall of Reconstruction our political status fell and rapidly subsided until it reached a level as low as that prior to the adoption of the War Amendments.

Now, the Negro in the South did not take his disfranchisement lying down. He had sublime faith in his lately bestowed constitutional guarantees, and persisted in going to the polls. When he was met there by denial and force, he took his case into the courts, relying upon those clauses in the Fourteenth Amendment which say:

> All persons born or naturalized in the United States and subject to the jurisdiction thereof, are citizens of the United States and of the state wherein they reside. No state shall make or enforce any law which shall abridge the privileges or immunities of citizens of the United States...

and upon that section of the Fifteenth Amendment which says:

> The right of the citizens of the United States to vote shall not be denied or abridged by the United States or by any state on account of race, color, or previous condition of servitude.

More than once he took his case to the Supreme Court of the United States, but the court pointed out that he had failed to show that the *state* had abridged or denied his right to vote or that persons who prevented him from voting had done so because of his *race, color, or previous condition of servitude.* So, unable to prove that the committee which had met him at the polls with shotguns was actuated by any such base and unconstitutional motives, he found his case thrown out. In the last analysis, he lost his vote because of the attitude of the Supreme Court.

The white people of the South pretended to believe and loudly proclaimed that the effort of Negro Americans to exercise their constitutional right was subversive and involved the overthrow of white supremacy and the blotting out of Anglo-Saxon civilization in the South, and the various quasi-legal expedients to prevent Negroes from exercising the right were devised and adopted. White people in the North depreciated the effort, feeling that the race could use that energy in making gains that would be more concrete. This was the period in which Booker T. Washington advised the race to eschew politics and devote its energies to acquiring property, especially farm property.

It is true that the power of the ballot is somewhat chimerical. White citizens who hold the unqualified right to vote do not find it a panacea for their ills. The image of the sovereign American citizen casting his ballot and determining the course of the nation and his own destinies is pretty much a rhetorically magnified figure. So, Negro citizens should avoid building exaggerated hopes on the right to vote. Nevertheless, we are eternally right in contending that, however great or small the power of the ballot may be, we need it. We are wise in understanding that we are not equipped to defend or hold any citizenship right unless we possess also the right to the ballot on a common basis with other citizens.

In my opinion we are farther along toward that point than we have ever been. The victories of the N.A.A.C.P. in the Texas "white primary" cases have knocked a big hole in the disfranchisement wall; it remains for us to widen the breach. The political position that Negro Americans have attained in the border states and in Northern and Western states goes far toward counterbalancing the conditions that still prevail in the deep South. There are those of us who look back on the Reconstruction period as a golden age. Those who do, need to realize that Reconstruction was, after all, an artificial situation. The one representative we now have in Congress, elected from the state of Illinois, and the dozens of Negro Americans who have been elected to state legislatures, municipal councils, and to other offices in Northern and Western states are, I believe, more significant as gains in citizenship rights than was the whole of the Reconstruction régime.

Full right to vote in the states of the deep South is yet to be won. It will be won. The wisest policy for Negro Americans in those states to follow is to qualify and vote as soon as they can in the Democratic primaries for the best candidates for local and state offices. For as long a time as may be necessary they should leave national politics alone. By leaving national Republican politics alone they will abolish all arguments about their being mere cat's-paws of alien Yankee domination.

In truth, if a Negro American in Mississippi cannot get equitable school facilities for his children or sanitary and other public improvements in his neighborhood, or is in danger of being railroaded in the courts, or mobbed or lynched, no President, Republican or Democratic, can help him one bit. In common sense, the only political concern at present of Negro Americans in the South is to have a voice in deciding who will be the judges of the local courts, the prosecuting attorneys, the sheriff, the members of the school board and the board of public works, and their congressional representatives. All of this is, of course, easier to say than do; for the astute leaders of the Southern Oligarchy know well that its accomplishment will lead to a real two-party system in the South, with both parties seeking Negro votes, and they will continue to resort to every device in their power to prevent such an outcome. But if Negro Americans use intelligent persistence, it will be done. It must be done; and not only for the good of the Negro but for the good of the South. For until it is done, the average Southern white citizen will remain with as little real political freedom as is possessed by the Negro.

I have expressed the opinion that the wise course for Negro Americans in the South to follow will be to go into the Democratic primaries as rapidly as they are able and vote for the best candidates for the local offices. In the North and West, Negro Americans should endeavor to maintain political independence. They should vote for Republicans or Democrats or Socialists or Communists, as they think best. Such a division of their votes will increase their political power and will also increase respect for them as citizens. To a fair degree they have done this. In more than one instance they have helped to elect the Democratic slate in state elections. But in national elections they have generally voted as a unit for the party of Abraham Lincoln—regardless of the fact that nobody who even slightly recalled the qualities of Lincoln was a candidate. In this policy there are elements of gratitude and sentiment, but the strongest compulsion is due to the fact that Negro Americans in the North and West feel bound by the situation of their fellows in the South, and they hesitate to place any more power over them in the hands of their oppressors. They feel that it is the better part of wisdom to stand with lukewarm and apathetic friends than with avowed enemies.

I think we might risk trying another technique, the technique of "boring from within." Not for decades have Republicans who have gone to Washington made any appreciable effort to ease the oppressors' load on the backs of Negro Americans. Their attitude and actions have been negative. For instance, when the Dyer Anti-Lynching Bill, after being passed by the House, was hanging in the Senate, a clear Republican majority sat by while the Democratic minority, led by a group of Southern senators, defied them to attempt to take action on the measure. I think it might be sound strategy to have a number of Northern Democrats in Congress who would be compelled to say to their colleagues: this must be done or that cannot be done, because we are here through Negro votes. It is likely that pressure of that sort would be more effective than any which our Republican friends have given evidence of being able to exercise.

The carrying out of a wise political policy will require wise political leadership. Policies do not carry themselves out; and no mass of people can be expected to carry out a policy unless it has proper leaders. The proper political leaders for us will need to be above the average of political leaders in general. They must be leaders who are not only sagacious but who are of unquestionable integrity. Leaders who can, if the necessity arises, make the sacrifice of putting the best interests of the race above their personal interests. Such men and women are rare, but we have a few; and without doubt, somewhere in our midst, there are others capable of intelligent and unselfish leadership. If they do not rise or if we fail to discover them, we shall not derive the fullest benefits from Politics as a factor.

LABOR AND BUSINESS

It may be truthfully said that heretofore we have given our attention almost exclusively to Education and Politics as factors for working out our problem. We had, it appeared, little or no comprehension of the basic importance of the economic factor. We knew, of course, that being poor had a great deal to do with our status, but we failed to understand clearly that there is a distinction between being poor and being without economic opportunity; that although the lack of money and the lack of economic opportunity may go together, they are not one and the same thing. We are just becoming aware of how much our status as a group is due to the existing economic order and our place in it.

Forty years ago Booker T. Washington perceived that the industrial color line in the South, that line on one side of which there were white men's jobs and, on the other, black men's jobs, was moving over. For many years there had been left on one side of that line a black industrial zone in which the Negro was practically secure. The mores of the South protected him. A white man in the South could then hardly have imagined a more humiliating calamity to himself than having to work at a "Negro job." Dr. Washington observed that that zone was constantly growing narrower and that the margin held by the Negro was becoming more and more precarious. On that observation he formulated the doctrine that was the basis of his teaching and his work. And it was that observation, despite any shortsightedness on any other phases of the race question, which entitles him to the order of statesmanship.

Today that black industrial zone in the South has vanished. There are no more traditional Negro jobs. Any job is a white man's job, from bootblack up or down. Forty years ago a Southern white man would probably have felt uneasy seated in a barber's chair with another white man standing over him sliding a razor round his throat. At that time the finest barber shops in the South were owned and operated by Negro Americans, and the men who ran these doubly inverted Jim-Crow establishments were among the most prosperous in the colored community. Whether it be considered a backset or a blessing, that particular field of employment is about lost. The ancient calling of the colored laundress is almost wholly taken over by steam laundries. White girls have largely supplanted colored men as waiters. In some Southern cities white men do not disdain to collect and cart away the garbage. The same sort of change has taken place in the skilled trades. With the immigration of native and alien artisans from the North and, perhaps, the awakening of the Southern white man to the dignity of labor, Negro artisans are in danger of being restricted to the work they may do for members of their own race.

The present situation is more difficult and more complex than the one which Booker T. Washington observed. No longer is there any point at all in the old saw, "A Negro can spend his money in the North, but he has to earn it in the South." The situation today comprehends not only the loss of industrial semi-security and the advent of fierce competition in the South, but also, largely because of the migration that followed the World War, the question of opportunity for employment over the whole country. To those who do not know our situation as we know it, it may sound more than captious for us to be uttering a special complaint about the difficulty of finding employment in these times. But we are justified in making a special complaint. We are not, we know, the only ones who are suffering from lack of employment. Many people of many classes are suffering. But there is this distinction: the hardship falls on those others, in general, as individuals; while we, because of the prejudice operating against us, stand threatened with economic strangulation as a group. Over and over the door is shut in our faces, not because there is no work, but because we are Negroes.

Most of us who have given thought to this phase of our problem think of it principally in terms of the relation of the Negro skilled and semi-skilled worker to organized labor. This is, probably, the key approach to the question. Organized labor holds the main gate of our industrial and economic corral; and on the day that it throws open that gate in realization of the truth that the cause of the white worker and the cause of the black worker are one, there will be a crack in the wall of racial discrimination that will be heard round the world. We have not yet found an effective means of convincing organized labor that this is what it ought to do. In one or two unions we have gained a somewhat firm footing; but the unions as a whole shut us out completely. The results of the arguments and overtures we have made have been practically null. The only pressure we control for backing them up is the more or less veiled threat of "scabbing." The unions, while barring us out, deem any effort to put that threat into effect as highly dishonorable on our part and a mortal blow at the best interests of the worker. This surpassing irony really passes over into the ridiculous. The union labor leaders are, probably, unconscious of this irony, and it is possible that they do not realize the crass cruelty of their position. Separate Negro unions have been suggested; but it is plain that this plan would only lead to organized "scabbing" and to driving in deeper the wedge between black and white workers. It is easy to see and understand that our chief trouble here, as in other phases of the race situation, is the lack of power to back up our demands. Nor are we able to summon any help. In education and general philanthropy the capitalist class has given us inestimable aid, but it would be silly to ask them to help us here. The great white middle class is not interested. The Communist party has in and out of season preached and insisted upon its tenet of workers' solidarity, but the Communist party is itself too weak to have any influence on American organized labor, except to make it tighter. At this point Communists will naturally ask: why do not Negro Americans strengthen the Communist party? I have already tried to state the case of Communism and the Negro, but I shall add: there is no apparent possibility that a sufficient number of Negro Americans can be won over to give the party the desired strength; and if the entire mass were won over, the increased proscriptions against Negroes would outweigh any advantages that might be gained. Every Negro's dark face would be his party badge, and would leave him an open and often solitary prey to the pack whenever the hunt might be on. And the sign of the times is that the hunt is not yet to be abandoned.

We are compelled to admit that this, the most fundamental question in our whole situation, the question of a fair and equal chance to earn our bread by our toil, is the most perplexing and unyielding with which we have to contend. It appears that for the present our main effort must consist in hammering the trade unions continually with the self-evident truth that they cannot advance or maintain standards and conditions for white labor while they leave on the outside a ready and almost unlimited supply of black labor. We must convince the white worker that our help is needed in the winning of the cause of labor.

In the meantime, we should devise methods of giving "workers' education" to our workers. We are not a part of organized labor—mainly because of the bar maintained by the unions. But our position is in some degree due to the fact that we are almost completely ignorant of modern working-class philosophy. For twenty-five years we have, by means of publicity, printed leaflets, mass meetings, legal action, and other methods, been effectively educating ourselves in the rights of citizenship. By similar means, and through organized effort, we should undertake to educate ourselves in the rights of labor.

But organized labor, though it may be the key, does not embrace the whole question of employment. There is the wide field of general employment, in which persons are hired and fired as individuals. More Negro Americans are dependent on this field for a living than are dependent on the field of skilled labor. In this field there are some remarkable exceptions to the laws of discrimination. We sometimes find a Negro American holding a job that puts our credibility to the test. The bar here is not so inflexible as it is in the field controlled by organized labor. The contacts between employer and employee are, in a sense, individual; and in instances the policy of discrimination gives way before influential recommendation or strong personality or exceptional capacity. But on the whole this is, too, a closed field to us. Take any city and look for the Negro employees in shops, in stores, in factories, in offices, in banks, in insurance companies, on street cars, on busses, and elsewhere. A curious observer in any American city might well ask: what does the Negro population do to make a living? One who observes the number of ways for earning daily bread in American cities that are barred to Negroes solely on account of race, and the few that are open, should be excused for marveling at the number of decent, law-abiding colored citizens these communities have. I believe that how we do manage is at times a mystery even to us.

As restricted as is the field of general employment, we do have some chance of branching out in it, and, little by little, of occupying new territory. By this process we have made up for much of the loss in the older and traditional lines. In several of the larger cities Negro Americans have attempted to take new territory by bringing power to back up their demand; the demand has been for the employment of Negro clerks in establishments where Negro Americans spend their money, and the power has been the boycott. In instances, the demand has been yielded to. But not yet have we demonstrated the efficacy of the boycott as a remedy or the wisdom of using it as a weapon. In our case it might prove a boomerang; on the very argument for the employment of Negroes where we spend our money, Negro employees may be let out where we spend no money. The boycott, in order to produce tangible and abiding results must have behind it real power and thorough organization. If it is merely a gesture of indignation or is carried on sporadically and without determination, it will fail. A financial boycott by the Jews of the world is in their hands a weapon to be dreaded by opposition of whatever strength because there is behind it real power and a perfected technique. It seems certain that it would be a sounder policy for us to insist upon the obliteration of the color line in employment. But there comes the question of power;

and lacking power to back it up, our *insistence* amounts to no more than a plea. Our economic and industrial experts should give the boycott close study. It is a matter that should not be left to mere enthusiasm, however well-meaning it may be, or to ignorance as to whether we are being benefited or damaged. If those who are qualified to judge assure us that we can actually gain ground by use of the boycott, let us by all means make intelligent and persistent use of it. If, on the other hand, they show us that while we may gain ground at one point we lose at several other points, we shall know that the boycott is a weapon for which we are not yet ready.

The exhortation, "Black and white workers unite!" is often made to us, but nobody, as far as I am able to learn, has yet come forward with a feasible method for bringing about this unity. Establishing a recognition of the unity of interests of black and white workers in the field of general employment presents a more difficult problem than it does in the field of organized labor. In organized labor an approach is possible. There are responsible people to whom we can talk, who will understand what we say, even if they do not comply with it. In the unorganized field neither of these conditions exist. Yet, the consolidation of interests and the removal of the color bar in this general field is of paramount importance, because so many more of us depend on the general field for livelihood than on the organized field. At the present time the only means we have for gaining ground or even holding our ground is by giving odds in competition. We are compelled to do our job not only as well as somebody else but better than anybody else. We have to set a pace for conscientiousness, steadiness, and willingness that other workers find hard to equal and impossible to exceed. We cannot ever yield to the temptation to mix having a good time with having a good job. We are under the necessity of breaking down an old stereotype that as workers we are shiftless, unreliable, and incapable. The only compensation for these extra demands is that they force us to build up a reputation for efficiency that will in the long run outweigh color.

There is another field of labor in which there are more Negro Americans than in any other. That field is agriculture, and close to seventy-five percent of Negro American farmers are share croppers. These share croppers are the most forgotten of all men. The majority of them are held in peonage, a system under which they are as unscrupulously exploited as ever they were under the system of slavery. They scarcely ever see money. Their experience for years has been that of being sunk deeper and deeper in debt, debt for which they may be exchanged, actually sold, from one landlord to another, without a possibility of clearing it off or of escaping physical retention by the landlord who holds it. These share croppers are ignorant and helpless; more helpless under the government's plan of aiding landowning farmers than ever before. Their condition is, however, unique in that it is subject to amelioration through legal processes: the investigation of practices of peonage and placing the findings before the proper federal authorities, and the securing of true accountings from landlords through action in the courts. This is work that could be easily done by the Greater Association for the Advancement of Colored People.

We have long been saying that we ourselves should raise our economic status by establishing businesses that would furnish us with the necessary capital and provide employment for our own people. That is a proposition that goes to the root of our trouble. It is a proposition about which we have tried to do something; and we have had a measurable degree of success. But we have not yet approached having an accumulation of capital or the provision of employment for any considerable number of our own race. There are obstacles that we have not been able to overcome. For one thing, business on a large scale has to be learned, and we get no chance to learn it. As an example, in some of the communities where Negro patrons are treated with scant courtesy there has from time to time been talk of opening a big department store. But the running of a big department store requires skill gained through long and wide experience. It is a business in which the buying and selling must be figured in fractions of a cent, and that is too narrow a margin to allow for the mistakes of ignorance and inexperience.

How are we under the present conditions to get hold of the knowledge and experience necessary for running, say, a big department store? We might follow the technique used by the Japanese in getting hold of things they wanted to know about the *inside* of Western civilization; well-born and well-educated Japanese served as butlers and cooks and chauffeurs in American and European families. We might organize a corps of our near-whites, have them go in and get the business knowledge, experience, and secrets, and bring them out to us. Something of this sort has already been done in the case of one or two secret societies—why should it not be done for more important purposes? I need not say that the carrying out of a plan like this would depend upon our being able to effect the correlation of our forces spoken of in the earlier part of this book.

Another obstacle in the way of doing business on a large scale is our lack of access to the main reservoirs of capital and credit. If a group of Negro Americans had a perfectly sound business project, where could they go to get a half-million or a quarter of a million or a hundred thousand dollars to finance it? Yet those sums, even in these days of depression, are not large in the world of big business. Several years ago, Dr. R.R. Moton made an effort to raise a financing fund of a million dollars. Negro Americans should have subscribed that million dollars, but did not.

Until these main obstacles are removed, we shall have to continue to do business on the smaller scale, while endeavoring to the utmost to develop it. We have had some success in this field, but it ought to be much greater than it is. That it is not greater is, in part, due to the fact that here there are some obstacles of our own creation. It is a common practice among us to go into business relying on "race pride." Now, "race pride" may be a pretty good business slogan, but it is a mighty shaky business foundation. A Negro American in business must give as excellent quality, as low a price, and as prompt and courteous service as any competitor, otherwise he runs a tremendous risk in counting on the patronage even of members of his own race. "Race pride" may induce them once or twice to buy from him a pair of shoes that cost more and wear out quicker, but it won't keep them doing it. The Negro business men who have succeeded have been those who have maintained as high quality, as low prices, and as good service as their competitors.

There is the common complaint about the failure of Negro Americans to patronize the business enterprises of members of the race. This complaint is so common and persistent that it has become almost a byword among us. I believe that a survey of the situation would show that this complaint emanates from those businesses that fail to meet competition. There may be an element among us that is still slave-minded enough to feel that anything white is better than anything black; that is crab-like enough to hate to see any one Negro getting out of the barrel; and so will pass by a Negro merchant only for the reason of trading with a white merchant. If there is such an element, it must be, I think, an insignificant one. If it is a significant one—well, we've got before us another field of education that will have to be worked.

And this brings us to another obstacle of our own creation: the unsound commercial principle of going into business *exclusively for members of our own race.* In practice it may work out that the bulk of the Negro business man's patronage may come from his race—there are, however, some notable exceptions—but his central and motivating idea should be: *I am out to do business with the general community, the entire country, the whole world.* Without this attitude, he will remain in spirit and in fact a petty business man. In so many ways the American Jews furnish us with splendid examples of policies and methods, which if we are wise we shall endeavor to study and follow. They conduct businesses all the way from pushcarts to international banks, businesses that give employment, I judge, to the greater part of their race in this country. But not one of them would dream of establishing a purely business enterprise and limiting the appeal to Jews only.

The development of business on sound commercial principles, business interlocked with business in general and connected with the lines leading to the main reservoirs of capital and credit, would make an addition to our forces and resources that would be beyond estimation. However, the prospects for the individual business man of any group are today far from being bright. Our greatest hope lies, probably, in our ability to adopt and make use of co-operative and collective methods.

INTERRACIAL RELATIONS AND CONTACTS

Interracial relations and contacts involve a policy upon which we are quite sharply divided. There are those who approve and cultivate these relations and contacts, and there are those who stand for limiting them to the smallest possible scope. Those of the second group—which I estimate is the larger of the two—feel and express distrust of all white people, and look with suspicion even upon friendly gestures from them. They frequently cast suspicion together with criticism at those of the race who do have contacts with the whites. An analysis of these feelings would, most likely, reveal them as a defense attitude. But whatever its psychology may be, the attitude exists; and good reasons back of it are easy to find.

Nevertheless, the attitude should be abandoned. For one thing, it rests in large part upon a fallacy; namely, that there are no white people genuinely interested in our highest welfare. Plain facts of our history in this country and our current knowledge refute that proposition. For another thing, this attitude runs counter to the course we must follow to reach our chief objective. Prejudice versus prejudice will not carry us very far along the way. We should establish and cultivate friendly interracial relations whenever we can do so without loss of self-respect. I do not put this on the grounds of brotherly love or any of the other humanitarian shibboleths; I put it squarely on the grounds of necessity and common sense. Here we are, caught in a trap of circumstances, a minority in the midst of a majority numbering a hundred and ten millions; we have got to escape from the trap, and escape depends largely on our ability to command and win the fair will, at least, and the good will, if possible, of that great majority.

The establishment and maintenance of friendly interracial intercourse cannot be brought about without overcoming difficulties. The accomplishment at once demands of both sides a considerable cosmopolitanism of spirit and intellect. It is easy to live within the strict limits of one's own group; one knows its language, its language of words and of ideas; one knows all the questions that will come up and the answers; one does not have to extend himself. Social and intellectual intercourse on even the outskirts of cosmopolitanism is a more strenuous matter; and that is one of the reasons why most human beings prefer parochialism. But time and time again the difficulties have been overcome and Negro Americans have been surprised to find how many white people it has been pleasant and beneficial to know, and white people have been, perhaps, more surprised to find how many Negro Americans it has been pleasant and beneficial to know. Out of these relations have come numerous fine and lasting friendships and an effect on the whole race situation that is far-reaching, though it may not be entirely manifest.

Many a Negro American is held back from such relationships because he feels that they put him in the position of seeking social equality. We should not be frightened by that bogy. The term itself has been so distorted that it makes no sense. In various states of this Union it means anything from intermarriage to breathing the same air in the same public park. No self-respecting Negro American should admit even tacitly that he is unfit to be associated with by fellow humans. Each one can stand manfully on the ground that there should be nothing in law or opinion to prevent persons whose tastes and interests make them agreeable companions from associating together, if they mutually desire to do so.

This matter is, naturally, more complex in the South than in other sections. There, interracial intercourse, when it does take place, is more often than not a one-sided arrangement. In such instances, the whites come into our midst, but, no matter how sincerely they desire the closer relationship, they fear to offend public sentiment by having us go into their midst. Few there are who dare defy that sentiment. The situation of those who genuinely wish to defy it and dare not is near to pathetic. The cultivation of social and intellectual intercourse between members of the two races in the South cannot progress very far until the whites are as free to act as we are.

I repeat that we should cultivate these relationships North and South whenever we can do so without loss of self-respect. We should be willing to take at least as many steps forward as the whites will take. Which does not mean that when a white person takes a single step forward we are to run a mile. If a white person takes that one step forward, let us not rail at him for not taking two or a dozen steps or not coming all the way; but let us give him due credit for the one step taken. In giving credit for that one step, however, we need not raise hallelujahs and try to make him feel that he has solved the race problem and brought in the millennium; and just that has been done more than once. Action of that sort is clownish shamming. Neither have obsequiousness and grinning any place. We could well take as an example the engaging and courteous but dignified manner for which native African chiefs are famed in their dealings with the whites. Treat white people just like humans; the sensible ones will appreciate it greatly. By the cultivation of these relations I do not mean a fostering of the old sentimental and patronizing regard for Negroes. We have reached the stage where that attitude is offensive. Furthermore, that attitude does not reach very far. I have frequently noted that with many white up-lifters the Negro is all right until he is up-lifted. The result we wish to gain from these relations is mutual respect and regard.

The cultivation of social and intellectual intercourse is an important part of the policy of commanding and winning the fair will and good will of the great white majority, but I do not wish to overemphasize its importance; for it is, after all, the smaller section of the field of interracial relations and contacts. Our major and more difficult problem in the field of interracial relations at present does not lie with the white man who disdains us and keeps us out of his club, but with the white man who fears us and keeps us out of his labor union. This man who fears that we may take his job, and fears that we may prove as capable in doing it as he is, and fears, too, that maybe he is not so superior as he assumes to be, we must also command and win his fair will, at least, and his good will, if possible. But we must constantly bear in mind that in commanding and winning the fair will and good will of all white America, conciliation is not the sole technique; there are times when firm opposition is the only effective means.

LEADERSHIP

Leadership can be made a very provocative topic. Lambasting our leaders is quite a popular pastime. Without question, since leaders are human, there is a great deal wrong with them—just as there is with followers—and, as every group of people has, we have the right and privilege of soundly and openly criticizing the words and actions of those who stand as leaders. It must, however, be admitted that the bulk of the criticism constantly heard comes from nitwits who have a mania for writing communications to the newspapers. This brand of criticism is neither sound nor sensible; the only apology for it is that frequently it is leveled at those of that considerable number who are not leaders in any recognizable sense of the term. The term "leader" has been greatly stretched, but real leaders are not and never were numerous. Leaders of the first magnitude are among the rarest of humans; God makes one only every so many centuries. We, as every other group, have on hand a large supply of self-set-up leaders. But real leadership is not a distinction to be assumed; it is an office to be achieved. Of the real leader the people some day become aware, and say: This man serves well, let us follow him.

We often utter hopes and prayers for a supreme leader, for a Messiah, one who will surely deliver us out of the hands of the Egyptians. He may come. Until he does, we must make the best use of all the elements of leadership we are able to develop. It seems to me that the present stage of our situation requires diversified leadership. I am certain that there are two elements which are necessary. We need an element of radicalism and an element of conservatism; radicalism to keep us from becoming satisfied and conservatism to give us balance; to the end that the main body will be steady, but alive, alert, and progressive. We should guard against being stagnant, on the one hand, or wild-eyed, on the other. The matter-of-fact conservative has in these days fallen into disrepute, a disrepute greater, probably, than is justifiable, and his low estate blinds us to certain weaknesses of the glamorous radical. There is an inherent weakness in the temperament of the radical which is not generally perceived. Through it, as through the temperament of the man of bravery, there runs a streak of cowardice. The man with a reputation for bravery lives in constant fear that at some time he may not appear in the eyes of his fellows to be making a brave enough show; the man with a known name for radicalism may live in constant fear that at some time he may be deemed by his comrades to have acted conservatively. The man who feels that he must take risks when no risk is warranted may make a heroic soldier, but he will not make a good general. The man who feels that he must be radical, whether the situation demands it or not, may be a stimulating force, but he will not be a wise leader. Neither professional radicalism nor stand-pat conservatism can alone provide the best leadership. Of course, if we produce the one man in whom these two elements are properly fused, the man not afraid to act radically when swift change is necessary, and not afraid to act conservatively when it is necessary to stand unmoved, we shall have the ideal leader.

Moreover, leadership involves more than individual leaders. There must be also a leading element, an element that can transmit and interpret to the greater mass the principles and policies that are formulated. This leading element should constantly draw on NEGRO YOUTH, in order to be kept quickened, and to safeguard against a vegetating leadership. If youth is not thus brought in and given a share in executing the work to be done, its ambitions, ideals, and energies will be largely dissipated. At many points in our social organism there is no life because of withered leadership. The thing to do is to cut out the dry rot and give the younger generation a chance. The impatience of youth to bring about changes should not be antagonized, it should be understood; it should not be curbed, it should be directed.

This kind of co-operation is not entirely easy to establish; for age is at bottom afraid of youth, and youth is at bottom disdainful of age. Youth prefers to work alone and not have its enthusiasms checked by experience. And age loves to hold on to its prerogatives. But we must seek to devise a co-operative scheme through which the new ideals and fresh forces of youth may be utilized to the highest degree. Such a scheme will afford youth a worthwhile objective on which to focus its surging energies, and will serve to keep the older generation invigorated. Such a scheme will do much to redeem our "lost generation." For Negro youth, like the post-War youth of the whole Western world, has its "lost generation," a generation for which the traditional sanctions no longer exist, a generation that is adrift, dissatisfied, disillusioned, and cynical—or is pleasure-mad. Such a scheme will put youth in touch with life's realities, and will provide an unsurpassed training ground for future leaders.

The question of leaders naturally brings up the question of followers. There can be no leaders unless there are followers. Followers have obligations and responsibilities, as well as leaders. As followers, we need to have intelligence, a sense of loyalty, and a sense of honor. We need to have enough intelligence to weigh and estimate men so that we can recognize real leadership when we see it, whether it is in high or lowly positions, and to detect the spurious from the genuine; enough intelligence to stimulate and help real leadership both by approval when it is merited and by criticism when it is deserved; enough intelligence not to be swept away by the winds of doctrine issuing from every loud-mouthed demagogue or smooth-tongued charlatan who comes along. We need a sense of loyalty that will impel us to give unstinted support whenever we find leadership that is capable and trustworthy, and to bear with it in its human weaknesses. And we need a sense of honor that will deem it an unworthy thing to seek to destroy a leader because of personal animosities or to crucify him merely to make a Roman holiday.

Unless we can be followers of this kind, we have no reason or right to look for great leaders.

STEREOTYPES, ART, AND MONEY

I mentioned stereotypes under another topic, but I wish to add a word more about them. The common-denominator thinking about the Negro in America—if we may call it thinking—is done in stereotypes. These stereotypes vary to the point of contradictoriness. "The Negro," and that includes *all* Negroes, "is lazy, shiftless, unreliable; he is an irresponsible child, a pathetically good-humored buffoon, a ridiculous caricature of a civilized man; he is an unconscious pilferer, he is incapable of mental and moral development, he is a brutal and degenerate criminal." One or more of these stereotypes enter into forming the ideas about Negro Americans held by the average white American. The anterior causes of these stereotypes need not be discussed.

These stereotypes have, for the greater part, been molded by what may be termed literary and artistic processes. Some of the most persistent of them were formed on the minstrel stage. For nearly three-quarters of a century black-faced minstrelsy was the chief and most popular form of American entertainment. Hardly a hamlet in the country was too small to be visited by a minstrel show. And it was from the minstrel show that millions of white Americans got their conceptions of Negro character. On the minstrel stage the Negro was represented as a shuffling, happy-go-lucky, banjo-picking, singing, dancing "darky," whose sole gastronomical delights were watermelon, 'possum, and chicken, and whose social outlet was a jamboree at which the chief diversion was expert razor slinging. To the minstrel stage can be traced the difficulty which white America finds in taking the Negro seriously. Much the same sort of thing was done in books about the Negro—with the further characterization of him as a base, savage, and uncivilizable being. In the earlier years the moving pictures carried on this tradition. All of which sounds ridiculous, and would be if these stereotypes did not color, influence, and constitute so large a part of national thinking about us.

Now, just as these stereotypes were molded and circulated and perpetuated by literary and artistic processes, they must be broken up and replaced through similar means. No other means can be as fully effective. Some of this work has already been done, but the greater portion remains to be done—and by Negro writers and artists.

For a number of years we have given vent to loud lamentations over the treatment we have received in literature and art. Well, what ought we do about it? Beg white writers and artists to treat us with more consideration? Of course not. What we need to do is to rear a group of Negro American writers and artists who can smash the old stereotypes, and replace them with newer and truer ones; who can produce work that will reach and affect many and many a white American who may never in a lifetime exchange a hundred words with a Negro; who can produce work that may affect people who will never even see a Negro.

How are we going to rear this group of writers and artists? By leaving them to get encouragement and support as best they can or by having them work primarily and definitely for us?

A New York publisher once said to me, "I would publish any good book touching on the Negro that came to me, if I felt that I could count on three thousand colored people buying it." I had to tell him that he could not count on three thousand; no, not on two thousand; not even on one thousand—not on one thousand out of twelve million!

We are not book buyers. We are not book readers. We lack intelligence about books. We show small interest even in books that vitally affect us, either for good or for ill. We have many cultured homes with elegant appointments, with grand pianos, grand victrolas, and grand radios, but not a bookshelf. If we had only twelve thousand Negro American book buyers—and I mean by "book buyers" persons who go regularly into a bookstore looking for a good book or who make up their minds about it from reading the literary reviews—the publishers of the United States would take notice, and as a consequence there would come into being a corps of Negro writers to set themselves to the task of changing and forming public opinion. But this demands the spending of money, some of our own.

We have tried a number of factors in the working out of our problem, and each of them has produced results in accordance with its applicability and the effectiveness with which we have used it. Nevertheless, one of the most powerful factors that could be brought to bear we have scarcely used at all. That factor is Money. If we were as far-sighted as we ought to be, we would raise a fund of at least a half-million dollars to be expended for the specific purpose of advertising our good points and making them familiar to America and the world. With a fund of that size we could begin and carry on for some time a systematic publicity campaign through books, periodicals, moving pictures, and other mediums in the United States, Europe, and Japan, a campaign that would gradually affect national and world opinion. Such a campaign would not need to be fictitious propaganda; the facts of our history in this country and of our struggles and progress would furnish an expert public relations council for us with all the material he needed. No intelligent person has to be informed of the power of skillful publicity. We have seen the demonstration that a sufficient amount of it can, on the one hand, foster a sense of admiration, respect, and friendliness between two nations or, on the other hand, stir up enough hatred to start them at each other's throats. We have stood by while we almost universally received unfavorable publicity, and trusted mainly to luck for what was favorable; we ought to make a planned effort to reverse this condition.

When we have been called on to safeguard our civil rights we have had to pass round the hat to get the money, and seldom have we succeeded in getting enough. We ought to have a trust fund of at least a half-million dollars for that purpose. From a fund like that, aid could be drawn for the Scottsboro defense. Other cases that will arise could be adequately taken care of. A part of such a fund could be used at this very time to follow up the decisions in the Texas "white primary" cases won by the N.A.A.C.P. in the Supreme Court. Supreme Court decisions do not enforce themselves; it is up to us to see that they are not disregarded.

I have here talked of raising funds amounting to a million dollars. That sum will to many be staggering. Many will say, "We are poor. We can't possibly raise a million dollars." We won't in our present disorganized state. But we could do it, and we would do it if we were sufficiently alive to the need. We spend greater sums than that for less vital things. One million dollars would average less than ten cents apiece; and there are individual Negro Americans who could make up for the contributions of a thousand, of five thousand, of ten thousand who would not give. I am constrained once again to quote that sad truth uttered by Professor Kelly Miller, "We pay for what we want, and beg for what we need."

CHAPTER IV

CONCLUSION

In these few pages I have made no attempt at a general consideration of social problems; rather have I sought to limit the discussion to the peculiar and immediate problems that confront us as a special group. I have also sought to project the discussion from the base of conditions as they are, and not from the base of conditions as we wish they were.

I have tried to show that the most logical, the most feasible and most worthwhile choice for us is to follow the course that leads to our becoming an integral part of the nation, with the same rights and guarantees that are accorded to other citizens, and on the same terms. I have pointed out that common sense compels us to get whatever and all the good we can out of the system of imposed segregation, to gather all the experience and strength that can be got from it; but that we should use that experience and strength steadily and as rapidly as possible to destroy the system. The seeming advantages of imposed segregation are too costly to keep. I have enumerated our principal forces and resources and set forth that none of these factors is a panacea; that we must correlate all our elements of strength to form a super-power to be centered on our main objective; that, knowing the rights we are entitled to, we must persistently use this power to defend those rights we hold, so that none may go by default, and to secure those we have not yet gained. I have stressed the vital need of plans and steps for uniting black and white workers. I have made plain the importance of interracial contact. I have pointed out the necessity of enlisting the energies of youth. I have shown that in addition to other factors there is an emotional factor to deal with. I have implied the fact that our policies should include an intelligent opportunism; by which I mean the alertness and ability to seize the advantage from every turn of circumstance whenever it can be done without sacrifice of principle. We require a sense of strategy as well as a spirit of determination.

To revolutionary elements it will no doubt appear that what I have outlined is too conservative. If it does, it is not because I am unconscious of the need of fundamental social change, but because I am considering the realities of the situation. Conservatism and radicalism are relative terms. It is as radical for a black American in Mississippi to claim his full rights under the Constitution and the law as it is for a white American in any state to advocate the overthrow of the existing national government. The black American in many instances puts his life in jeopardy, and anything more radical than that cannot reasonably be required.

Much that I have here written I have stated before. In what I have said I have sought to avoid being either academic or lyric. I have spent no time with analyses of the psychology of race prejudice. I have suggested no quick or novel cure-all, for there is none. There is no one salient to be captured; our battle is along a wide front. What I have outlined is a plan for a long, hard campaign. A campaign that will demand courage, determination, and patience. Not, however, the patience to wait, but the patience to keep on working and fighting. This may seem far from a cheerful prospect; but why should we utter wails of despair? Our situation is luxuriously easy to what former generations have endured. We ought to gain fortitude from merely thinking of what they came through.

And we ought to gather inspiration from the fact that we are in the right. We are contending for only what we are entitled to under the organic law of the land, and by any high standard of civilization, of morality, or of decency. Black America is called upon to stand as the protagonist of tolerance, of fair play, of justice, and of good will. Until white America heeds, we shall never let its conscience sleep. For the responsibility for the outcome is not ours alone. White America cannot save itself if it prevents us from being saved. But, in the nature of things, white America is not going to yield what rightfully belongs to us without a struggle kept up by us. In that struggle our watchword needs to be, "Work, work, work!" and our rallying cry, "Fight, fight, fight!"

I offer now some words of caution. We are in constant danger of growing to feel that all the ills we suffer are due to race prejudice, and so, of falling into the habit of framing excuses for our own shortcomings. We must try to avoid that danger. We should squarely face our failings. And, too, we should remember that, if race prejudice were abolished today, there would remain to us tomorrow all the ills that are common to humanity. That, however, is exactly the point we are striving to reach, the point where we can enter the race, not handicapped back of the line, but starting from scratch.

In the situation into which we are thrown, let each one of us, let the whole race, be ceaselessly on guard against the loss of spiritual integrity. So long as we maintain *that* integrity we cannot be beaten down, not in a thousand years. For instance, we suffer the humiliations of Jim-Crowism; but we are not vitally injured so long as we are not Jim-Crowed in soul. If it is necessary for me to travel on the railroad in a Jim-Crow state, I am in all probability forced to climb into a Jim-Crow car; but the injury inflicted on me is only external, unless I should feel within myself that I am in my right place, that I am where I belong. Each time one of us *voluntarily* and *unnecessarily* Jim-Crows himself, he is undermining his spiritual integrity. We often permit mere timidity to undermine our spiritual integrity. We must throw off timidity and break through the barriers whenever we are able to do it. We often take discrimination for granted where there actually is none or where it is so indefinite that a little courage and pressure would sweep it away. Each time we break through or sweep away discrimination we make it easier for the next time and the next one.

This is a struggle in which time after time we are compelled to yield ground; let us never yield ground spiritually.

The pledge to myself which I have endeavored to keep through the greater part of my life is:

I WILL NOT ALLOW ONE PREJUDICED PERSON OR ONE MILLION OR ONE HUNDRED MILLION TO BLIGHT MY LIFE. I WILL NOT LET PREJUDICE OR ANY OF ITS ATTENDANT HUMILIATIONS AND INJUSTICES BEAR ME DOWN TO SPIRITUAL DEFEAT. MY INNER LIFE IS MINE, AND I SHALL DEFEND AND MAINTAIN ITS INTEGRITY AGAINST ALL THE POWERS OF HELL.

Selected Bibliography

WORKS BY JAMES WELDON JOHNSON

The Autobiography of an Ex-Coloured Man. New York: Sherman, French & Co., 1912.

Fifty Years and Other Poems (Boston: Cornhill Company, 1917).

God's Trombones: Seven Negro Sermons in Verse. New York: The Viking Press, 1927.

Black Manhattan. New York: Alfred A. Knopf, 1930.

Along This Way. New York: Viking Penguin, 1933.

Saint Peter Relates an Incident: Selected Poems. New York: The Viking Press, 1935.

Negro Americans, What Now? New York: The Viking Press, 1938.

WORKS EDITED BY JAMES WELDON JOHNSON

The Book of American Negro Poetry. New York: Harcourt, Brace & Jovanovich, 1922.

The Book of American Negro Spirituals, with J. Rosamond Johnson. New York: The Viking Press, 1925.

The Second Book of American Negro Spirituals, with J. Rosamond Johnson. New York: The Viking Press, 1926.

SELECTED COLLECTIONS OF WORKS BY JAMES WELDON JOHNSON

Andrews, William, ed., *James Weldon Johnson: Writings.* New York: The Library of America, 2004.

Bond, Julian, and Sondra Kathryn Wilson, eds. *Lift Every Voice and Sing: A Celebration of the Negro National Anthem.* New York: Random House, 2000.

Wilson, Sondra Kathryn, ed., *The Selected Writings of James Weldon Johnson.* New York: Oxford University Press, 1995.

———, ed. *In Search of Democracy: The NAACP Writings of James Weldon Johnson, Walter White, and Roy Wilkins* (1920–1977). New York: Oxford University Press, 1999.

WORKS ABOUT JAMES WELDON JOHNSON

Andrews, William. "Introduction," *The Autobiography of an Ex-Colored Man.* New York: Penguin, 1990.

Baker, Houston A., Jr. *Singers of Daybreak: Studies in Black American Literature.* Washington, D.C.: Howard University Press, 1974.

Bell, Bernard. *The Afro-American Novel and Its Tradition.* Amherst: University of Massachusetts Press, 1987.

Brown, Rae Linda. *Music, Printed and Manuscript, in the James Weldon Johnson Memorial Collection of Negro Arts and Letters.* New York: Garland Publishers, 1982.

Byrd, Rudolph P. *Generations in Black and White: Photographs by Carl Van Vechten from the James Weldon Johnson Memorial Collection.* Athens: University of Georgia Press, 1993.

Fleming, Robert E. *James Weldon Johnson and Arna Bontemps: A Reference Guide.* Boston: G.K. Hall, 1978.

———. *James Weldon Johnson.* Boston: Twayne Publishers, 1987.

Gilroy, Paul. *The Black Atlantic: Modernity and Double Consciousness.* Cambridge: Harvard University Press, 1993.

Johnson, Charles. "Lift Ev'ry Voice and Sing," *Turning the Wheel: Essays on Buddhism and Writing.* New York: Scribner, 2003.

Kostelanetz, Richard. *Politics in the African-American Novel: James Weldon Johnson, W.E.B. Du Bois, Richard Wright, and Ralph Ellison.* New York: Greenwood Press, 1991.

Kutzinski, Vera. "Johnson Revises Johnson: *Oxherding Tale* and *The Autobiography of an Ex-Colored Man,*" *I Call Myself an Artist: Writings by and About Charles Johnson,* ed. Rudolph P. Byrd. Bloomington: Indiana University Press, 1999.

Levy, Eugene D. *James Weldon Johnson, Black Leader, Black Voice.* Chicago: University of Chicago Press, 1973.

Price, Kenneth M., and Lawrence J. Oliver. *Critical Essays on James Weldon Johnson.* New York: G. K. Hall, 1997.

Skerret, Joseph T., Jr. "Irony and Symbolic Action in James Weldon Johnson's *The Autobiography of an Ex-Coloured Man." American Quarterly* 32 (1980): 540–58.

Smith, Valerie. *Self-Discovery and Authority in Afro-American Narrative.* Cambridge: Harvard University Press, 1987.

Stepto, Robert B. *From Behind the Veil: A Study of Afro-American Narrative.* Champaign: University of Illinois Press, 1979.

Tate, Ernest Cater. *The Social Implications of the Writings and Career of James Weldon Johnson.* New York: American Press, 1968.

The statements and observations made by such figures as Sterling A. Brown, Horace Bumstead, Charles W. Chesnutt, Countee Cullen, Owen Dodson, Aaron Douglass, Frances Grimke, George Schuyler, Joel E. Spingarn, Carl Van Vechten, and others that appear in the headnotes of this volume are from the correspondence of James Weldon Johnson that is part of the James Weldon Johnson Memorial Collection of Negro Arts and Letters at the Beinecke Rare Book and Manuscript Library of Yale University.

About the Editor

Rudolph P. Byrd is professor of American Studies in the Department of African American Studies and the Graduate Institute of the Liberal Arts at Emory University. He has written essays and reviews on various aspects of American and African American literature, culture, gender, and sexuality for such publications as *Callaloo, African American Review, Los Angeles Times, The Washington Post, The Atlanta Journal-Constitution,* and *MELUS.* His books include *Jean Toomer's Years with Gurdjieff: Portrait of an Artist, 1923–1936* (1991), *Charles Johnson's Novels: Writing the American Palimpsest* (2005), and, as editor, with Beverly Guy Sheftall, *Traps: African American Men on Gender and Sexuality* (2001).